Living in Turbulent

The Story of a Remarkable Life

FRANK VIELBA

Translated from Spanish by

Holly Kay Davies

Copyright © 2016 Frank Vielba

All rights reserved.

ISBN -10: 1537602357
ISBN-13: 978 - 1527602356

Copyright © Frank Vielba 2016

The right of Frank Vielba to be identified as the Author of the Work has been asserted by him in accordance with the Copyright, Designs and Patents Act 1988

All rights reserved. No parts of this publication may be reproduced, stored in a retrieval system, or transmitted, in any form or by any means without the prior written permission of the author, nor be otherwise circulated in any form of binding or cover other than which it is published and without a similar condition being imposed on the subsequent purchaser

ISBN-13: 978-1527602356
ISBN -10: 1537602357

In memory of Trinidad and Nicasio,

For teaching me who I am.

This book is dedicated to them

And to all those who suffered

In the Spanish Civil War

For Carlos and Isabel,

So that they may know their roots

And carry on with the journey

Contents

ACKNOWLEDGEMENTS 7
PROLOGUE 9
1. A SPECIAL DAY 11
2. THE PARTY 16
3. LA ROMANA 24
4. THE FAMILY HISTORY 32
5. ADOLESCENT YEARS 49
6. THE OPPORTUNITY 55
7. THE CAPITAL 60
8. MARÍA'S WEDDING 66
9. DOMESTIC SERVICE 72
10. STORM CLOUDS 79
11. MILITARY REVOLT 98
12. MADRID RESISTS 102
13. PARALLEL LIVES 113
14. THE LAST DAYS 143
15. VISIT TO HERVÁS 150
16. REPRESSION 175
17. IN SEARCH OF A HUSBAND 185
18. POST-WAR 204
19. UNCERTAIN YEARS 214
20. CHILDHOOD MEMORIES 222
21. DREAMS AND REALITY 235
22. FRANK EMIGRATES 242
23. THE TRANSITION 252

24. A NEW LIFE 259
25. ALONE 267
26. FAME 273
27. ONE HUNDRED YEARS 290
EPILOGUE 296
APPENDICES 302
    MAPS 302
    CHRONOLOGY..311
    MAIN CHARACTERS (in order of appearance in the text) 321
    BIBLIOGRAPHY...325
    BIBLIOGRAPHY (WEB) 333

ACKNOWLEDGEMENTS

This book would not have been possible without the help of many people; I would like to mention some of them here. Firstly, my companions in the Instituto Cervantes Reading Group in London: Pablo Peris, Begoña Pérez, Raquel Hernández and Lydia Bernardello whose constant readings and suggestions spurred me on throughout the entire project. I am equally indebted to Magdalena Tirado from the *Centro de Escritores de Madrid* [Madrid Writers' Centre] for her advice and guidance at the start of my journey as a writer. I would also like to express my gratitude to: Carlos and Marie Ruiz, Albert Marra, Eugenio Pastor, Filomena Urbano and José Luis Enebral, who offered details and suggestions that made my book a more rounded and complete piece of writing.

For the English text I am also grateful to Dewey and Elizabeth Hill, Keith McClellan and Stuart McIntyre for their helpful comments and feedback. Special thanks are due to Holly Kay Davies who did magnificently translating the Spanish text.

From within the family circle, I would especially like to thank my cousin Mari-Tere who appears in the book on several occasions and spent many a long day researching this project with me. I would also like to mention my other cousins Trinidad and María who recounted many details that I would not otherwise have known.

Last but not least I would like to single out my wife Carol, who has provided sage advice on many different aspects of the book (including English text translation), and given me unconditional support throughout, helping me over the finish line.

In writing this book every effort has been made to trace all the copyright holders but, if any have inadvertently been overlooked, the author will be pleased to make the necessary arrangements at the first opportunity

PROLOGUE

This book tells the story of a humble working family in Spain in the twentieth century. The main character is my mother; Trinidad. She lived a remarkable life surrounded by people and events that defined Spain's history over the last one hundred years. The other characters in the book, although not quite as remarkable as her, also tell an important story and echo the experience of many other Spaniards at the time.

In telling these people's stories I wanted to bring to light their humanity and positivity, whilst also not shying away from the reality of their existence. Each character has their own rhythm, their own light and shade, which reflects the evolution of their life. Each character stands out in their own way, however they all have one thing in common: they are real people, they all existed in the flesh; they are not a product of my imagination, or just characters in a good yarn. However, some names have been changed to protect individual's identity.

Their respective stories cover a time period of over one hundred years, starting in the nineteenth and ending at the beginning of the twenty-first century. Why does the story span such a long period of time? Well, because, I think, that in order to understand someone you have to know where they have come from, the environment they were born into, their life and the lives of the people most important to them.

The narrative thread in the book centres on Trinidad who, over her one hundred years (or actually one hundred and three years) on this earth, guides us through Spain's most important historical events during a difficult time in her own life. Later on, the stories of characters such as Nicasio (my father) bring the Civil War to the fore, along with all the tragic events that marked not only the lives of those who lived through it, but the lives of their children and grandchildren too.

In my research I relied upon two primary sources of information: memories as recounted to me by the characters themselves, or sometimes by their children, relatives or friends; and also official documents from historical archives. In order to limit the degree of subjectivity, and to verify facts and provide context, I consulted a fair amount of secondary sources of information which are listed in the bibliography.

My main reason for writing this book was to tell the story of Trinidad and her family, not because of how interesting and valuable it may prove to future generations of our family (although that may be the case). Rather, I did so because I believed it could be educational and entertaining for a wider audience; perhaps even provoking critical reflection. If after reading this story, readers follow my mother's fine example of optimism, hope, and love, I will be glad that I have written this tale.

London, August 2016

1. A SPECIAL DAY

Age is an issue of mind over matter.
If you don't mind, it doesn't matter

Mark Twain

Madrid, 14*th* April 2007

Trinidad didn't know what was going to happen. Her son had told her that everything was organised and she was not to worry about a thing. She tended to forget details from time to time, but she wanted to give the impression that she was on top of everything this time; she wanted to appear calm. Ever since she had woken that morning, however, she seemed to have this nervous tic. It was a recent phenomenon that made her mouth move as though she were chewing something. Her niece, Mari-Tere, had warned her that she should behave and not move her mouth that way as it 'looked ugly' and today was a 'special' day, after all.

Trinidad made an effort to control her tic whilst she played with the Our Lady of the Pillar necklace she was wearing. She looked at herself in the mirror in her room and thought herself elegant in her Scottish wool jacket, a present from her niece Trini, in honour of the occasion. Amidst a head of white hair, black locks fell on her forehead lending her a youthful air. It was a contrast that had caught the attention of more than one person in her friendship group, and she always repeated to them what the doctor had told her: *"Trinidad, that's just you getting younger again."*

She took another long look at her face in the mirror, with her penetrating, dark brown eyes. She did not like her large ears, nor the deep wrinkles on her face and neck that had gathered over time. She did like her small-framed glasses though, they made her look like a university professor. She decided that she was suitably presentable for the occasion, but she wanted to make sure.

"Mari, come and see what you think," she called to her niece.

"Yes, very nice, you look beautiful. You'll be the belle of the ball, and rightly so," said Mari whilst planting a kiss on her cheek.

"Do you think my son will be proud of me?" Trinidad asked.

"Well of course he will, we're all really proud of you," came the response.

"And when we get to The Casino, what should I do?"

"Nothing, you just be good as always. Don't do that thing with your mouth and it will all turn out great, you'll see," Mari-Tere replied.

Trinidad sensed that her niece was more nervous than she was, but wanted to appear as if she knew what was going to happen so that Trinidad didn't worry herself. As extraordinary as this occasion was, it was not a one-off. They had been through it all before in 1965, when her father had celebrated his hundredth birthday. He was so much in her thoughts today. She would have dearly liked for him to be with her. Would he be proud too?

At first she hadn't thought this day would come, but as time went on she began to believe it might, especially once she reached 95. After all, she was the frailest of all of her siblings and no one ever imagined that she would live to be a hundred years old. Now, as Fate would have it, she was set to join that special club of people who, like her father, had lived for a century.

She took after her father in her small stature and frail body. Like him, she was slow to develop. She was the only one in the family that her mother took to the doctor; something that, being poor, they couldn't afford. Her mother had said 'Doctor, my daughter has just turned fifteen and yet she has still not become a woman, can you give her a pill or something to make her develop faster?"

Trinidad still felt panic when she remembered that embarrassing moment, like the panic she felt when she had to go to confession for the first time at her communion. "Father, I confess…" She would have liked to have seen that priest's face behind the partition, to see what he thought of her sins. Now she smiled when she remembered that moment.

Her father's height had always been a topic of conversation among people in his hometown. At her parents' wedding, the parish priest that married them had said, "Francisco, how have you managed to end up with such a slim and beautiful woman, being as short as you are?" Francisco didn't reply to the priest, he just winked and smiled roguishly. There must have been some tacit understanding that passed between the priest and Francisco; maybe something to do with his fame as a ladies man, because the father never again asked that question.

She couldn't recall much about the celebration for her father. Was it in Madrid? Who had come to the party? She remembered they gave him a pocket watch and a new *bilbaína* hat, the typical black beret worn in the North of Spain. That was it; times were different then. The family's financial situation was not particularly buoyant; all her siblings, apart from Pepe (José III), were living 'on their uppers with barely enough to keep the wolf from the door'. That's what her husband Nicasio used to say, he was from Castile and he talked that way.

The Casino scared her a bit. She had heard good things about it; a very elegant and refined place, where members played bridge (an English card game that she didn't understand), and the social gatherings were legendary. She had never been inside though; her familiarity with it was only through photos she had seen in the newspapers.

Thinking about it, she was almost certain that her father's celebration had been held at her sister Teresa's house in Madrid and it was a simple affair, with wine, cake and lemonade. Some journalists from the newspaper *El Diario Madrid* came and asked questions for a piece that appeared in the following day's paper. Because he mentioned he had heard Seville was a very beautiful city to which he had never been, the paper offered to pay for her father to fly there. In the end though, he didn't dare go because he was scared of flying. Don Emilio González de Hervás, her father's fellow countryman and a poet who also lived in Madrid, came to the party. He brought one of those *Partagás* cigars that were her father's favourites. However, what moved him the most was receiving a telegram from Prince Juan Carlos and Princess Sofía, congratulating him on his special birthday. Francisco had been a monarchist all his life.

This comparison with her father led her to recall some of the ways in which, to her mind, they were similar. They were both fragile in their physical appearance. They were both optimists. They both had a certain sparkle in their eyes. They were both monarchists. They had also both surprised their doctors with genes that let them reach their hundredth birthday. Ever since they were born, they had both given the impression that, like the thin branches on a tree, they would break whenever the wind blew. However, great hurricanes had blown on many occasions in their lives and those branches had remained intact, still there, defying the passage of time.

Taking another look in the mirror, Trinidad saw herself happy and proud to have reached the age of a hundred. What's more, she was confident that she could beat her father's record of **one hundred and one years, 10 months and 5 days.**

2. THE PARTY

The clock in the nearby Puerta del Sol had just struck midday as Trinidad and her family walked into The Casino. Guests had already started to gather in the grand and spacious entrance hall. Some had come from as far as England, others from Madrid, Barcelona, Cáceres and Valladolid.

As Trinidad entered the grand revolving doors, the noise of the traffic from the street disappeared. The April morning chill that she had felt only moments before eased. New sounds and their sources became apparent. First she noticed the soft murmur of a fountain which was ahead of her in the centre of an indoor patio resplendent with plants and flowers. But there was another murmur which was coming from behind the ornate central staircase. This sound was the conversation of the recently arrived guests awaiting the happy centenarian. With her family by her side Trinidad made her way towards the source of this second sound. Voices began to quieten once they saw her, and soon there was total silence.

The smiling faces of the guests went unnoticed by Trinidad who, feigning calm, struggled to remember who all of these people were that had come to greet her. Their faces were different from how she remembered them. Time, unforgiving as it is, had changed their physiognomy. It must be the same for them with her face, she thought, (which made her look at herself anew in the mirror as she had before she left the house).

"This is your niece María, the one that lives in Barcelona, I know it's been ages since you last saw her," said her son.

"Hi auntie, how are you? You look beautiful, what's your secret?" her niece asked.

"Hi María, it's so good of you to come. Secret? No secret. Just luck, pure and simple," said Trinidad, whilst moving her mouth anxiously.

The encounter with María made her think of old times when her niece had arrived with her mother and siblings to take refuge during the bombings in the Civil War. Back then, her sister María, along with her four children, crossed el Parque del Retiro every day from the Pacífico neighbourhood to the Salamanca neighbourhood where Trinidad lived. Salamanca was an area respected by military aircraft. Those were long and difficult days. There were various military barracks in Pacífico, which made living there impossible; the bombardments were never-ending. At night, María and her children stayed over at Trinidad's until the morning came and the sky was once again free of bombers.

Her attention soon became fixed on the next guest, this time her nephew Manuel. Manolo (as everyone called him) was the eldest son of her sister Josefa. As Trinidad looked at Manolo, she thought of that sister. What an extraordinary woman Josefa had been. In a rural environment, where infant mortality was extremely high, Josefa had managed to bring up a family of ten children without losing a single one. Trinidad, on the other hand, had married late and had only managed to have one child who was almost left motherless as a result of a difficult birth.

Trinidad instantly recognised the next person; her sister-in-law Julia who suffered from Alzheimer's which gave her a strange grimace. Despite this, Julia still had her mischievous smile, and her small eyes danced like sparks in a fire. Her clear, high-pitched voice still retained her Valladolid regional accent. She was no more than a metre and a half tall, and because of her height had always had a 'small girl' complex; something which she reminded everyone of when they went to take a picture of her. Trinidad and Julia had worked together during the war. Julia had always been good to Trinidad and Nicasio when things were difficult for them in the post-war years. As she didn't have children, Julia could always afford a few luxuries, and she had helped them with food and clothing.

The Puerta del Sol clock chimed twelve thirty. The Casino hall started to fill up with guests who moved to join those who had congregated in the middle of the patio, next to the fountain. Their party clothes added colour to the décor and their faces lit up as they recognised relatives or friends. Waiters went back and forth with trays of drinks and canapés. Conversations were held in small groups and the accents that could be heard illustrated the cultural and geographical variety of those in attendance. Trinidad was the centre of the party and she was greeted by kisses at every turn, without necessarily knowing who it was that had given them to her. These displays of affection enveloped her in an emotional cloud which made her move her mouth non-stop. Every so often, she would remember her niece's advice and try to regain her composure and control her nervous tic, only to revert to her previous expression moments later.

After she had received all the guests, Trinidad and her relatives started to move towards the dining rooms on the upper level. The white marble staircase was resplendent beneath candelabras that reflected in decorative mirrors. The glass dome in the centre of the roof, allowed sunshine to flood in, throwing light upon the columns that supported the internal balconies above the staircase. Red carpet, bearing the letters CM of The Casino's insignia, covered the main staircase and the adjoining corridors that housed statues of illustrious men. It was a shame that Trinidad's cataracts prevented her from seeing all of these details, but she was smiling so much as she walked arm in arm with her daughter-in-law, that she seemed to be enjoying every second.

As the guests arrived upstairs, they saw the banquet hall which looked magnificent. The tables were lined up with geometric precision. The theme was white, with the tablecloths and covered chairs matching the white of the inside of the window frames and the roof. The pale colour of the walls contrasted with the dark of the picture frames and the red of the carpet. Flute music could be heard in the background which ever so slowly began to be lost in the noise of the dinner guests' conversations.

Tables bearing the name of each family were positioned strategically, around the head table at the centre, radiating out to the edge of the room. The sensitive task of arranging who sat where had fallen to Trinidad's son and Mari-Tere. With a great sense of responsibility, they had meticulously organised a seating plan placing the Martins, the Vielbas, the Gonzálezes and the Lópezes in their rightful place, according to family protocol.

The feast began and was savoured by all; at which point Trinidad's face returned to normal. She had eaten her vegetable timbale with langoustines and her grouper with mushroom, and she was proud not to have got the tablecloth dirty at all. The chardonnay, which she loved, had left her with a calm and serene expression that illuminated her whole face. Around the table, she could hear conversations in English between her grandchildren and her daughter-in-law. It made her think of the evenings that she had spent in England in years gone by which, together with everything else, made her feel content, as if she were at home.

Almost without her realising, time had passed and they had reached dessert. The head waiter brought over a birthday cake and placed it on the table in front of her. It was a chocolate cake and it had little red candles with the number 100 on. Everybody got to their feet to sing *'Cumpleaños Feliz'* and 'Happy Birthday' in Spanish and English at the same time. Realising the importance of this moment and not wanting to disappoint her guests, Trinidad threw back her body to gather momentum, and in one big breath she blew out the three little candles. Then everyone started to sing her name amidst a clamour of cheers and applause, sharing her joy in the emotion of the occasion. Blowing out those birthday candles symbolised a historic moment in the lives of Trinidad and her family.

Suddenly, she found herself surrounded by people who approached the table to hug her and wish her well. They also all wanted to capture this big moment with their camera. The flashes and clicks of the digital machines went off at incredible speed and she seemed to be in a cloud again, this time a cloud of happiness. Her nervous tic had disappeared and in its place was a bright, friendly and extremely contagious smile.

Given the merriment of the guests, their greetings came in all forms, and some were even poetic.

If after this experience, Auntie,
My soul still feels,
Eternal, eternally,
I will carry on loving you"

This was passionately proclaimed by one of her nieces. Another one pronounced dramatically:

"I love you with my soul,
And with my soul I die.

The poems and photos went on. Each family group would take a turn to be in the photo. The Gonzálezes presented her with a commemorative plaque from the Town Hall in Hervás (her birthplace). It was handed to her by Manolo, her nephew, along with a letter from the mayor of Hervás, which Manolo read aloud, much to everyone's delight.

Then the party reached the point that Trinidad feared most: the speeches. Her son had asked her to get up and say a few words as well. She hadn't slept well the night before, going over and over again in her mind what she should say. Her son had given her a few ideas, but now in the moment she found she had forgotten everything.

Without being conscious of it, she started to think about Nicasio. Of everyone in the family, her husband had been the undisputed master of public speaking. His sister Julia had called him 'the Lenin of Ceinos' because of his Marxist speeches. Trinidad could almost see him right there, on his feet, offering up eloquent phrases left and right, with his easy way of speaking and his Valladolid accent. In theory, she could probably have learnt a lot from him in this respect, but unfortunately after forty-six years spent as his constant audience, she had grown to detest anything vaguely resembling a speech.

While she was reflecting on this, her son, Frank, got to his feet and began his speech. "To summarize a remarkable life, such as my mother's, is no easy task…" he began. She listened intently and when her son made a mistake with a fact or a date, she interrupted him to say "No, that's not right, what happened was…" and all the guests laughed.

Finally, it was her turn. She got up without any help and, fixing her gaze on the centre of the room, she started off by saying:

"Thank you so much to everyone for coming and making me very happy on what is such a special day for me. It has been emotional to see some old familiar faces; I almost didn't recognise some of them after so many years. I never thought I would turn a hundred and still be enjoying life. One thing's for sure, my life isn't remarkable at all, my son made all of that up…"

3. LA ROMANA

Hervás, 5th April 1907

Dawn was breaking. The sun started to burn through the morning mist that hung over the rooftops of Hervás. Mount Pinajarro, with its snowy peak, looked down from on high upon the lush, green countryside of the Ambroz Valley. The Santa María de las Aguas Vivas Church sat at the top of the town[1]. It peaked through the low-hanging clouds that gathered around its bell tower. In the lower part of town, which was home to the poor, the morning silence was shattered by a cockerel crowing. It was six o'clock.

At number 5 Calle del Rabilero, in what would formerly have been the Jewish quarter, a tiny girl could be heard crying. Two people looked down at the new born baby. The mother's face lit up when she saw her new daughter; for a moment she forgot that this was her eighth birth. The neighbour who had helped with the delivery was smiling as well; all the effort that she and the mother had put in had been worth it. She was a beautiful child, but she did not weigh much (5lbs 8oz). Her body, wrapped in a knitted shawl, was burning hot like bread just out of the oven. Her mother looked at her and the emotional bond between them, one that would last a lifetime, was instantly formed.

"Do you know what you'll call her, Dorotea?" the neighbour asked.

---

[1] See map 1.

"Yes, we'll call her Trinidad."

Trinidad had been born into a family of twelve children. José I (1893-1902) and Felisa (1894-95) had already died by the time she entered the world; the first of polio and the second of gastroenteritis. The children had been born like clockwork, on average one every eighteen months, as shown in the table below.

Offspring of Francisco Martin Calzado and Dorotea Gómez Montero

José I, (22.02.1893)	Felisa (20.08.1894)
María Josefa (30.09.1896)	Francisco (09.10.1898)
Jesús (23.01.1901)	José II (19.02.1903)
Teresa (05.05.1905)	Trinidad (05.04.1907)
Antonia (21.03.1909)	Josefa Antonia (20.12.1910)
Petra (18.06.1913)	José III (03.09.1915)

Their mother lay awake at night, wondering how they were going to get by with such a big family and hardly anything to live on. Conversations with her husband Francisco on this matter hadn't succeeded in dampening his desire in the bedroom. Dorotea gave a resigned sigh and thought that perhaps it was God's will for her to have such a red-blooded husband.

Trinidad's arrival in the world was going to make her parents' financial situation even worse. The family home where they lived was tiny with only three rooms; two on the ground floor, including the kitchen, and one room on the top floor, where all the family slept. The hardships grew with every new child they brought into the world. So, it was no surprise that her parents would look for a solution to their problematic living situation. Her aunt Felisa (Dorotea's sister) was in a better financial position than them and, like a guardian angel, she offered them a finca, or small holding, that she owned just under two miles away from Hervás[2]. It even had its own cottage. And that is how, one month after Trinidad was born, the whole family moved to the country.

It was a sunny morning in May when the family and all their worldly goods, which didn't amount to much, finally locked the ancient door of their home on Calle del Rabilero. As they were climbing up Calle de Abajo[3], one of their neighbours passed them.

"Dorotea, is it true you're going to live in the middle of nowhere? Don't you know it's dangerous to live in the country when you have such a small child?" she asked, fixing a distinctly judgemental stare on Dorotea's family.

"Yes, I know, but we'll just have to put up with it, what else can

---

[2] See map 2, the finca was known as La Romana.
[3] See map 1.

we do?" Dorotea replied.

The neighbour's warnings weren't justified however, and happily Trinidad survived her first few months. Yet, as their neighbour rightly predicted, life in the country was in no way easy. Dorotea would rise at the crack of dawn and make breakfast for the little ones. This was usually goats' milk with dry bread from the day before, and some fruit during summer or chestnuts in the winter. For her older children and her husband, Dorotea would make garlic soup with an egg and, occasionally, a piece of blood sausage. On really special occasions, such as after the pig slaughter, she would give them a bit of bacon. Once they had all eaten breakfast, Dorotea would eat whatever was left over. Sometimes that was just bread and milk, but at other times, really most of the time, it was only a bit of milk. This would be her only sustenance until midday.

After breakfast Dorotea milked the goats. Their milk made up a large part of the family's livelihood. She sold the milk in town and used the money to buy bread and groceries. On days when there wasn't much milk, she had to ask for credit from the business owners (this was common practice for families of modest incomes, above all in years where the harvest was lean). Fresh meat was very expensive and was only eaten once in a blue moon, that's to say, once a year and then only if it had been a good year in the fields.

In the afternoons, Dorotea went to a nearby stream to wash clothes for one of the innkeepers in town. It was hard work and there was risk of accident or illness. In winter, she had to break the ice to reach the water and often, after two or three hours washing, her hands were left red-raw and she got chilblains. In summer, on the other hand, she had to fight off the mosquitos that bit her incessantly. Sometimes one of her daughters would accompany her. Although the pay was negligible, at one cent for every piece of clothing washed, at least she was contributing to the scarce income of the family. At the same time, she was also preparing her daughters for a job that was one of the few available for poor people in the town in those days.

Despite these financial hardships, Trinidad grew up healthy and happy in the company of her parents and siblings. She liked life on the finca. She quickly learnt to run around the land freely, like a rabbit through the meadows. The finca had three plots that followed the geography of the land, and which the family had aptly named 'the top bit', 'the middle bit' and 'the bottom bit'. The cottage where they lived was situated on the bottom bit and it was, if possible, even smaller than the home they left behind in Hervás. It was made up of two small rooms, with a pen connected to the back of the house, where they kept the animals. The house didn't have electricity, running water, or sewerage, which was not uncommon in 1907. The family would carry water in jugs from a plentiful natural spring that was nearby; there was always water flowing even on the hottest days of summer. All the daily chores, from the housework (cleaning the house, cooking, drawing water from the well), to the farm work (preparing the furrows for planting, feeding the animals, picking fruit), were done during daylight hours. When night fell, they used an oil lamp for light. During winter, to save oil, the family would gather around the little fireplace which gave a small amount of light, and they would talk in the darkness, telling each other about things that had happened in the day, and talking of the jobs that had to be done the next day.

The ground was only ploughed every other year, to allow it to rest in the traditional ways of the region. In the top field, and in the middle one, they planted corn, wheat, rye and alfalfa; crops which they later harvested and sold at market. The lower field had the most fertile soil, so there they planted vegetables, such as potatoes, beans, lettuce and tomatoes, to feed the whole family. Their diet was supplemented with hens' eggs, the odd rabbit or pigeon, and the milk produced by the few goats which, at that time, were the only animals that the family owned.

There were fruit trees on their land; apple, pear, cherry, fig and peach. They added colour to the landscape in summer and also lent a certain variety to the family's diet. In the top field, one of the vine arbours produced some extremely sweet grapes that Francisco took care of; he mainly used them to make his home-made wine.

The finca was separated from the Monte del Castañar by a public path which bordered the pine trees and chestnut trees that gave shade and cool in summer months. This path was the only route linking the finca with the town and at the other end it finished at Gargantilla, a village hidden in the middle of the valley. The area was called La Romana and from there you could just make out the Ambroz Valley to the west, with its fertile orchards and reservoir where the blue water shone on sunny afternoons. To the east, you could see the Cabrera mountain range, with the peak of Pinajarro dominating the whole region[4]. It was some of the most beautiful countryside around.

In summer months, Trinidad woke to the sound of birdsong in the morning. The jays were really rowdy; sometimes they competed with the cockerels to see who could make the most noise. At night, the cicadas and crickets shattered the silence with their chirps. Her father often used to say that when the crickets chirped like that it meant that the weather was on the turn. At night, she became engrossed looking at the stars and contemplating the vastness of the sky. Although she didn't understand the mysteries of the natural world she thought it a beautiful thing to be able to look at the sky all lit up and to listen to the sounds of animal life around her. For her that was important and it made her happy.

In winter, the countryside took longer to wake up. Birdsong was replaced by the bellowing of the bulls, the jangling of cowbells or the whinnies of horses in nearby fields. When night fell in the coldest months, you could hear wolves howling as they came down from the mountains in search of food. One winter night while coming back from the town with her mother, they crossed paths with a wolf before they got to the finca. During those few moments, mother and

---

[4] See map 3.

daughter stood expectant and stiff with fear.

On market days, Trinidad climbed the stone wall at the entrance of the finca, and watched the herds of cows and goats pass by as the farmers took them to market. Sometimes she saw wild bulls accompanied by leading oxen, at which point she would shout for her family to come and see them. Really, all she wanted was not to be alone because she was terrified the bulls would stray off the path and enter into the finca, so she would quickly close the gate. At other times, she saw neighbours from Gargantilla pass by, some on horseback and some on foot. On summer afternoons when it was really hot, some would stop to let their animals rest, rolling a cigarette in the shade and chatting with Francisco or Dorotea while they waited.

As Trinidad grew up, her relationship with her mother grew stronger. With the curiosity of a five-year-old child, she asked many questions, to which her mother always tried to find an answer. It was in this way that, little by little, she got to know the story of her town and of her family.

4. THE FAMILY HISTORY

Oh Hervás, if I only could!
If I only could, Hervás, return you to the grace
of the mill and the glowing fields,
and the ancient beauty of your vineyards,
overflowing with light red wine.[5]

According to Trinidad's mother, the town of Hervás was quite old; it dated back to the end of the twelfth century. It was at that time, according to scholars, that the town gained its name. Prior to the twelfth century, its geographic location close to the Silver Trail[6] meant that its denizens were of many different cultures and ethnicities: Phoenicians, Carthaginians, Romans, Visigoths, Arabs and Mozarabs. There were also Jews who moved into Hervás at the start of the twelfth century. During the reign of Alfonso VIII, the Knights Templar built a chapel dedicated to San Gervasio, next to the Santihervás River. Before the town gained independence through a charter in the year 1816, Hervás had been owned by the Duke of Béjar.

By 1870, after the birth of Trinidad's parents, Hervás had a population of more than three thousand. As was the case in other places in the region, wealthy families owned the majority of the land and some of them had residences outside of Hervás; in Béjar,

---

[5] Emilio González de Hervás, "Mis Versos de Ayer y Hoy" [My Verses of Yesterday and Today], Librería Raíces (Alicante), 1971 [quote translated from Spanish by Holly Davies].
[6] See map 3.

Salamanca or even Madrid. The middle classes worked in business, as artisans and in small industries. Some of these inhabitants were farmers or landholders with their own plots. The remainder of the population were workers, day labourers or tenant farmers, the latter worked the land and also lived on it. Many of them also provided domestic and manual labour to the more powerful classes. At that time Hervás had five cloth factories, two furniture factories and several windmills that together employed the rest of the population.

Hervás was divided into two parts[7]. Houses in the higher part tended to be better constructed; this was the habitual home of the wealthy. Its heart was the Santa María de las Aguas Vivas Church, where there had previously been an ancient castle in the Middle Ages. From its watchtower visitors were treated to a panoramic view of the whole region. The medieval lower part of the town had worse-quality housing, and was a maze of narrow, dark, badly-designed streets; although they were at least cobbled and moderately clean. This was the part of town in which Trinidad's whole family had been born.

Trinidad's father, Francisco Martin Calzado, had been born on 29th January 1865 at number 41 Calle de Abajo. Her paternal grandfather, Sebastián, had been a weaver, and years later Francisco would follow in his footsteps. Her paternal grandmother, Evarista, had married Trinidad's grandfather in 1864 and they had both died before Trinidad was born. Apart from Francisco, there were five other children from the marriage: Margarita, Antonia, Mari-Cruz,

---

[7] See map 1.

Juana and Felipe.

Francisco was to serve the King, Alfonso XII, and it was while on service in La Coruña that he got his first look at the sea. As soon as he could get an overnight pass, he returned to Hervás to check that his beloved Dorotea was still waiting for him. He knew the wolves were circling; Dorotea had other suitors. Trinidad had heard someone say to her mother that a cousin of theirs had been after Dorotea and wanted to win her away from Francisco. Whether or not that was true, the fact of the matter is that once his military service was over (at that time marriage was not allowed while a conscript was doing his service), Francisco asked for Dorotea's hand in marriage and her parents agreed.

The wedding was held in the Church of San Juan Bautista, in the Plaza del Convento, on 23rd January 1892[8]. The bride wore a dark-coloured percale dress with a black veil. The groom wore a coffee-coloured woollen suit with a matching hat. A small group of family and friends attended the wedding. Francisco was about to celebrate his twenty-eighth birthday and Dorotea was twenty-one years old.

Although small in stature, Francisco was a good-looking lad. He had bright, shining, green eyes; a mocking demeanour and a long moustache like King Alfonso, which lent him a jokey, happy appearance. He had an aquiline nose, thin lips, and his face was always bronzed from the sun. His wide forehead was often covered

---

[8] **See map 1.**

by a black peaked cap. He had a sweet temperament and a soft, melodious, almost birdlike, voice. In his younger years, he drove the girls wild with his Cheshire cat grin, and his jokes and silliness. He was called Tío Fuste (because that was the second surname of his grandfather) and his fame as a ladies man was well-known among the young, and not so young, ladies of Hervás. As a man, he had three vices: wine, cigarettes and women. The order changed somewhat depending on the season, but those three elements were constants throughout his entire life.

Although he had never been to school, Francisco had a great memory for numbers and dates, and he could recite poetry, verses, folk songs and couplets effortlessly. His verses almost always revolved around sex. Some of his favourites were:

"For your thighs and on high I do beseech,
Let me take my sword and place it in your sheath"

---oOo---

"Ooh Mamma, I broke my little jug at the village fountain!
Never mind the jug, just what will people think then"

---oOo---

"They say they will bury me under your bush
A happy death it will be, for death I will push"

One of Francisco's other talents was his knowledge of the countryside. With no training on the subject, he had learned the names and lifecycles of the plants and trees in the region. This meant that people in the town would often come and find him to ask questions on the matter. His fame extended as far as the forest rangers, who had also been known to seek him out in search of help.

Trinidad's mother Dorotea Gómez Montero had been born in Hervás on 28th March 1874, at number 10 Calle del Rabilero. She was the fifth of eight children in a poor family. Dorotea's father, Ruperto, worked as a weaver in one of the factories. Trinidad's maternal grandmother, Petra, was very dedicated to her work as a mother and a housewife. She had one mission in particular: to imbue all of her children with Christian faith. It seems she was quite successful, as one of her daughters, Constancia, became a nun. Another of her daughters, Felisa, also tried to enter religious service after losing her husband and daughter, however she finally abandoned the idea for health reasons.

Francisco and Dorotea were neighbours and it didn't take them long, over the years, to get to know one another and fall in love. Their courtship began in the year 1889. Dorotea was eighteen years old and she was a good-looking girl. Her neat, elegant waist had turned more than one head while she walked along the street with her friends. Francisco wanted to marry her before he completed his military service so that other boys didn't steal her away, but Dorotea's parents didn't want her to marry so young.

Dorotea was tall and slim, with serious, delicate features. Her large, dark eyes shone like embers and lent an intensity to her gaze that captivated men, as did her long, fine, silky hair. As a girl, she already showed signs of having a sweet and peaceful nature, always ready to help her fellow man. From a very young age, her mother's religious teachings had begun to take root in her and she was a fervent Catholic. Her faith was unwavering; she never doubted, not even in the most difficult of times. Quite the contrary, her belief in God grew stronger as time passed. "If it weren't for my belief in God, I would not have been able to cope with so much suffering", she often used to say to her children.

At the start of the marriage, everything was good. Francisco followed in his father's footsteps, working in the cloth factory which he had joined a few years before. He earned eight reals (two pesetas) a day there, a salary that allowed them to live modestly in 1893. After the wedding, they rented the house at number 5 Calle del Rabilero, where Trinidad and all of her elder siblings were born. Their maternal grandparents still lived at number 10.

In 1900, a day labourer's wages were four reals (one peseta) a day, and it was necessary to work from sun-up to sun-down in order to earn that. In the summer months, labourers would work 14 hours every single day of the week; then in winter there was no work at all. Francisco's wage was double that of a day labourer but with their changing circumstances it soon hardly saw them through to the end of the month. Feeding and clothing a family of four children took an annual salary of 600 pesetas.[9] With only Francisco's salary, they just

---

[9] La provincia de Cáceres, situación socio-económica y condiciones de vida

didn't have enough and it showed at mealtimes. The children would fight about the contents of the lean stew; screaming and complaining that one or other of their siblings had eaten more than their fair share. The situation only got worse as more children arrived.

When the factory closed in June of 1900, Francisco was left without work. Dorotea remembered that tragic day well. It was early in the morning, and she was hard at work doing the household chores when she heard noises out in the street. She leant out of the window and saw that her neighbours were talking in an agitated manner, as though something had happened.

One of them saw Dorotea approach and said to her, "Dorotea, you'd better run down there quick, the factory where your husband works is on fire".

Dorotea hardly had time to take off her apron before running down to see what was happening. As she rounded the corner, she realised that a lot of people were heading down Calle de Abajo towards the Fuente Chiquita bridge[10] where the cloth factory was located. Some others were climbing the fountain in the middle of the hill, holding buckets which they filled with water before running down to where the fire was.

(1883-1902) [Cáceres province, socio-economic situation and living conditions (1883-1902)], Luis Carlos Sánchez Bueno, Revista de estudios extremeños [Extremadura Studies Magazine], ISSN 0210-2854, Vol. 58, Nº 1, 2002, pp 93-138.

[10] See map 1.

As she grew closer, Dorotea began to see smoke rising next to the bridge where the factory was. In the middle of the street, once she managed to get past a house that had been blocking her view, she could see that the cloth factory building was going up in flames at great speed. The flames and smoke rose in spirals that climbed higher and higher, eclipsing the clear blue sky of that hot summer's day. The fire was opening up gaping holes in the roof and you could see the blackened wooden rafters on the inside of the factory. There was hardly any mortar holding up the building's stone walls, leaving them leaning dangerously to one side.

The neighbours, acting as firemen, tried to supress the blaze. At the same time, the factory foreman was giving orders to his workers to evacuate the building. Between the din of voices and orders from on high, nobody knew what to do with themselves. Dorotea searched the crowd anxiously for her husband. Some tense moments passed and she prayed with all her heart that nothing had happened to him. Finally, amid a group of people that were leaving hurriedly, she saw Francisco appear. He was safe and sound, although his face was black with soot and his long moustache was lightly singed.

The full extent of the tragedy only became apparent when firemen from Béjar eventually arrived and managed to put out the flames. The damage was extensive and the factory was mostly ruined. The worst part wasn't the material damage however, but the two workers who died in the fire: a young boy of 15 and a man the same age as Francisco. Dorotea felt a huge sadness for the relatives of the victims, and not just because they had lost their loved ones. In the case of the widow, who was poor, Dorotea knew that she would now be left completely and utterly destitute. In those days, workers were defenceless. Nobody received any type of help or financial compensation after the death of a relative in a work accident. If that weren't enough, there was a rumour going around that the fire had been set intentionally, because the textile industry was in crisis, and the owners didn't have the money to pay wages.

The loss of Francisco's job coincided with a turbulent period in the labour market. One day, when Trinidad went down to the town with her mother to see her grandparents, she noticed that the streets of Hervás were full of people shouting and holding up huge placards that she couldn't read. She had unknowingly borne witness to a clash between the peasants, workers, employers and the police. It scared her so much that she didn't return to Hervás until her First Communion some years later. When she got back to the finca that day, still a little shaken up, she asked her father what had happened and what this thing called a strike actually was. He told her the following story.

"A long time ago, before your grandparents were born, there was a very important man called the Duke of Béjar. Just so you understand, a Duke is a very rich man who owns lots of properties, including in those days our town. So then, this man likes industry a lot. By industry I mean making or building things that are then bought in shops, like blankets, tables and shoes. One day he sent for an Englishman known as Juan Cortés to help him build a fine-cloth factory. Mr Cortés was a very clever man who had already built factories in his own country and, with the help of the Duke, he soon began to do the same in Hervás.

"Little by little, our cloths and blankets gained a reputation that spanned the whole region, and they were of such good quality that they often competed with goods from Béjar[11] in markets in other areas. The year before the fire, La Colonia, the factory where I worked, won an international prize for the quality of its cloth. But, unfortunately, now things have changed. The army, which was our main client – a client is someone who buys our products – doesn't buy them from us anymore and, in a short time, factories have started shutting down due to a lack of clients. And that is how I was left without work.

"In the year your sister Teresa was born, there was really bad weather and a really bad harvest. Poor people didn't have any work, not in factories, not in the fields, and people were very hungry. We were in a bad way too, but thanks to the help of your aunt Felisa and her husband, we were able to put food on the table. That winter was also extremely cold; a lot of people died, mostly elderly people and children."

At this point her father tried to explain what the demonstrations that she had seen on 13th November 1912 had been about:

---

[11] See map 3.

"The placards you saw in town and the demonstration that scared you so much today, are to do with all of this. When a factory closes, people are left without a job and they can't feed their families. If the bosses, that's to say the owners of the factory, don't do anything to open it up again, then the authorities try to force them to do so. But when that doesn't happen, the workers have nobody to turn to, so that's why they must take to the streets and protest against a situation that they think is unfair.

"You asked me what strikes are. Well, strikes happen when workers and the owners of the factories don't reach an agreement to resolve their differences. The workers get together and decide not to go to work until their proposals are accepted.

"The employers, on the other hand, don't want to negotiate with the workers and this means public order is disturbed, as it was today. There is a lot more to explain about all of this but that's enough for today. You'll start to understand better when you're a few years older."

The fact that Trinidad didn't go to school made the task of understanding what went on in the world, and why things were the way they were, much trickier for her than it was for girls that were able to attend classes.

In the mornings, she watched enviously as the neighbour's two young girls passed by on their way to school. However, in keeping with the family tradition, neither she nor any of her siblings received primary education. Rates of illiteracy in Cáceres[12] were among the highest in the country; 70% of men and 80% of women were illiterate. State school wasn't free and, as was the case in many other families, Trinidad's family didn't have enough money to pay for it.

From a very young age, her job had been to take care of the baby goats and of her younger brothers and sisters. She took care of her sister Petra, six years her junior, until Petra sadly died of childhood convulsions. Another sister, Antonia, who had been born two years after, died as well, of pneumonia at just three months. She got on really well with her sister Josefa, who was younger than her by three years. Between the two of them they took care of José III, born in 1915, who was the last of their siblings.

José II was the most intelligent of all of her brothers and sisters. Although he had never been able to go to school he managed to learn to read and write all by himself and wanted to study to enter a seminary. However, in 1909, when he was six years old, José II had an accident when out playing which injured his spinal column. The family couldn't take him to the doctor because you had to pay for that. So, without treatment, José II's injury developed complications. He died three years later, without being able to fulfil his dream of entering the priesthood.

The family had seen many tragedies in a short time. By 1915, after the birth of José III, five out of their twelve children had died.

---

[12] See map 3.

The eldest, Francisco, had turned 16 and he worked in one of the wood factories near the railway station. Maybe it was seeing the trains go by every day in front of the factory, or maybe Francisco just had dreams of a better life, but for months he dreamt of leaving Hervás. One day he decided to talk to his parents about it and put the idea to them.

"Mother, Father, I would like to go to Madrid this year to try my luck and find a better job."

"Son, you're still very young and you have a job here," his father had answered. "Things in Madrid are not good. According to what they say in town, there's a lot of unemployment and the political situation is really unsettled, what with the war in Morocco and the fighting in the Great War."

His mother had added, "And what's more, how could you leave us when we need you so much! Who will help your father work the fields? Don't go son, I beg of you."

Francisco had spoken to his fiancée and she wanted to go to Madrid with him, but had similar problems with her parents who wouldn't allow her to leave. What with one thing and another, in the end Francisco decided to stay in the town, at least for a little longer.

The family had still more tragedies to deal with though. Trinidad remembers that day, 3rd March 1915. She was on the finca playing with her puppy Lulú, when one of the neighbours came running asking where her parents were. Even though she was only very young, Trinidad had the feeling that something bad had happened. The news could not have been worse. Her brother Francisco had been in an accident in the factory. He had been caught in one of the machines and died in the most tragic way.

The loss of Francisco was a tragedy for the whole family. Her father had lost the physical help of his son. Trinidad, on the other hand, had lost her big brother whom she had adored; and as for Dorotea, as a mother she didn't know what to do with herself. The loss of her son had left her broken. She replayed their conversation from a few days ago over and over in her mind. Knowing what she now knew, Dorotea asked herself why she couldn't have just let him leave. Her Christian faith told her that it was a punishment from God and she couldn't stop thinking about her 'sin'. She took a long time to get over that tragedy.

With Francisco's accident, the family's financial situation became even more precarious. Trinidad's father was now fifty years old and could not find suitable paid work except work in the fields. This physical work was hard, almost a death sentence for an older person especially one who wasn't used to farm labour. However, after the loss of his son, the entire family was depending on his skills as a farmer to survive. Sometimes he went wandering in the nearby forest not able to forget his son's accident; asking himself the same questions as Dorotea. Like her, he felt he was to blame for his son's death.

Jesús was now the only one of the older boys left, given that José III was still very small. Jesús had always been different from the others; he had a withdrawn, reserved character and didn't talk much. However, at the same time, was very caring and he had a big heart. He worked as a shepherd, watching over a flock of sheep; taking them to the mountain where they could graze in the common sheep pastures. Jesús spent most of the year away from his family. However, he sometimes came down from the mountain to lend his father a hand working the fields. His younger brother and sisters admired his huntsman-like qualities, as he often brought them some animal or other that he had trapped in the mountain. Snakes and lizards were his speciality and many members of the family had eaten these delicacies in Dorotea's soups, without even realising.

María, the eldest of the sisters, started out looking after children and at sixteen years old she went to work as a servant in one of the taverns in Hervás. There she met a family who lived in Madrid; they were looking for a maid so she went with them to the capital.

Teresa, the second eldest of the girls, followed in her sister's footsteps and started looking after children when she was barely twelve. There were several children in the house where she worked and one day Teresa came home crying. When her mother asked her what was wrong, Teresa said that the lady of the house had fired her because she had let the youngest child, who was only a few months old, fall onto the floor. Teresa had to look for another job.

Through all of this, Trinidad was taking in everything that went on around her. In her young mind, she didn't understand why her parents were poor and had to work so much, while others didn't want for anything. Although she hadn't been to school, her natural intelligence told her that it wasn't fair that some people had so much money and didn't want to share it with those who had little. After all, she always saw her mother helping those in need, even though she didn't have enough to get by. Her mother explained to Trinidad that Catholicism taught us to help our fellow man and that it was right for there to be both rich and poor people; after all, God had made the world that way. Trinidad didn't understand why God had made it that way but she listened to her mother's advice respectfully.

Trinidad was very close to her sister Teresa and when they shared their views on this situation, they found they were in agreement. They both wanted to be rich, as it meant they would work less, and so would their parents, who were getting older now.

Trinidad loved animals. Apart from her puppy Lulú and her kitten Ágata (each of the children had their own favourite cat), she was very close to the goats she looked after. Sometimes they had to sell one of them in order to pay off the bills they owed in the town. When that happened she grabbed hold of the animal like it was her child, and tried to stop her father taking it away. The animal didn't want to leave her either, and it bawled as though it really were losing its mother

In the month of August, she would go with her father to a neighbouring town, Aldeanueva del Camino[13], where the livestock markets were held. There she saw how the merchants bought and sold animals. Trinidad was amazed when she saw the buyers open the horses' mouths and look at their teeth to check their age. She also liked to see the pigs (normally sows) who made lots of noise and sold for a good price. The cows and wild bulls scared her, she latched on to her father when she saw them.

After she had been to the market a few times she realised that it was always the same. The process ended with her father selling the goats that they had brought; the youngest ones that Trinidad had seen being born and had looked after with so much love and care. After using some of the money to pay off debts, there was at most enough to buy a sow or swap the donkey for another younger one. Other times, around Easter, her father chose one of the youngest goats to be served as a special meal for the whole family, but Trinidad refused to eat it because she felt so bad.

---

[13] **See map 3.**

5. ADOLESCENT YEARS

By the age of eleven, Trinidad had been helping her mother to wash clothes in the river for three years, and she started work looking after children as well. At first, she cared for the children in the Manglano family, who lived in Calle de la Estación[14]. Then, she went on to care for some rich and very naughty children, who made fun of her and called her names. Trinidad had to come up with ingenious ways to deal with them. The children's mother gave her an approving look, no doubt admiring her expertise. Despite her young age, she used to say, "I was forced to grow up because I took care of children."

Trinidad was contributing to her family through her work as a nanny and she also used to help her mother sell milk. Once, when milk production was higher than normal, her mother told Trinidad to go through the streets calling out, "get your fresh milk at a good price - fresh milk."

Trinidad's only day off was Sunday, when she went to mass with her mother and her sisters. There were two churches in the village, but the family always went to the Church of San Juan Bautista, where Trinidad was baptized and received her First Communion. All of the women went to mass; some of them went more than once a day. Father Antonio, the very strict priest, counted the parishioners on

---

[14] See map 1.

their way out, like a shepherd would his sheep to make sure he hadn't lost any. Catholicism was the only religion in Hervás, and was followed by almost all of the inhabitants.

After mass, Trinidad visited her aunt and godmother, Felisa, at her house in Calle del Comercio[15]. Felisa asked her if she had gone to confession and if she was free of sin. Trinidad always replied yes and her aunt would give her some money to buy sweets. Felisa had married her cousin Saturnino after getting the necessary permission from the archbishop. Eugenia, their only child, had died of pneumonia at the age of eight; it was quite a common childhood disease at the time. The couple weren't hard up, mainly because Saturnino had inherited land from his parents.

Time went on, and Trinidad continued to grow up. At thirteen, despite her slim frame she was already being noticed by a lad or two who would ask her whether or not she was going to the dance. Her aunt had forbidden her from going to the dance, however, as she said, "It was a mortal sin."

One day Trinidad asked her sister Teresa, "Tere, why don't we go to the dance in Villa Rosa? There's this boy that I like and he's asked me to the dance but I can't go alone."

"Does Mother know?" Tere replied.

"No, but you won't tell her, right?"

---

[15] **See map 1.**

Teresa, who was two years older than Trinidad and was very 'go get-em', said she would go to the dance with her little sister, risking both the fury of her parents and her good reputation.

Once there, boys immediately began to approach the two sisters to ask them to dance, but they just laughed and said no. Most of the other girls were with their mothers who were acting as chaperones, monitoring the boys that approached. Although Trinidad and Teresa were very young, they knew how to look after themselves and there was no need to bring their mother along. In the end, they accepted some invitations to dance and had a great time. Trinidad never did get to dance with the lad that had flirted with her that day, because he wasn't even there.

Time rolled on, and the situation at the house on the finca was becoming ridiculous. The whole family slept in one big room with absolutely no privacy. Both boys and girls slept in one bed together. What had been acceptable when they were children, was now becoming more difficult. The girls were all between the ages of ten and fifteen, whilst the boys were aged between five and nineteen. For the eldest siblings, the process of dressing, washing and going to bed were becoming a complicated operation involving the phrase "please don't look at me while I'm changing". They lacked the physical space needed for a family of seven people, and so living together gave way to arguments and fights. Their difficult living situation wasn't easily solved; on that much everyone agreed. It took an unforeseen, natural event to speed up the decision that had to be taken.

It had been a typical August day; extremely hot. As the afternoon drew in, storm clouds began to cover the sky. At dinnertime, there was thunder and lightning in the distance although it was quite a way off still. At eleven thirty at night, with all the family in bed, the storm could be heard, but it was still more than a mile away. Nobody could sleep, especially not the littlest ones who held onto each other tightly for comfort. Finally, all was quiet. Everyone drifted off to sleep until, at four in the morning while the sky was still dark, the storm arrived with ferocious intensity. In a matter of minutes, the heavens opened and a downpour drenched the dry fields. At first the parched fields drank up the water like a sponge. However, as the rain grew heavier, the water began flowing like a river down towards the lower ground where the family house was. Suddenly, the flood gathered momentum and became a torrent that carried along trees and rocks as though they were nothing. Then, in a flash, the water breached the front door, which the storm pushed opened effortlessly. The screams of the children that slept near the door woke their parents, who instantly realised the danger they were all in. Struggling against the storm, they managed to get their children out of the house before it was left completely submerged. Working together they were able to scale the wall that separated their house from the neighbouring meadow, it was more than three feet high. From there, with panic and tears in their eyes, they watched the storm pass until, at last, it abated completely.

When dawn broke and they saw what was left of the house and its surroundings, the family were heartbroken. Once again fate had dealt a cruel blow to a poor, humble, country family. At least this time the family had survived. So it was decided that instead of repairing a half derelict house, they would build a new one; this time on higher ground.

The entire family took part in the build. They laid the foundations with the help of a relative who was a bricklayer. The stones that were left from the old house were moved to the new site. Even José III, the youngest of all, was seen carrying wooden planks that were so big he almost toppled over. The girls helped carry pails of water from the nearby well, so that their brothers and parents could mix cement. The operation lasted until March the following year. In the winter months, the family slept in town at Aunt Felisa's house; as always, she was ready and willing to help them in any way she could.

Like their previous one, this new dwelling didn't have water or electricity, as bringing power was very expensive even from the closest point in Ermita de San Andrés[16]. The family just didn't have the money to pay for that. Putting in running water was difficult for the same reason and their plentiful natural spring continued to be used as before.

The new house was built with granite that was native to the region and had a solid, compact structure. The outer walls were white and the roof red. The attic had a window that looked to the west

---

[16] See map 2.

letting in light, although it remained closed in winter to dry fruit. Inside there were three rooms; two small ones which were used as a kitchen and dining room, and one large one which was divided into a living room and a bedroom. There were three wrought-iron beds, two of them in the bedroom; Francisco and Dorotea slept in one and the eldest girls slept in the other. The third bed was in the living room, next to the back wall, and it was where the littlest ones slept. In the eastern part of the bedroom there was a large, tall window with iron bars, this let in the only light that reached the inside of the room. It was only in the summer that this provided enough light to see by, in the winter you had to carry a candle. The wooden shutters were kept closed in summer to keep the area cool and in winter to keep out the cold and the rain. The main door, made of two sections joined together with iron nails, had a latch that was opened with a big key, which they kept behind a stone at the back of the house. The new house didn't have a pen for the animals. Francisco had decided to carry on using the old one, as it had suffered the least damage in the storm.

6. THE OPPORTUNITY

It was Sunday 5th September 1920 and there were only a few days to go until the local festival in Hervás. Everyone in the family was talking about it and making preparations to enjoy the celebrations. Even Jesús came down from the pastures to enjoy a few days off. It had been a hot and airless day. After he finished his work, and before changing to go down to the town, Jesús bathed in a well in a nearby wood. It was a deep, dark well surrounded by trees, so it hardly saw any sunlight and the water was always icy cold.

After bathing, he got dressed in his Sunday best and set off to Hervás. A few hours into his walk back to the finca, he started to feel unwell, with shivers and chills. At first, the family didn't pay any heed to his complaints, thinking that he had just drunk too much. However, the following morning his condition hadn't improved, in fact, it had deteriorated quite rapidly. The family didn't know what to do. Dorotea tried several homemade ointments, giving them to her son in an attempt to make him better. This wasn't something that you called the doctor for and the family didn't have an *iguala*, or financial arrangement that would have covered the cost of his visit. Despite the home remedies, Jesús's health didn't improve, and seven days later, at 11 in the morning on Sunday 12th September, he died of triple pneumonia. He was 19 years old. And thus, instead of putting on their party clothes, the family went into mourning.

Jesús's death came as a crushing blow to Trinidad. At thirteen years of age, she began to see death in a different way. It was not something that happened in other families, or at least that's how it seemed to her. She asked herself, why her family? What had they done to deserve so much bad luck? She couldn't understand how the world could be so cruel. Her mother, who after so many tragedies appeared almost saint-like, said 'Jesús has joined your brothers and sisters in heaven". However, Trinidad didn't want to listen to her mother, and she cried for her dear dead brother.

A year had passed since Jesús's death, and the news that the family's eldest daughter, María, was to get married in Madrid, lifted everyone's spirits. The family wanted to send someone to the wedding, but neither Dorotea nor Francisco could leave the finca or the small children unattended. What's more, the train ticket was a small fortune for such a humble family. Nevertheless, María could not be alone on her wedding day; someone from the family had to be there. In the end, Aunt Felisa, who was María's godmother and was better off financially, decided to go and take Teresa and Trinidad with her. For the two sisters, the journey had a dual purpose. Firstly, they would go to their elder sister's wedding. Secondly, they would do something to help their family's living situation. In light of the financial hardship they were all living in, Francisco and Dorotea saw this opportunity to go to Madrid not only as a way of representing the family at the wedding, but at the same time as a way of offering their daughters a better place to live and an opportunity to carve out a future for themselves.

After what had happened to their eldest children, their parents thought that it was important for the girls to have a future. As a result of conversations with influential people in the town, Francisco and Dorotea found two respectable, well-to-do families in Madrid that were looking for a 'country girl' to take into domestic service. And that is how the journey to Madrid for María's wedding, ended up being a one-way trip for the two sisters.

On the day of their departure, Trinidad and Teresa were very excited at the prospect of seeing their sister María again, and going to a wedding for the first time. They looked at each other as if to give one another strength. Neither of them could comprehend the enormity of the step that they were about to take. From this moment on, their lives would never be the same and in some way they sensed that they would be forever united by this move.

The whole family went with them to the station. The train was about to arrive. Felisa tried to cheer the two sisters up, even though it was also her first time travelling to Madrid. However, Trinidad cried and clutched her mother, as though it was the first day at school that she never had. Josefa and José III, who were 11 and 6 years old respectively, understood that something new and significant was happening there at the station, but they didn't realise that they wouldn't see their sisters again for a long time. Their parents tried to hide their feelings and keep their daughters' spirits up. However, the emotion of the situation was reflected on their tense faces. The memory of their beloved son Francisco overwhelmed them at times like these. Fate had decided that it would not be Francisco, but instead Teresa and Trinidad, who would take this journey. Their parents looked at one another, silent understanding passing between them. It was as though they were watching Francisco waiting for his train. They wanted to give Teresa and Trinidad the opportunity that he had never had. The girls had been model daughters in every way and they deserved this. It was only the idea of not seeing their daughters that saddened them.

For their part, Teresa and Trinidad were dreaming of a better world; where work was dignified and gratifying; where life was fairer. Neither one of them anticipated the challenges and dangers that lay in wait for them in the big city. Trinidad was excited about boarding the train which was already coming into view in the distance, the same train she had seen pass so often from the bridge near the finca. Teresa, on the other hand, was more excited about striving for a dignified future and about being able to marry someday, like María. Both sisters dreamt of a better future, and they expected to see those hopes and dreams fulfilled in the capital.

The train entered the station to a buzz of excitement from the few passengers that were waiting on the platform. The din of the engine blowing and letting off steam from its sides made everybody step back. The noise of the carriage wheels screeching as they braked and slid down the tracks made the two sisters cover their ears and smile. The three women boarded their third-class carriage, with its wooden seats, while the rest of the family stayed on the platform. Lulú the puppy had also come to see Trinidad off and at the noise of the train she jumped and leapt about, seemingly excited by the bustle of people getting on and off the train. Halfway down the carriage, through one of the small windows, the family saw first Teresa and then Trinidad, lean through to wave anxiously, and their family responded by waving their white handkerchiefs. Moments later, the engine gave a sharp whistle and started to move off. Teresa and Trinidad kept their eyes on their loved ones who were still waving their handkerchiefs in the air. Little by little, the familiar figures shrank until they were lost in the horizon. As they left Hervás, there was a sign that read, **"Madrid 191 miles."**[17]

---

[17] See map 2.

7. THE CAPITAL

Madrid has three graces,
Along with a fierce loyalty,
Heart, thankfulness
And pride in its hospitality[18]

It was five o'clock in the afternoon, one December day in 1923, when *El Lusitania* arrived at Estación de Delicias in Madrid. Caught up in the moment, the three women (Felisa, Trinidad and Teresa) looked through the small window astounded to see such a big station. There was a glass and wrought-iron roof, and it was so different from the station they had left in Hervás. Pressed up against the window, as the train slowed, the two sisters and their aunt searched the crowd for a familiar face. People seemed different here: the men wore black toppers and the women wore colourful hats. It seemed to Trinidad that she was looking at one of those postcards the rich people in town sent to their relatives; the ones they sent when they had been on holidays to cities and met people from far-flung places that Trinidad had never seen in real life.

The third-class carriages were at the rear of the train. The sisters didn't know where to turn their attention, given that the platform was so long and full of people. It was pure coincidence when Felisa glimpsed a small figure in a grey cotton suit and a matching hat. He was a short man with a moustache, and he was waving at them. He smiled at them as though he had recognised them. By his side, there

---

[18] Ángel J Olivares, Historias del Antiguo Madrid [Stories of Old Madrid], La Librería, page 321 [translated from Spanish by Holly Davies].

was also a girl of around eleven years old, that nobody recognised. The man took off his hat and then Felisa recognised him as Demetrio; María's future husband. She said to her nieces, "Oh look it's Demetrio!" and she shouted to him, waving her hands, "Demetrio, Demetrio!"

They got off the train and hugged Demetrio and the girl, Paquita; Demetrio's daughter from his first wife. At a slow pace, because the crowd took up the entire platform, they filed towards the exit with the rest of the passengers. The noise of voices joined with the horns of *simones* (taxis) and the porters shouting as they passed, "Careful, careful, let me through, let me through. Ladies and gentlemen I have a full load, mind out!" while passers-by parted to make way for them. Trinidad looked at all the people moving forward, lost in thought and looking slightly dazed. When they made it outside Demetrio looked up at the overcast sky and said, "We're not going far, but we should get a move on - it looks like it's going to rain," They started walking, and while Teresa and Felisa started a conversation with Demetrio, Paquita asked Trinidad:

"Is this the first time you've been to Madrid?"

"Yes," replied Trinidad.

"It's really pretty, you'll like it, you'll see," Paquita reassured her new friend.

"You think? I'm a bit frightened, it's all so big and so different here."

"No, don't you believe it, my area is tiny and everything's really close by."

"But I don't think I'll be living in your area," Trinidad said with a frown.

"Aren't you going to live with us?"

"No, I'm going to a place called Calle de Bordadores."[19]

"And where's that?"

"I don't know, they've told me it's near the Puerta del Sol."

"Oh, yes that area is very big and there are lots of people; it's near the Palace, where the King lives."

"Where's that?"

"It's in the centre of town, I'm sure my father will know," Paquita said and called out to her father. "Dad, where's Calle de Bordadores?"

Demetrio looked at his daughter, a little surprised by the question, and said to Trinidad that she wasn't to worry about finding all of that out, as her sister María had everything arranged for the next day.

The morning was grey and the sky was leaden, it looked as though it might snow. Trinidad didn't have a clock so she didn't know what time it was; only that she was awake and it was early. She hadn't slept well the night before, due to a mixture of excitement from the journey, nerves at starting a new job in the capital where she didn't know anybody, and a dry cold in the air that she wasn't accustomed to. She mulled over the advice that her mother had given her before she left Hervás, "My daughter, you must be on your best behaviour and think of us. Always be polite, honest and honourable,

---

[19] **See map 4.**

and always do what they tell you. Things will be difficult at the beginning, but it will all work out well, you'll see, because your older sisters will help you."

In spite of her mother's advice, Trinidad was scared to leave her sisters and be left alone in a house where she didn't know anybody. Of course, the people she was going to work for were nice people that her parents knew, but she just wasn't sure. She had never left the countryside before and now the big city scared her.

Nevertheless, the interview with her new mistress that morning went well, which went some way to soothe her nerves. Doña Luisa explained the jobs that were to be done. In the mornings, she would have to take care of dressing and giving breakfast to the two children: Luisito and Jorge. Jorge was the oldest, he was five years old and he very much liked making mischief. Luisito was two years younger, a lot quieter, and a little bit lazy; it was hard to get him out of bed in the mornings. Sometimes Luisito let himself be led by his brother and between the two of them they could cause quite a rumpus at any given moment.

In the afternoons, she was to take them out to play in the Parque del Retiro or the Palacio Real gardens[20], which were close to where they lived. As well as looking after the children, Trinidad was to lend Fernanda, the maid, a hand with the household chores. She was from Galicia, middle aged with a weak constitution and easily prone to fits of exhaustion. That bit she didn't hear from Doña Luisa, but she worked it out for herself later on.

---

[20] See map 4.

The first day that she took the boys out for a walk, Jorge let go of her hand and went running off to cross the road. Trinidad shouted at the boy and a passer-by, realising what was happening, grabbed Jorge before he could cross the road which was at that moment full of cars. After that scare, Trinidad was more careful.

That same morning, doña Luisa asked her if she liked to eat squid in ink. She didn't know what that was, but remembering her mother's advice about not causing a fuss, she said yes. Later she realised that she didn't like it and so went hungry as there was nothing else to eat.

Going out in the streets right in the centre of Madrid scared her. Calle de Bordadores was located between Arenal and Mayor[21]; two of the biggest roads in the old town. The three-storey houses were beautifully built, with wide doorways and light internal courtyards. The street was short and narrow, with shops down both sides. All of the neighbours knew each other. To begin with, they stared at her and the young men shouted compliments like, "Hey girl, look at how well you move; you rotate better than the earth." Another one said to her, "Miss, if beauty was taxed your parents would be ruined." She turned red and ran to the safety of the doorway.

The noise of the cars flustered her. Often she looked the wrong way when she crossed the road. Doña Luisa had explained how she should get to the park with the children, but sometimes she still got lost and ended up having to ask someone the way back.

Getting on the Metro frightened her at first. Her small-town

---

[21] See map 4.

mind marvelled at the invention, how was it that a train could possibly go underground! However, she soon got used to it and she loved taking the Metro to go and see her sister on the days that she had off. For twenty cents she could get on at Sol station and get off at Pacífico,[22] and it only took 5 minutes.

The physical work was often exhausting. One of the chores that doña Luisa had given her was to help Fernanda polish the wooden floor in the apartment. The two of them had to do this with a chammy leather and a hard wax that was very difficult to apply. After hours spent polishing with their hands and their feet, doña Luisa came to inspect it and she would scold them if the floors didn't shine. Years later, Trinidad complained, *'They certainly took advantage of me in that house."*

---

[22] See map 4.

8. MARÍA'S WEDDING

María and Demetrio's wedding was held on 29th December 1923, in the San Antonio de la Florida chapel[23], which is now a church. The chapel had always been very popular with brides because, according to tradition, young girls of marriageable age would go to the chapel with thirteen pins[24] in their hand, placing their palm into the basin of holy water, only to then remove it and see how many pins remained, which would tell them how many boyfriends they would have that year. It was rumoured within the family, although Trinidad could never confirm it, that María was a regular at that place and she used to go there every year to ask the saints for a suitor. True or not, María had dreamt of getting married in San Antonio de la Florida and she did.

Following their older sister's instructions, Trinidad and Teresa boarded the tram for the first time. At Puerta del Sol they took the number 8 and they got off at 'La Bombi'[25] which was right outside the chapel. It was a cold day and the Manzanares River was covered with a dense fog that looked as though it wouldn't lift all day. Of the two of them, Teresa felt the cold the most; so she drew her Hervás wool shawl tight around her to keep out the chilly breeze that was coming across the river. The two of them started off on the short walk to the chapel, taking care not to get mud on their clean shoes.

---

[23] See map 7.
[24] Echoing the tradition of the wedding coins (thirteen coins which are exchanged by the bride and groom during a wedding ceremony).
[25] A neighourhood in La Bombilla or 'the lightbulb', so called because it was at the end of the tram line and the tracks went back on themselves to change direction, forming a sort of lightbulb shape in the line.

All along the Florida path, long lines of tall and ancient arbutus trees spread out before them.

The two sisters went into the lit chapel. They walked towards the front left row of pews and sat themselves behind the bride and aunt Felisa, who was the maid-of-honour. María was dressed in black tulle, enhancing her height. The delicate comb placed in her hair, a long lace shawl and black gloves gave her outfit an elegant touch. Demetrio was wearing a dark grey suit, with a matching tie and a white shirt. His full, black moustache stood out against his tanned complexion. Paquita was the bridesmaid.

***

After María's wedding and during their first few months in Madrid, Teresa's help was crucial for Trinidad. In those moments of weakness that she had, when she missed her parents and she sobbed to see Hervás again, Teresa was there to console her. She gave Trinidad the strength to go on.

Just like her sisters, Teresa had that certain family look. She had black hair and eyes; a penetrating gaze; full lips that transformed into a sweet and attractive smile. Teresa had inherited her strong will and generosity from her mother, and she too had a huge willingness to love and defend her family. From her father she had inherited his forceful character. Teresa didn't let anyone encroach on her territory. Just like the rest of her brothers and sisters, Teresa hadn't been to school but she had great problem-solving skills. On one particular day, when Trinidad was having a hard time because she couldn't get Jorge to behave and she didn't know what to do, Teresa taught her some games that she knew for five-year-olds and Trinidad tried them on Jorge with great effect. Teresa was also working as a nanny on Calle del Arenal, really close to Calle de Bordadores, which meant the sisters saw each other almost every day and shared all their experiences and problems.

The two sisters had arrived in a Madrid that was going through huge upheavals. Two years before their arrival, the city had seen the assassination of the President of the Government, Eduardo Dato, at Puerta de Alcalá[26]. After the assassination, the press blamed the Catalan anarchists who were unhappy about the heavy hand the Madrid government had taken against people on strike. The truth was though, that the social and political situation in Spain in 1923 was complex. Spanish colonial politics in Morocco were entering a decisive phase after the Anual Disaster[27] and Alfonso XIII's system of liberal monarchy was at crisis point. People were afraid to go out in the street in case they were mugged and there was even talk of a military coup.

The sisters tried their best to forget the rumours and bad news, distracting themselves with visits to María and her family. They also used to go to the cinema to see Charlie Chaplin films, and others like 'Snow White and the Seven Dwarves'. Or they would take walks in el Parque del Retiro, Recoletos or La Castellana. One of their other favourite things to do was to go window shopping in the centre of

---

[26] See map 4.
[27] Huge defeat for the Spanish military against the riflemen commanded by Abd el-Krim near Anual in Morocco, on 22nd July 1921, which led to Spanish colonial politics being redefined in the Rif War.

town. They spent hours looking in department store shop windows (shops like *Madrid-París, el Bazar X, el Bazar de la Unión, El Águila*). They also peered into shoe shops on Calle Preciados and corsetry shops on Calle Conde de Romanones and Calle Magdalena (places like *Casa Code, la Corsetería Ezarque*).

Trinidad earned 12 pesetas per month; a sum you couldn't buy much with. For example, a pair of shoes cost between 10 and 15 pesetas; a women's jacket suit made by a dressmaker, 35 pesetas; a ticket to see a film, one peseta; and a lipstick, 75 cents.

Madrid's own landscape was also changing at that time. Buildings like the Telefónica[28] or la Casa de la Prensa jutted out into the skyline, over a hundred feet high. The work going on to remodel the Gran Vía and the Ensanche[29] started to change the face of the metropolis. The Metro and numerous tram lines that crossed the city in all directions allowed the people of Madrid to travel for a modest sum; it took them to areas in the newly-forming suburbs, like Tetuán de las Victorias, Cuatro Caminos and Vallecas.

El Parque del Retiro was popular and Trinidad and Teresa used to go there often. They liked to go and watch the skating, which was a fashionable sport back then. It was also rumoured to be a place you could find a suitor. There was a rhyme that went:

If you go to Retiro to have a good time,
Don't go skating in a hurry,
Because it has been said by more than a few
That many a visitor ends up getting married

---

[28] See map 4.
[29] Expansion plan to allow more urban growth in Madrid by neighbourhood and social class.

The best places to find a suitor were fairs and dances. In the local area, there was the Santiago fair (in Plaza de Oriente) and, a bit further away, the El Carmen fair (in the Chamberí area). As for the dances, Teresa and Trinidad had heard people say that in Calle del Barco (to the north of the Gran Vía[30]) there was a dance at The Costanilla, which was a decent one because it had a *bastonero,* or a master of ceremonies, who called the dances and also wasn't afraid to let the boys know if they were going too far with the girls. Trinidad and Teresa liked the idea of going but they had to take care that their mistresses didn't find out, because dances were not well thought of and they could lose their good reputation in an instant.

Another thing they chatted about was the strange way that people from Madrid talked.

"Trini, I don't know if you understand what the people in this town say to you but I find it really difficult. My mistress, who's a marchioness, talks to me in a very posh way and the butler, who's from Madrid, is trying it on with me the whole time," complained Teresa.

"Well, look, it's the same for me," Trinidad assured her. "And, the same happens to Fernanda, who's from Lugo, and she's been in Madrid for twenty years. Yesterday she asked me if I knew what 'tie this fly by its tail for me' meant."

"Ugh, what utter nonsense," responded Teresa, without realising she had just captured the exact meaning of the idiomatic phrase in

---

[30] See map 4.

question, "so what did you say?" she asked.

"That I didn't know anything about the local lingo; what about you, do you know what it means?" Trinidad asked full of curiosity.

"No, but with the amount of flies that there are in Madrid in the summer, it can't be a difficult thing to do," came Teresa's innocent reply.

Trinidad went on, "Fernanda is a bit like a 'stuck record' and makes stupid remarks as if they 'come out of her ears', as Valentín says."

"Who's Valentín?" Teresa demanded to know.

"The fruit seller in the shop below where I live," came Trinidad's reply. "The other day he had an argument with one of his customers and he told her she 'wasn't a proper woman' and told her she was 'older than the monuments'. He's a bit 'loopy'."

"Well girl, it seems to me that you are 'vay advaanced' in learning to talk posh." Teresa joked.

"Right, we'll have to hunt them while they're flying even though we don't know how to trap them (the flies that is)."

9. DOMESTIC SERVICE

Trinidad had been in the capital for three years now and she was starting to feel at home. In that time, she had changed jobs on more than one occasion. The way to find a new job, according to Pilar (who she had worked with in her last house), was to go from shop to shop looking at the wanted adverts. Pilar, who knew how to read, also looked in the newspapers and often found some work ads like these:

'Able girl needed to serve, Montera, 23, 3rd floor'

'Maid needed for everything, 25 pesetas, Victoria, 10, 2nd floor'

'Charming young girl available for everything apart from cooking, Hermosilla 42'

'Wanted: attractive thirty year old maid, bachelor, Preciados 42'

'Presentable young girl seeks gentlemanly protection, Carretas 3'

Trinidad soon learned to tell the serious offers from those that offered that questionable 'something extra' and she would look out for offers that had better pay and were in a good area. She found out about some jobs through other servants; as they knew her they would tip her off if they saw there was a vacancy. And that was how she came to work at a civil servant's house in Calle de San Quintín[31].

The civil servant was called don Luis and he lived with his wife and four daughters. Trinidad started as a servant this time, as she no longer liked working as a nanny. Also, she wanted to start climbing the career ladder in domestic service, where you did everything. She would work 12 hours every day, with one day off every two weeks.

---

[31] **See map 4.**

Her salary was 25 pesetas a month. Once every three months she would count up her savings and send money home to her parents with Demetrio. At that time he was acting as the bank. He often travelled to Hervás using a concessionary ticket[32] since he worked for the railways.

She liked the Palacio area more than being in the Centre. It was the home of high-society, people there had very good manners that she hoped to emulate someday. The house where she served seemed a palace to her. The red granite building was well-built and had four floors; their floor had five exterior balconies overlooking the Plaza de Oriente, next to the Palacio Real[33]. When she opened the balcony doors in the mornings, she could see passers-by walking through the gardens and queuing in front of the Royal Opera House to reserve their seats. In the afternoons, she would take don Luis's young daughters down to the square to enjoy the sun, while Trinidad talked with the other servant girls. She loved to sit on one of the benches near the central fountain and listen to the sound of running water, it was like music to her. She thought it a very romantic place.

She served with don Luis and his family for two years. After that she had two more jobs; one on Calle Campomanes and the other on the Cuesta de Santo Domingo, both in the same area. Throughout all of this, Teresa had been working in an army general's house on Calle Monteleón (next to Plaza de San Bernardo). The two sisters continued to see each other as usual and they visited María who now

---

[32] A ticket issued by the rail companies to their employees allowing them to travel for free.
[33] See map 4.

had two sons: Demetrio (born in 1924) and Francisco (born in 1926).

In 1927, her new friend Alejandra, who she had worked with in another house and with whom she had become good pals, told her that she had seen there was a vacancy on Calle Arrieta[34] nearby. Trinidad went along and, as she had such good references from previous colleagues, she got the job.

The position was second maid in a house where, apart from her, there was one other servant, a nanny and a cook. Don Saturnino (the master) was an admiral and he lived with his wife doña Luisa and their daughter Carmen, who was seven. Don Saturnino had an assistant called Felipe who would visit the house frequently for work matters. Felipe was doing his military service in the Ministry of the Navy and he hoped to complete his architecture degree when he finished his service. He was a nice, clever boy and he had the gift of the gab.

One afternoon, while Trinidad was with Carmen enjoying her favourite spot next to the fountain, she saw Felipe appear.

"What does the water in this fountain have that it can attract the most beautiful rose in this garden?" he said to Trinidad.

"Hi Felipe, I didn't see you there," said Trinidad, pretending that she hadn't seen him approach. "You gave me quite a fright!"

"Well I saw you," came Felipe's reply. "Ever since I met you, not a day goes by that my heart doesn't ache for you."

"Come on, don't be silly," Trinidad replied disbelievingly. "Tell me what you're up to, how did you know I was here?"

---

[34] **See map 4.**

But Felipe hadn't finished yet, "You are the sun that brightens my morning, the star that guides me by night, the drink that quenches my thirst…"

Trinidad blushed, "Well well, hark at you, you're very romantic today…"

"Do you love me? If you love me, give me a kiss," Felipe said while he moved in closer to Trinidad and tried to kiss her.

Trinidad, remembering what her mother had told her, moved backwards so that the boy couldn't reach her face and she slapped him.

He had been pursuing her for a while, and wanted her to be his. She didn't think it was a bad match but she thought she was still too young to settle down with a partner. What's more, she doubted the boy's true intentions. Right after she slapped him she regretted it, but it was too late to take it back. Felipe didn't forgive her and he never discovered Trinidad's true feelings towards him. The chance of a future romance vanished when Felipe was moved to another post in the Ministry of the Navy.

The following year, Dorotea came to Madrid for the christening of María's first daughter. María had given birth to a girl and she had named her after her. The baptism was on 7th April 1928 and Trinidad was godmother. When Trinidad saw her mother again it gave her the courage to open up about her scuppered romance with Felipe. Dorotea listened to the story and sympathised with Trinidad, telling her that she'd done the right thing by rejecting him so that he didn't take advantage of her. However, she said that at the age of 21

Trinidad wasn't that young anymore and so she could start having a formal relationship with a young man. Before quickly adding the proviso that he must have good intentions and that Trinidad must take care to look after her reputation.

Her conversation with Dorotea made Trinidad think about the best way to get a suitor. The truth is that in her day-to-day life she had very few opportunities to meet a man. She got up at seven in the morning and she never went to bed before eleven at night. No sooner had she woken up than she had to serve breakfast to don Saturnino, who liked to be up early, so that he had time to read his papers and prepare his paperwork before going to the Ministry. At eight o'clock she woke doña Luisa, who would immediately ask for her hot chocolate with pastries. As soon as Trinidad had finished with breakfast, she cleaned the house, scrubbed the floors (at that time this was done with a straw scourer and on your knees), she made the beds and dusted the furniture. The flat had seventeen rooms including the servants' rooms, so Trinidad had to divide up the work carefully, to ensure she had enough time to finish everything. At midday, lunchtime, she would set the table and then collect the dirty plates. In the afternoons, she collected the clothes and ironed them. At five o'clock she put on her afternoon uniform to receive guests, of which there were many. Doña Luisa belonged to a social club and there were meetings at her house on many an afternoon. The mistress and her friends took tea in the afternoons, which Trinidad served them. At night, the master and mistress often had guests; she would serve them dinner, then clear the table and stay around until they dismissed her for the night. Trinidad's work day only came to an end when she received instructions from doña Luisa that she was no longer required. So, some days it was long past midnight when she returned to her bedroom, utterly exhausted.

This daily work routine only varied once every two weeks, on Thursday afternoons, when she had three hours off. Doña Luisa was very demanding and wouldn't stand for Trinidad returning late. What's more, Trinidad knew of friends that had been dismissed for being late. The standards and rules of your masters were to be followed to the letter.

Which is why, in her daily life she only came into contact with the opposite sex on her days off or when she went to the market. In order to attract potential suitors she started to take more care in the way she dressed. The fashion among young people of the well-to-do classes, was to wear your hair short in a boyish style. However, it wasn't very well-regarded for servants to have that style. Dressing outside of her class would be motive enough for doña Luisa to sack her.

Trinidad copied the way Teresa dressed. Short hair, in so far as it was allowed for servants, jacket suit, with a handkerchief in the top pocket, long earrings and light makeup that you would hardly even notice. Proper girls were not allowed to wear lipstick or nail varnish, as only women of loose morals wore those. In summer months, Trinidad swapped suits for silk dresses in colours or florals that were lighter and daintier, and suited her body shape better.

She now earned 40 pesetas a month, but the money in her

savings didn't give her enough to buy many clothes. One day she tried her luck with the lottery and, as she couldn't read, she asked the building's doorman if he could look in the paper to see if she had won anything. A few days went by without hearing from him, before he finally told her that she hadn't won anything. Slightly suspicious, Trinidad asked him to give back the ticket, but he said he'd thrown it away. She stopped playing the lottery after that.

10. STORM CLOUDS

The political situation in Madrid was becoming more violent every day. The streets around the Palacio Real were the battlegrounds of Monarchists and Republicans, workers and bosses, students and policemen. On more than one occasion, Trinidad had been forced to take refuge in a doorway as she witnessed workers pursued by the *Guardia de Asalto*, the blue-uniformed urban police force of the Republic. At moments like that she remembered the story her father had told her when she was little, just after she had seen her first street protest in Hervás. Just as they were back then in her hometown, tensions were running high in Madrid and there seemed to be no willingness to resolve the increasingly politicised labour conflicts.

In view of the overall state of the country, prime minister Primo de Rivera stepped down on 30th January 1930. The King decided that the Head of his Military Chamber, General Berenguer, would become Prime Minister in his place. Wanting to distance himself from the politics of his predecessor, Berenguer established a *dictablanda* or toothless dictatorship (as the press dubbed his government), however his regime didn't last long. Elections were held for the Spanish *Cortes* on 31st January the following year, with the aim of restoring public order. However, the Republicans and the left-wing parties boycotted the elections, leading to Berenguer's resignation on 13th February 1931. He was replaced by Admiral Aznar on 18th February that year, but it was too late to save the monarchy which was already undoubtedly lost. After his 27-year reign, Alfonso XIII found himself to be increasingly isolated and he was without the support that he had once enjoyed from the military, politicians and the people.

The *Alianza Republicana* or Republican Alliance parties won the election that had been held on 12th April and the Second Republic was proclaimed in Spain. The following day, Admiral Aznar said something that would be quoted time and again in subsequent years: "Spain went to bed as a Monarchy and woke up as a Republic". A few days later the King set off on his journey towards the port of Cartagena, and into exile.

Trinidad and Teresa had been talking about the political situation for a while. One day, shortly after the Republic's electoral victory, the two sisters met in el Parque del Retiro and chatted about the subject over a delicious glass of *horchata*, or almond milk.

"In my house everyone's happy that we're a Republic," said Teresa. "I've heard my master, who as you know is a general but of a liberal persuasion, say that this is going to be good for the country."

"I don't know Teresa. In my house the Admiral says the election was rigged and that the Right had just as many votes as the Left."

"Well, of course," responded Teresa. "That's because your master is a monarchist and he doesn't want us poor people to stop being poor."

"I don't think that's it Teresa," Trinidad replied thoughtfully. "I think that under Primo de Rivera people had a better quality of life, at least there was order on the streets."

"Yeah, see and what good did it do us? We're worse off than before," said Teresa.

"Listen my love, I don't understand much about politics," said Trinidad, "but what I do know is that it's not safe to go out in the streets now. Last Monday the bakers were on strike, on Tuesday there was a transport strike and yesterday all the students were going around all worked up, singing that French revolutionary song."

"The Marseillaise?" asked Teresa.

"Yeah, that's the one. Well whatever," Trinidad sighed. "I think it's a shame the King has gone, you know."

"Look, the King didn't leave," Teresa said testily. "Haven't you heard people singing that song? 'The King went on his way, when we told him he couldn't stay'!"

"Poor him. Alejandra told me that he left because he was scared he and his family would be killed, you know, like what happened in Russia."

"Never mind Trini, be realistic. The King is on the side of the rich, that's why he supported Primo de Rivera's coup. So be it, let him hit the 'rue' and leave us in peace."

Trinidad thought about it and said "I agree with my Master. It's the politicians that are the problem. They're always on the radio giving speeches and inciting the 'rabble', so of course people are going to get all worked up."

"Well I've heard that the problem is the Church siding with the bourgeoisie, and not wanting poor people to learn to read or write, just so they don't make trouble."

"Well that's not true, because don Tomás, the parish priest of the church where I go, told me where I can go to learn to do sums."

Trinidad said shyly.

Teresa was surprised, "Really? I didn't know you were thinking of going to school."

"Well, I can't go now," Trinidad said quietly. "Doña Luisa won't let me. She says it won't do me any good; that I already know enough".

"Just what I was saying to you - us poor people aren't going to get out of poverty until some of us are actually in charge." Teresa went on passionately.

"Well, we'll see what happens, obviously the situation's at boiling point."

"Ok darling, see you tomorrow, and take care – don't catch that flu that's doing the rounds."

"Same to you. Cheerio."

***

It was a sizzling morning on 11th May 1931. The nanny had been taken ill and Trinidad had to take Carmencita to school, something she'd done once before. As they walked down Calle Bailén[35], they saw people leaning out of their terraces and balconies. It seemed as though something was happening. When they reached the edge of the Plaza de España they saw a cloud of smoke rising into the blue morning sky.

At the other end of the square, on the corner of Príncipe Pío (or Ferraz as it's known today) a building was on fire. Trinidad squeezed Carmencita's hand tightly as she noticed the place on fire was the

---

[35] **See map 4.**

Padres Carmelitas Convent. She knew it well as she sometimes went there to listen to mass. As they got closer they saw a hoard of people were also headed for the same place.

The flames had shattered some of the building's windows. Noises could be heard from the inside; bangs alongside small muffled explosions, and the crash of heavy objects, as though they were falling from a great height. The heat of the fire, not to mention of the sun and the crowd of spectators all gathered in one place, made Trinidad keep her distance. She saw her own feelings of astonishment mirrored on Carmencita's face. With eyes open wide the little girl looked at everything incredulously, as though she were not in fact an onlooker witnessing such a momentous event, but merely a child reading a fantasy story in a comic book.

People from all walks of life were flooding into the Plaza de España[36] to see what was happening. There were street vendors, doubtless hoping to make a killing from the bystanders. There were also policemen, housewives, business workers, rag and bone men, women and children all rubbing shoulders in a tide of people that was growing by the minute. One man was telling anybody who would listen that the fire had been the work of some shirtless hoodlums. He said he had seen them enter the holy building by the back door, armed with blocks of wood that they had found in the construction sites on Gran Vía. They had an oil drum with them which they used to set the chairs and pews of the church alight, starting the fire.

One street vendor was selling churros and donuts; another, ice

---

[36] See map 4.

lollies and ice creams; a third had shoelaces for sale and was offering three shirts for a peseta. Some of the onlookers bought a churro; a little boy looked up at his mother beseechingly "Mummy, will you buy me an ice cream? It's really hot." A young bank employee leant against the wall and polished his shoes while he watched the fire. The odd remark could be heard from the crowd:

"Down with the priests!" shouted one of the onlookers.

"No sir, that's not right, it's not their fault," came the response from a woman with a prayer book in her hand.

"Well, actually ma'am it is, this country is free - finally! And we don't want them telling us what to do anymore. And after what the Cardinal[37] said last Sunday, they deserve it!"

"Goodness gracious, what a tragedy," muttered the religious woman.

"Come on now, out of the way, let the firemen through", shouted one of the policemen; his gruff voice booming as he used his arms to force open a path through the crowd.

Trinidad headed away from the scene filled with a sense of panic, and more anxious than ever to reach the school. As they made their way there, they heard snippets of conversations on the streets saying that other churches and convents were burning too. Trinidad lifted her head and saw it was true, black smoke was rising from several buildings in Madrid's skyline. The smell of burnt wood hung in the air. Trinidad took a handkerchief out of her dress and used it

---

[37] Reference to a pastoral letter written by Cardinal Primate Pedro Segura on 1st May 1931. The Republican press and left-wing parties interpreted this missive as a declaration of war on the Republic.

to cover Carmencita's mouth so she wouldn't breathe in that awful smell. She started to walk faster. Thinking back to the conversation she had had with Teresa only a few days before, Trinidad crossed herself. If this was the beginning of the Republic there were bad times ahead.

***

Two years had passed since the churches had been burnt down, and Trinidad decided to change jobs again. This time she started as a cook on Calle de Castelló in the Salamanca neighbourhood[38]. Don Carlos lived on the main floor, whilst his brother don Fernando had the second. Don Carlos was a bachelor and don Fernando was about to get married.

When Trinidad started in her new post don Carlos was thirty. He was a tall man of stocky build, with a pleasant face and of a calm nature. Although he was a native of the Toledo province, he had grown up in Madrid and was an engineer by trade. His late father had been a lawyer and his mother had come from nobility. Don Carlos was very religious; every day before going to work he would pray in the chapel he had in his house.

Like his brother, don Fernando had also been born in the province of Toledo[39]. From a young age he found he was drawn to the military and after graduating from the Infantry Corps of the Toledo Military Academy in 1912 he served the King at several points along the Iberian Peninsula, as well as in Africa. He had received the Military Service Cross (with red badge distinction) for

---

[38] See map 5.
[39] See map 7.

his services at Ceuta and Tetuán. At the age of 33 he was promoted to the rank of Chief Commander, but was then assigned to the Reserves for health reasons the following year. There was talk that this move hadn't really been down to his health, which was in fact good, but was instead the result of military reform brought in by the new Republican government.

In don Carlos's and don Fernando's homes the staff was made up of Trinidad who was the cook, Alejandra who was a maid and Emilia who was housemaid. There were more than 23 rooms spread over the two floors and these needed to be seen to and cleaned every day.

As part of her new role, Trinidad would go out each day to do the shopping in Torrijos market on Calle de Hermosilla[40]. The first thing she had to do was order the milk for the following day; the milkman would then deliver it directly to the house. After that she went down Príncipe de Vergara, which in those days was a promenade with trees, benches and an array of shops.

On her morning walk she would take in the world around her: the nannies passing the time swapping gossip and romantic tales, while also keeping an eye on the children in their care as they played; the housewives who stopped to chew the fat with their neighbours, analysing events and news of the previous day; the shopkeepers complaining about price rises from their suppliers.

She turned right where the road met Hermosilla and headed for the market, which at that time of day was crammed as usual. The din

---

[40] See map 5.

was deafening: the continuous hollers of shopkeepers calling out their wares; the remarks from the, mainly female, customers on the price and quality of the goods and their arguments about who was first in the queue; the loud voices and booming sounds from the stream of people and shopping-carts, all came together in a jumble of echoes making it practically impossible to hear anything. However, Trinidad was used to this cacophony. She visited all her usual stalls and bought the items she needed. By now she was well-known to the stall-holders. At first when she was still a new face they hadn't given her a good price, but she bought so much and came to the market so often that she soon became one of their best clients. Juanito, the greengrocer, saved his best pears and grapes for her, since those were her employers' favourite fruits. Pedro, the fishmonger, had always been courteous and attentive to her since the very first day. Cod *al ajoarriero* was one of don Carlos' favourite dishes, Trinidad would often cook it for them on a Thursday. Pedro knew this and so he would keep back the best pieces of cod for her on that day.

Each time Trinidad went out shopping she would wonder at the streets in the Salamanca neighbourhood. Their modern straight design, which stretched out into the distance as far as the eye could see, meant that cars travelled along them at great speed. The wide, well-kept pavements made for a pleasant walk at any time of the day. The trees gave some shade in the hottest times, although the tall buildings in the area meant that there was always shade on one side of the street or other.

Most of the stately houses were actual palaces built at the end of the previous century. The entrance halls were wide and luxurious; they had marble staircases and huge mirrors. Each time she walked into the entrance hall of the house where she worked Trinidad stared in wonder at the main lift. It was only for her employers and their guests but she was fascinated by how it worked; just one more of those modern inventions that she so loved. In the mornings, when she came down early, it stood waiting on the ground floor; she wondered if she would ever be able to ride in it. While the doorman was away from his usual post on cleaning errands, she would take advantage of her solitude to examine the lift at length: the wrought-iron outer doors featured elegant designs and made a metallic sound on opening and closing; the inner doors were made of glass and they gleamed when the light was turned on. As she stepped into the lift car she breathed in the fragrant air, like in the cinemas on Gran Vía that she loved to visit. Mirrors hung on the side walls seemingly expanding the space within, although this was only an optical illusion. The buttons that took you up and down were black with a white surround, one click and you were taken to any of the property's five floors. In many buildings of the era, those not as grand as this one, the lifts could only be used to travel up. The lift seemed to Trinidad like a portal that transported her to a fantasy world, just like the cinema. It was a world where money, power and beauty were all interlinked. Trinidad dreamt of one day becoming part of that world, but all the while she knew that could never happen because of her social standing. That was when she remembered the gap between the rich and the poor in her village.

Trinidad finished her daily rounds with a walk up one of the biggest roads in the area; Calle Goya.[41] By chance, one morning she walked into a new butchers that had opened and she met Juan, one of the shop assistants. As they chatted she found out he was also from Hervás. Juan immediately took an interest in her and invited her to the dance. She said yes, and they went out a few times but she soon lost interest and eventually stopped accepting his invitations. When Alejandra asked her why she was no longer going out with him, Trinidad replied: "I just don't like him…and he smells like a butcher".

***

It was June and Madrid was getting hot. People were starting to leave the city to go on holiday. Trinidad had been gathering provisions for a few weeks as don Carlos had told her that things were deteriorating and war could break out at any moment. The sad reality was that it wasn't safe to go out on the streets anymore. Food had to be ordered by telephone and brought to your house. However, now the shopkeepers had begun warning her that some foodstuffs were already running out. The government-controlled media constantly repeated the message that there was no need to panic, that there were plenty of goods in the markets as usual. The reality was starkly different for Trinidad though, and she often asked herself if these reporters were actually living in the same country as her.

After lunch one afternoon, the three servant girls gathered in the

---

[41] See map 5.

kitchen to catch up on recent events. Alejandra, stood leaning against a cupboard looking over at Trinidad and Emilia, who were sat next to each other on two chairs in the middle of the room.

"There's no way out of this. Things are getting worse and worse," Alejandra started off.

"You're right. Who knows where this will end. We can't leave the flat or go out on the streets, we're like prisoners," Trinidad responded.

"Well, that's your choice you know you two. Me - I come and go and as I please," Emilia added.

"Well of course you do, you're in your element. Just look at the way your lot are now, it's ridiculous!" responded Trinidad.

"No Trini, it's just that I don't listen to the bosses when they talk among themselves about what a bad state the country's in," came Emilia's reply.

"What are you talking about?" said Trinidad, "when I come into the room to get anything they all hush up so I don't hear what they're saying. I mean, the other day doña Concepción started talking to don Fernando in French as soon as she saw me come into the room."

"Of course they did, it's like they don't trust us," responded Emilia.

"Well, most of all they don't trust you, Emilia!" blurted out Alejandra. "And they don't even know about your boyfriend."

"What's wrong with my boyfriend?" Emilia asked.

"Nothing love, don't worry," reassured Alejandra. "He's a good guy, but him being secret police - it frightens people."

"Don't talk rubbish, Alejandra, my Luis is as good as gold," exclaimed Emilia.

Trinidad said pensively "I think since Primo de Rivera went we haven't been able to relax."

"You're right Trini, since then things have gone from bad to worse. First there was Castilblanco,[42] then the Casas Viejas massacre[43] and in '34 the Asturian miners' strike[44] which was a hair's breadth from unleashing chaos."

"Wow, you're so well-informed, Alejandra. And to think you don't even know how to read," Emilia wondered, giving her friend a warm smile.

"Well, a girl has her sources. You didn't think you were going to be the only one in-the-know did you, just because you can read the papers?" came Alejandra's quick reply.

"Talking of papers," continued Emilia. "I read in *El Heraldo de Madrid* that fifty-five percent of the land in Don Benito, Extremadura is owned by just eight landholders, and the rest is owned by more than four thousand people."

"Well, it's not like that in Hervás," said Trinidad, "of course there are some, but the land is more shared out."

---

[42] Conflict between local people in this area and the police force or *Guardia Civil* on 31st December 1931 during which four police officers were lynched.
[43] Events in the Casas Viejas neighbourhood in the province of Cádiz on 10th January 1933 during which members of the CNT, or National Confederation of Labour, were killed by police officers.
[44] Workers' uprising organised by the UGT (General Union of Workers), PSOE (Spanish Socialist Workers Party) and CNT (National Confederation of Labour) against the Gil Robles government of October 1934. The insurrection, also known as the revolution of October 1934, was dealt with severely by General Franco. At the final count there were 1,335 dead and 2,951 injured.

"I'll carry on shall I," said Emilia with a flourish. "It's even worse in Jerez de los Caballeros in Badajoz.[45] Ninety-two percent of the land there is in the hands of only ninety men. What do you think of that?"

"Well, where I'm from in La Mancha," interjected Alejandra, "there are hardly any landholders either, and if you don't believe me ask don Carlos' family."

"And to finish off, listen to this. On page 11 they printed a list of the largest estates.[46]

Duke of Medinaceli 195,633 acres.

Duke of Peñaranda 129,058 acres.

Duke of Alba 89,630 acres.

Marquis of Comilla…"

Alejandra jumped in here, "Well whatever love, that's your lot's fault. Didn't they say they were going to bring about 'Land Reform' and all that?"

"No, Alejandra, it wasn't our people's fault, it was the right-wing government's," countered Emilia. "Ever since Azaña left, they blocked everything we had suggested."[47]

"And that's why I don't want to hear any talk of political parties," Trinidad interrupted. "I've already lost count of how many Presidents we've had since the Republic fell."

"Well, it's at least eight or more," Alejandra said sagely.

---

[45] See map 3.
[46] List published in the press in 1936.
[47] Reference to the fact that 'land reform' which was voted in during the first Republican term (Azaña's government of 1931-1933) was dismantled during the second term (governments of Lerroux and others 1933-1936).

"Let's see," said Emilia, counting them off on her fingers "Niceto Alcalá Zamora, Azaña, Lerroux, Ricardo Samper, Lerroux (again!), Azaña (again!)… yes, that's at least six, maybe more."

"Well, however many there are, all I know is that there are more strikes each day, more people out of work, prices go up and the country is ready to explode at any moment," said Trinidad.

"Whoa, Trini, you're such a pessimist!" said Emilia.

"No, I agree with Trini," said Alejandra. "You just have to look at what's happening in the streets. You can't go out, there are guns going off everywhere, murders and if things go on like this anything could happen."

"I mean, look at the number of unemployed people there are everywhere," Trinidad went on. "A friend of mine who just got married, her husband is a builder and he's been out of work for six months. They're desperate - thankfully her boss let her carry on working after she got married, if not they wouldn't even have food on the table."

"Well, I have friends who are out of work too, Trini," said Emilia. "That's the bosses' fault, ever since the CEDA[48] joined the previous government, they've refused to negotiate with the unions."

"The most important thing for me Emilia, is that nobody's controlling the damn country, I mean, just who's in control?" snapped Alejandra.

---

[48] Reference to the period from October 1934 to September 1935 during which four members of the CEDA (Spanish Confederation of Autonomous Right-wing Groups) formed part of Lerroux's government, including CEDA's leader Gil Robles.

"Of course, people are saying that the military will stage a coup any minute now. That's why the bosses have asked us to start gathering provisions, because of what might happen," Trinidad interjected.

"Yes, well everybody is doing just that," Alejandra pronounced knowingly, "that's why all the shops are empty".

"That's why workers should support the *Frente Popular* or People's Front. The time has come for a revolution. It's them or us! Come on girls, let's go to the Puerta del Sol!"

"Come on now, hush up! I wouldn't go to the Puerta del Sol even if they gave me a box at the Royal" said Alejandra. She loved the opera but had never been to the Royal Theatre.

At that moment one of the service bells in the kitchen started to ring. The three of them realised that it was coming from the dining room.

"That'll be doña Concepción ringing for someone to bring up her five o'clock tea," said Trinidad.

"Will you look at that, the country is on the verge of collapse and the only thing on that woman's mind is her tea" blurted out Emilia.

"Get real, Emilia. There are always going to be poor people and rich people. No revolution is ever going to change that," Alejandra said emphatically.

"Well, we'll see. It wouldn't surprise me with people like you two around. I, on the other hand, don't plan on being a maid all my life."

"Well, go right ahead. Man proposes but God disposes,"

Alejandra blurted out.

"Don't you go mentioning me to God and the Saints, that's all we need."

"Come on girls, finish up the chat for now - the time for daydreaming is over, it's back to real life. I've got to take doña Concepción her tea before she starts to get annoyed. So come on, let's get to work!" said Trinidad, as she got up and headed towards the sitting room where doña Concepción was waiting for her.

***

Some days later, Trinidad heard reports on the radio that soldiers had risen up against the Republic's government. A number of politicians[49] had been killed in a wave of attacks, triggering a military uprising led by General Franco on the 18th July 1936. It wasn't unexpected, and the news didn't spread panic among the people of Madrid. Like most people, Trinidad didn't expect the uprising to last long; all the others had ended after a couple of days, and with that thought in her head she went to bed.

It was hot when dawn broke on 22nd July. The sun burned through the gaps in the blinds and the temperature had already reached nearly thirty degrees. Trinidad had been awake for a while; she took a small handkerchief out of her bedside table and dabbed at the sweat that trickled down her face. She looked at her alarm clock and turned it off before the bell went. It was about to turn seven

---

[49] On 12th July 1936 Police Lieutenant José Castillo was killed by a Falangist cell. In revenge for this attack, conservative representative José Calvo Sotelo was gunned down by a member of the Assault Guard or *Guardia de Asalto*. According to historians these two murders were the catalyst for the Spanish Civil War.

o'clock and so she got up and dressed quickly, as usual. Don Carlos was an early bird, and he liked to have his breakfast at half past seven; but he didn't like to be kept waiting.

She was making coffee in the kitchen when Alejandra walked in complaining that she hadn't slept the night before because of the heat. In the early hours of the morning she thought she had heard whispered voices but then it all fell quiet. Trinidad asked Alejandra if she had seen or heard anything from don Carlos, to which she replied that she hadn't. That wasn't normal. Neither was it normal for doña Concepción not to have rung for her coffee, as was her usual way; she was always so meticulous and timely with her habits.

The kitchen clock had just struck half past seven. Trinidad headed towards the dining room with a breakfast tray for don Carlos and coffee for doña Concepción. Within a few minutes she hastily returned and, with a look of surprise on her face, told Alejandra that the bosses weren't in their lodgings. They looked at one another and then went up to see if Emilia, who lived on the floor above, had seen them that morning. Emilia confirmed that she had seen neither hide nor hair of any of them.

They went down to ask the doorman if he had seen anything, but they couldn't find him either. When they went back up they rang on 2B's doorbell – their next door neighbours. The housemaid opened the door to them with frightened eyes, then immediately broke down in tears.

"What happened?" asked Alejandra.

"Last night the *Checas*[50] came - they took my employers and the doorman away," answered the girl from next door.

[50] A *checa* or *cheka* was a soviet institution created as an instrument of terror. During the Spanish Civil War they used Republican militiamen to arrest, interrogate and summarily try and execute those suspected of sympathising with the other side. In general the *checas* were given the name of the street where they were located or the name of their leader.

11. MILITARY REVOLT

War is too important to be left to the generals.[51]

George Clemenceau

Getafe, 20th July 1936

Dawn was breaking over the Toledo countryside. It was going to be a hot day, typical of the end of July. The city seemed to be sleeping, although there was an electric quality to the air; and a strange, almost surreal, calm.

Like most of his neighbours in Getafe[52], Nicasio had not slept the night before. The military uprising against the government of the Republic had forced the mainly working population into a state of war. Nicasio was worked up about the mission that had been entrusted to him. The moment he had spent so long waiting for had finally come. It was time to put his political ideals to work, for the good of the people.

Troops loyal to the government along with a group of civilians, including Nicasio, were positioned outside the barracks- armed and ready for the attack. Nicasio was proud to belong to this group of young socialists and communists. Like their comrades in arms *La Guardia de Asalto* and the militia, they were all willing to give their lives if necessary for a cause they blindly believed in.

---

[51] https://en.wikiquote.org/wiki/Georges_Clemenceau.
[52] See map 7.

The fascist rebels were billeted in the artillery barracks awaiting orders to go out on to the streets and join the military coup. All forces loyal to the government had issued an ultimatum and the deadline for the rebels to surrender themselves had now passed. The tension was evident in the faces of those awaiting the attack. Among the rebels other battles were raging in the subconscious of some soldiers, should they follow their superiors' orders, or remain loyal to the ideals of their class.

At four in the morning, when dawn was about to break, a squadron of airplanes appeared in the sky having taken off from the nearby airfield; the air force and *La Guardia de Asalto* had remained loyal to the government. The airplanes neared the barracks and suddenly started to drop bombs on the rebels. Caught by surprise, the rebels moved their artillery pieces and trained them to the skies above, trying to follow the paths of the planes.

Inside the barracks, the officers barked orders at their soldiers. The soldiers meanwhile looked up to the sky and ran scared trying to hide from the bombs that were falling. The projectiles didn't have enough precision to hit the munitions dump and the fuel depots as they had only been launched by hand, however they did cause fear and losses among the rebels.

Outside, the forces loyal to the government were preparing for an attack. No sooner had the bombardment finished than the officer who led the attack unit, approached the entrance to the barracks and demanded that the rebels surrender. This request was met by a shot at close range which knocked the officer to the ground. At that moment, upon a pistol signal, the soldiers outside and the machine gunners in the watchtowers opened fire on those inside.

When Nicasio saw one of his own men fall, he pulled down on the trigger of his rifle filled with a white-hot rage, joining the tirade of his comrades. It was the first time he had used a weapon for real and it gave him a strange feeling. He was filled with a disconcerting mix of fear and excitement, and he couldn't tell which was stronger.

In a matter of seconds the sky was ablaze with the lightning flashes of machine gun fire and the bright explosions of cannons. The noise was deafening: bullets whistled by in every direction, flying over the attackers' heads and landing in the walls of nearby buildings; Republican machine gun fire rained down on enemy positions from at least three hundred feet; the screams of their comrades "Fascists! Bastards! Long live the Republic!" all jumbled together with the cries of the wounded and fallen.

For the first time in his life Nicasio felt an unfamiliar fear. His heart was racing and it felt as though hundreds of tiny butterflies were darting around his stomach. In one particular moment, he feared he might die and instinctively thought of his family. However the moment soon passed and the clamour of battle brought him out of his reverie. With great effort he regained control of his movements and fired his rifle in the direction of the enemy. All the while, thoughts of his revolutionary ideals gave him the courage to overcome any fears.

The battle didn't last long. The rebels came to the conclusion that it was impossible for them to defend their position. The threat of enemy air power together with the greater numbers in the government forces, the desertion of some soldiers under siege that had been loyal to the Republic, as well as the prolonged gunfire from the machine gunners, soon led the rebels to surrender.

Nicasio went from feeling utter terror to absolute euphoria. He was so happy he could burst; they had defeated the fascist forces. He didn't think that any of the small number of bullets that he had actually managed to fire correctly had hit the enemy target; after all his army training had been very limited. However, the battle allowed him to try the art of war on for size. As he would say years later, "Getafe was literally my baptism of fire."

12. MADRID RESISTS

Madrid, Spain's Heart
Beats feverishly.
If yesterday its blood was simmering
Today with more heat it boils

Rafael Alberti [53]

After talking to the servant from the second floor, Alejandra and Trinidad trudged back up to their floor with a sinking feeling in their hearts. How could their bosses have just disappeared without leaving any trace, and without saying anything? Emilia, being the most daring of the three, said she would ask her boyfriend if he knew anything about it. Luis was a communist and he was also rumoured to be part of the *Checa* in Lista.[54] [55] The servant from upstairs had told them which police station their bosses and the doorman had been taken to; however they wanted to wait for the results of Luis's investigation before making their way over there.

By the following day, any fears that their bosses might have been 'disappeared' were calmed somewhat. The previous night, guys from the *Checa* in the Buenavista Police Station[56] came to the door in the early hours asking after the owners of the flat. Petrified, the three

---

[53] Defensa de Madrid, Milicia Popular, Diario del 5º Regimiento. 4 Nov 1936.
[54] *Checa de Lista* was located in the cloistered convent building that was formerly home to the nuns of *Concepción Jerónima,* on the corner of Calle Velázquez.
[55] See map 5.
[56] This *checa* was located in the Salamanca neighbourhood, as was the Calle Castelló house.

servants said that their bosses had disappeared and they had no idea where they were. The young militiaman didn't seem convinced, thinking that the three maids could be hiding their bosses. With this in mind, he said they were to accompany him to the police station to make a statement. Emilia had other ideas however. Being, as she was, an attractive woman and knowing, as she did, how to treat young militiamen, she gave him an alluring smile and convinced him not to take them away.

Some days later, Alejandra decided to go to her hometown to be with her family while she was still able to travel. Trinidad and Emilia stayed where they were. In the morning, as had become their custom, the two girls met in the kitchen to catch up on things. They talked about how they were going to survive this situation which was becoming increasingly difficult and uncertain.

"Have we got many supplies left?" Emilia asked.

"Some," said Trinidad, "don Carlos asked us to stock up quite a bit. And it'll be easier now there are only two of us; but the supplies situation is only going to get worse, and fast".

"Yeah, the mayor keeps on giving out orders that basic necessities shouldn't be hoarded, but there are still queues outside shops from about six in the morning," added Emilia.

"Yup, and there's a big hoo-ha about vouchers. Loads of shops aren't taking them anymore because they say they're fakes," said Trinidad with a resigned sigh.

"It's the same old story, Trini," said Emilia with a world-weary look, "I think it's the shopkeepers who don't want to actually sell their stuff, so that they can hawk them on the black market later and get more money. We should report them!"

"I don't know Emilia, the fact is we've just got to cut back on everything. If we carry on like this, we'll have run out of supplies in a few weeks, tops," said Trinidad. "The other big problem is our wages. That's the main reason Alejandra went back to her hometown. At least there her parents can feed her."

"Yeah, at least I've got Luis to help me out a little for now, but what about you?" said Emilia with a worried glance.

"I've got a few savings but they won't last long to be honest. Anyway, I've always got my sisters," said Trinidad pensively, "but they're worse off than me. María has four mouths to feed after all".

"Well, lady, we'll just have to look after each other," Emilia responded, linking arms with her friend. "And if that doesn't work we'll become militiawomen, then we'll never go without food."

"Yes girl, sign me up now," Trinidad said rolling her eyes, "the stuff you come out with Emilia!"

"Why not though? My cousin Rosa did, she's at the front in Somosierra. From her letters it sounds as though she's doing very well," Emilia carried on.

"Yeah I'll get my gun now, what do you think?" said Trinidad sarcastically.

Emilia saw Trinidad was upset and she gave her a smile. Trinidad had a natural calm about her, and Emilia enjoyed pushing her buttons to see her get worked up. On this occasion however she decided to change tack and steer the conversation to something less contentious.

"Ooh, did I tell you that Luis took me to meet his Mum yesterday, I like her - she seems like a good egg. She and her four sons all belong to the Spanish Communist Party, just the way I like it," Emilia said proudly.

"Well, everyone's either a socialist, a communist or an anarchist nowadays. We live in different times," said Trinidad boldly. "The first question anyone asks is always, what party do you belong to?"

"Well that's how it should be. For us working women, the SCP is the only party that defends our rights. You should join too."

"Not a chance!" said Trinidad. "I don't want anything to do with politics; like my mother says 'a person that gets into politics is like a cat that gets into a chimney; they come out either blackened or burned!'"

The two girls carried on their daily debate like this, without either one claiming victory. They never let their political differences get in the way of their friendship though; they knew that the future was uncertain and one way or another they would need each other's support to survive.

Things had moved quickly in Madrid. The government's initial euphoria after defeating the rebels in the capital had been followed by a slew of Republican defeats. By the end of August, the rebel forces controlled a third of the country.[57] Those in the Republican media gave a favourable account of the war's progression, but most people in Madrid didn't believe a word they said. Instead, they began to tune

---

[57] *Madrid en la Guerra Civil [Madrid in the Civil War], Volume I,* Pedro Montoliú, Silex, 2000, pp. 122-23.

into the forbidden *Radio Burgos* so they could at least get the other side's biased account of the war's development too.

The first few weeks after the rebel uprising had been awful in Madrid. Every suspect and enemy of the Republic was rounded up, resulting in more than sixty-six murders every day.[58] Places like Casa de Campo,[59] the Cementerio del Este, the Pradera de San Isidro and even the Mercado de Legazpi were flooded with people looking for lost relatives. Trinidad prayed not to find her employers listed among the names of the dead.

Trinidad didn't go out on the street much during that time, but each time she did she saw huge change. The streets were now full of armed militiamen, all dressed in blue overalls. There wasn't a hat or tie in sight; those items of dress were associated with the bourgeoisie and so wearing them was enough to get you reported. It was rumoured that anyone who made a big thing about being Republican was surely a fascist and only dressed that way as a disguise. There was a shift in the way people spoke as well: no more 'sir' and 'goodbye', it was 'you' and 'see ya'. The militia salute of raising your closed fist became very popular with people. Relationships became more casual: it was more acceptable for couples to live together before marriage, or even for the woman to be pregnant before they tied the knot. Civil weddings became all the rage; people could be married by civil servants, union representatives or army officers.[60] Emilia and Luis had a civil wedding in the Fuencarral neighbourhood[61] but Trinidad

---

[58] Montoliú 2000, Op. cit. pp. 85-93.
[59] See map 7.
[60] Montoliú, Op. cit. pp. 146-148.

didn't go to the wedding.

After taking Toledo, Franco started to close his net around the capital and by the end of August he had begun to bomb the city. Trinidad remembered the evening well. She had been to see her sister Teresa as Friday was her day off; Teresa still worked in the Republican general's house. She had come back about half past nine on 28th August and at quarter to twelve that night the bombs began to hit. She could hear the sounds of the planes, the sirens and the explosions, whilst flares lit up the sky in central Madrid. Trinidad was petrified and unsure where to go or what to do. She heard later, on the radio, that three 20lb bombs had been dropped. One fell on the Plaza de Castelar in Cibeles, another on the gardens of Buenavista Palace (in the Ministry of War) and the third on Calle Barquillo on the other side of Paseo de la Castellana close to where Trinidad lived.

Things didn't get much better through September or October either. In fact, Franco's grip on the city tightened even more. The rebels' success in the areas surrounding Madrid (Toledo, Guadalajara, Ávila and Segovia) created a stampede among those in the countryside who were loyal to the government; they all fled their homes to seek refuge in the capital. Throughout those two months Madrid had to provide refuge to half a million people. Trinidad knew first-hand what was happening in the areas that had been invaded by the rebels, thanks to the various refugees that she housed in the flat. Following a government order, all flats in Madrid had to take in refugees from the invaded areas and Trinidad had taken in a family

---

[61] See map 4.

from the country including the elderly parents, their daughter and two small grandchildren. On top of that, Luis's mother and grandmother had also come to live with them in the flat. The Salamanca neighbourhood was a no-fly zone for rebel aircraft, making it the perfect place to house families that lived in those dangerous areas that were subject to non-stop bombings. So, the flat in Castelló went from housing two people to fifteen. María came and went with the children but her husband Demetrio, who worked in the Paseo de Pacífico,[62] chose to stay put and take his chances.

By the start of November, it had been generally assumed that Madrid would be captured by Franco's forces. The international press corps in Spain sent news to their home countries that the capital was about to fall. Many of them already had press releases prepared recognising the *Gobierno de Burgos* or Burgos Government. There was also talk of the Republican Government moving to Valencia, rumours which proved to be true on 6th November. That same day, Pedro Rico, the Mayor of Madrid addressed the people of Madrid on the radio. He said, "The Government wishes to speak truthfully to you and to prepare you for a great challenge. The enemy is at the gates. Madrid, we are sure, will fulfil its duty as capital. We are now in a combat zone." [63]

As she listened to the mayor's words, Trinidad started to think about the meaning of the word 'enemy'. Who was the real enemy? Franco and his followers were obviously the enemy of the government and of the parties that formed the *Frente Popular* or

---

[62] See map 7.
[63] Montoliú, 2000, Op. cit. page 193.

People's Front. However, for many right-leaning Spaniards the enemy was the political parties that were leading Spain to the brink of disaster to serve their own interests. The majority of people, including Trinidad, don Carlos and many other Spaniards, were pacifists and they didn't want war. However, in little more than three months their country had become a maelstrom of hatred, rancour, reprisals and murders. A place where buildings and convents were pulled down; where revolutionary ideas awoke class struggles that had laid dormant for centuries. Trinidad couldn't stop thinking that she had been born into both a significant and a very dark time in Spain's history.

Looking around her as they listened to the news on the radio, Trinidad saw her own fear reflected in the faces of the refugee family in her flat. She had talked to them and now knew that they had fled their village escaping the Falangists, who were killing anyone that they deemed to be red, regardless of gender or age. Trinidad looked at Emilia, whose eyes were burning with emotion and anger as she heard how Largo Caballero, whom she greatly admired, had abandoned these people to go and join the new government in Valencia. Trinidad looked at Luis's mother who, with her fist aloft, shouted '*No Pasarán*' or 'they shall not pass'. She looked at her sister María and her four little children and she felt sorry for them. What possible future could they hope for in this country that was destroying itself before their very eyes? So much tragedy and desolation.

On the seventh day, the city awoke in a state of tense

anticipation. In some branches of the *Juventudes Socialistas Unificadas* or Unified Socialist Youth a poster was pinned to the door saying, 'Closed - gone to the front'. Whilst in some other branches there was unprecedented activity because unions had called their members to form battalions.[64] Madrid's salvation or its fall would ultimately depend on the events of the 24 hours that followed.

Despite the raised expectations, the day passed relatively uneventfully as General Varela, the head of the rebel troops, had not planned for the big assault to happen until the following day. This fact was only found out due to one of those simple twists of fate that can end up shaping history. The Republicans captured an enemy tank in Casa de Campo and the driver had a document with him, detailing all the plans of attack for the following day. After weighing up whether or not the document could be trusted, or whether it was part of a trap, the Republican command gave the order to position troops at those points in the city that Varela and his forces had planned to attack.[65]

The rebels didn't achieve the aims they had planned for day eight. Although they reached the gates of the Ciudad Universitaria[66] (to the North), they entered around Casa de Campo (to the West), and they stopped half a mile from the Puente de Toledo (to the South), they didn't manage to take control of the situation and they were repelled by the defenders of the capital. The *Junta de Defensa de Madrid* or the Madrid Defence Collective requested reinforcements

---

[64] Montoliú 2000 , op. cit. pp. 198-199.
[65] Montoliú 2000, op. cit. page. 199.
[66] See map 7.

from Valencia and in the days that followed, the people of Madrid saw the first members of the International Brigades marching down Gran Vía.

Trinidad and Emilia went out into the street to watch the soldiers pass. The fear that everyone had felt earlier had by now turned into a contagious joy. There were shouts of excitement as women waved from windows on high, and crowds filled the pavements to witness the arrival of these brave foreigners, willing to give their lives in the fight against fascism. A sea of flags fluttered in the breeze, some red, some a mixture of red and black; and fists were raised in the air to salute the parade of courageous soldiers, while the crowd sang the Internationale:

Stand up, damned of the Earth
Stand up, prisoners of starvation
Let us all rise up and shout
Long live the Internationale!

Madrid did not fall in November 1936, nor did it fall in the following month, not even in the following year. In subsequent months, after three failed attempts to conquer the city, Franco opted for a different strategy; ordering his troops to occupy any remaining territory that was still in hands of the Republican Army. The people's chant of *'No Pasarán'* or 'they shall not pass' held true. The courage and bravery of the people of Madrid had saved the day for now; they had resisted an enemy invader, one that was not welcomed by many

Spaniards. However, Madrid would now face a different kind of war; one that the city was not at all prepared for.

13. PARALLEL LIVES

Madrid, Chilean Embassy, 1936

The refugees arrived a few at a time. They were worn-out, often emaciated and they came with nothing but the few clothes that they stood in. It was no surprise that their spirits were at rock bottom having spent days or even weeks in hiding by that point. Most of them had tried their luck elsewhere before they came knocking at the embassy's door. Some had been detained by the *Checa* but were lucky enough to have been released due to lack of evidence; a simple twist of fate that kept them from being 'disappeared' as so many others had been. They had moved from place to place, always on the move trying to outrun that fateful knock at the door. Others had sensed that they wouldn't get a second chance, and had simply fled their homes without a trace.

The Ambassador don Aurelio Núñez Morgado personally saw to the needs of many of the new arrivals.[67] In order to gain entry to the embassy, a refugee had to be recommended by someone or to know someone who had contact with the diplomats inside; or, they had to prove that their life or liberty were at risk. After being allowed in, each refugee was assigned a place in one of the embassy safe houses.

The refugees were a diverse group; made up of soldiers, noblemen, engineers, lawyers, business owners, shop-keepers, priests,

---

[67] *Los sucesos de España vistos por un diplomático* [Events in Spain as seen by a diplomat], A. Núñez Morgado, 1947.

nuns, women and children. The one thing that bound them all together was that they were a part of the 'other' Spain. These were the people that Franco saw as the epitome of traditional Spain; people from the Catholic faith, from the large estates, from the 'command and control' ideals of his Generals. They represented both the virtues and the sins that had governed Spain for centuries.

Don Carlos had arrived at the Chilean Embassy at the end of September, along with his two brothers Fernando and Antonio and their families. Armed with a protection order signed by the ambassador, they were 'housed' at the Decanato.[68] Not long after the uprising began don Carlos, don Fernando, doña Concepción and their daughter Conchita, had sought refuge in don Antonio's residence in the Salamanca neighbourhood. As an ex-Commander of first rank during the Monarchy, don Fernando was a prime candidate to be arrested; his life was in danger.

Those first days were full of anxiety and unease. The brothers had a friend in the Ministry of War, he told them that the *Checa* had gone to the house in Castelló to look for them. Having left without success, it was obvious the *Checa's* next move would be to visit the houses of any of the brothers' relatives in Madrid. In the middle of August they received word from a 'spy' that worked undercover in the police ranks of the government. He said that the brothers were on the Buenavista *Checa's* list for don Antonio's neighbourhood.

One night a relative called (the telephone was still a secure mode

---

[68] Former palace of the Countess of Gavia on the corner of Paseo de la Castellana and Calle Marques del Riscal, one of the buildings owned by the Chilean delegation.

of communication at that point) and informed the brothers that they must leave the flat because the *Checa* had worked out where they were hiding. That same relative then offered them a safe place to spend the night.

At the crack of dawn that morning, heavy boot steps could be heard climbing the stairs at don Antonio's building, and voices boomed from behind his front door. On hearing 'Police! Open up!' don Antonio obediently opened the door. A group of militiamen accompanied by an Inspector started to question him as they searched the flat for signs of the fugitives. In a state of frustration when they didn't find what they were looking for, they demanded don Antonio accompany them to the police station.

Don Antonio was an engineer with a long and illustrious list of achievements at the *Escuela de Ingenieros CCP* or School of Engineering (Roads, Canals and Ports) where he was a professor. He worked for the Ministry of Public Works and Transport and he was held in high regard by both liberals and conservatives alike. Just like the rest of his family, he was a very religious man and this is perhaps the only thing that put him in danger. Luckily for don Antonio, after he was arrested there were people on the Republican side that vouched for him and he was released soon after his arrest.

When he returned home, the first thing he did was check that his brothers, wife and children were safe. He then made contact with some fellow engineers who were already safe in the Chilean Embassy. Through one of them he got the ambassador's permission and led all of his family to shelter at the embassy.

Somosierra Front, November 1936

From the bunker you could just about make out the Somosierra Front, in the form of a faint line just over a mile away. From this vantage point in hills of Buitrago de Lozoya, the Sierra de Guadarrama stretched out into the horizon. To the right was the Puentes Viejas reservoir,[69] which was of huge strategic military importance as it supplied water and electricity to Madrid. To the north, not far from the village of Buitrago, you could make out the Coruña Road which linked Madrid with the north of Spain.

Following an impressive advance at the start of the battle, General Varela's troops had been neutralised by the *Frente Popular* army to the north of Madrid. The Buitrago sector had been the site of continuous battles between the two sides, however neither one had made great advances. The main site of battle was the elevated ground of Cerro Piñuecar, to the north of Buitrago, where the Republicans had succeeded in holding their front line after many a bloody battle.

The sector had quietened down since the start of the war a few months ago. The scuffles that occasionally broke out now, lacked the intensity of those first days. The front line had moved to the Segovia-La Granja axis where the clamour of battle could still be heard. It was winter and the nights were bitterly cold. Soldiers stationed in the trenches warded off the chill with a type of brandy that, though effective, left a distinctive metallic taste in the mouth. During the day

---

[69] See map 8.

however, the sun's warmth made temperatures almost pleasant inside. The bunkers themselves were made of reinforced concrete and were surrounded by a wall nearly two-foot thick. These thick walls held up substantial roofs, covered by a solid mass of stones to shield any direct hits from the air and enemy fire. The small interior served as an observation point; from its tiny window enemy movements could easily be tracked.

Nicasio watched for even the smallest of movements and he noted down any events on the ground in a special notebook, which was then handed to his commanding officer at the end of the day. It was monotonous work and required a lot of concentration, which is why the soldier on this duty was relieved every two hours. To pass the time while he gazed at the expansive horizon that opened up before him, Nicasio often thought about how the war was progressing. This led him to think back to his childhood and how his political ideals had matured with time.

When he enlisted in the army and was assigned to the *1ª Compañía de la 26 Brigada Mixta* he was happy to be surrounded by young Communists like himself. In the *Extremadura* and *Juventud Campesina* battalions there were many party members and even some fellow country folk from Valladolid.

From a very young age Nicasio had sympathised with the parties on the left, which wasn't surprising given his roots. Nicasio Vielba Pastor was born in Ceinos de Campos in Valladolid[70] on 2nd March, 1915. His father, Francisco, was a day labourer and his mother,

---

[70] See map 9.

Felisa, was a dressmaker. He attended the village school until he was fourteen. He was always one of the brightest students at the school and his teacher wanted him to continue with his studies. However, being the oldest of eight children in a farming family, there were other priorities. His mother was an intelligent and cultured woman; an avid reader of both novels and more serious tomes, she had imbued Nicasio with a love of reading, poetry and culture in general. His father was a hard worker and he knew farm work as well as anyone. Francisco had inherited a small patch of land from his parents before him but it wasn't enough to feed his large family, so he had to earn money as a day labourer. Francisco had a calm temperament and a placid character: he was a peace-loving man, who didn't mess with anybody, as fellow Ceinos folk would say. Always ready to help those in need; he was socialist in his beliefs but he didn't want to get involved in politics. However, his fellow townspeople persuaded him to stand in the town's 1932 elections for the Spanish Socialist Party (PSOE) and he ended up as the president of the PSOE for Ceinos de Campos.

At 23 years old, Nicasio was a young man of medium height; he had blond hair, pale eyes, an aquiline nose and attractive features that lent him a trustworthy look. He was a great public speaker and he could convince anyone who listened to him, with his oratory. His control of the Castilian language was impressive, even more so given that he was for the most part self-taught.

When he finished school, Nicasio took the decision not to work in the fields; it was back-breaking work that provided hardly enough money for food. He had watched how his father lived, and over time he came to the conclusion that being an agricultural labourer would earn as much as being a shepherd with no sheep. One of his uncles in town was a nurse practitioner and a barber, as well as being a labourer. Seeing as Nicasio didn't like the idea of working as a nurse or working in the fields, he decided to be a barber.

Over a two year period he learned the trade from his uncle, and through living in the village Nicasio came to understand the workers' dilemma. Ever since he was a boy he understood that being an agricultural worker in the region of Tierra de Campos[71] was difficult work. He remembered going to the threshing floor with his father. At that time all jobs were still done by hand. For example, to plough the earth they hooked up animals (normally mules that his father had rented for that particular job), to the plough using yokes and halters. Once the ground was ready for sowing, this was done by hand with the help of a seed drill. The workers walked up and down scattering the seeds across the land. Harvesting was also done by hand, with sickles and scythes. When the harvest had been cut, the grains were hauled to the threshing floor, they were spread out and then threshed by a thresher, after which the grain was cleaned in machines with winnowing forks.[72] Once the grain and the straw had been separated, the grain was poured into sacks with the help of a wooden funnel and the straw was taken to the hayloft. This whole process took days to

---

[71] Natural Spanish region located in the autonomous communities of Castile and León, the region covers the Palencia, Valladolid, Zamora and León provinces.
[72] Iron filters of different lengths, some with twists, which when they turn push the straw towards the outside.

complete, and was often done under a blazing hot sun that scorched the skin as well as leaving you dripping with sweat. The working day lasted until sundown and if you were to avoid sunstroke you had to wear a straw hat. Nicasio struggled with the work and callouses formed on his hands in no time. He soon realised that he wasn't born to be a labourer.

On top of the physical hardship that the workers went through, the financial reward they received in return was pitiful. The price of wheat rose and fell from year to year and the bosses took advantage of any opportunity to reduce the day-workers' salaries. As a case in point, Francisco's daily wage wasn't more than 10 pesetas on the days that he did work, and he was never given more than fifty days' work a year. The wages were also dependent on the harvest, so in a bad year they all had to tighten their belts and the family went hungry. There was hardly any job security and young people had to leave the area in order to find work. All in all, there was no future in the fields and his own father was living proof of that fact.

At the age of sixteen, Nicasio finished his apprenticeship with his uncle and went to work as a barber in Medina de Rioseco[73]; a sizeable town about 12 miles away from Ceinos, where there were more opportunities for work. In 1931, Medina de Rioseco was a socio-political pressure cooker. The 1904, 1921 and 1923 strikes had given rise to a revolutionary climate which was nearing its peak when Nicasio arrived in the town. As if that weren't enough to fire him up, being a barber also meant he met a diverse range of people from all

---

[73] **See map 9.**

walks of life. All the latest news and events were discussed at the barbers.

"Good afternoon comrades, farmers and other family, in that order," said Fermín when he walked in that morning. Fermín was one of the workers on the 'burra' train.[74] "Is there a long wait?"

"Not as long as we had to wait for Land Reform," said Juan the officer, a chatty man who always had an anecdote at the ready.

"I hope Largo Caballero delivers us the Land Reform that Pablo Iglesias promised us,"[75] added Pablo, another regular (farmer and member of the local *UGT* or General Workers' Union), as he watched Nicasio shave his soap-covered face in the mirror.

"It's now or never!" said Fermín.

"According to reports in this morning's *El Socialista* newspaper, Azaña's new government has already started to 'tighten the screws' on the owners to get them to accept the concessions they made during the last strike," said Nicasio, speaking up for the first time.

"As if, man! We should do to them what we did to the King – throw them out! Let them go to Paris and leave the land for the people who work it," said Pablo passionately. He got so worked up underneath the cape that Nicasio looked at him in surprise and moved the blade out of the way quickly to avoid cutting him.

"Well now you come to mention it, that's not a bad idea. Let them stay in Paris, we're sick to the back teeth of capitalists," said

---

[74] Nickname given to the small-gauge railway that linked Medina de Rioseco with Valladolid.
[75] Reference to a visit that Pablo Iglesias made to Medina de Rioseco in 1904 to attract new members to the party.

Fermín emphatically.

"Another report in the *Norte de Castilla* newspaper this morning said that a particular chant is gaining popularity in Madrid," Nicasio went on, "it goes like this: 'Where are you going, Alfonso XIII, where are you going, so sad and put out? I'm getting the express train 'cos Madrid kicked me out'."

"Talking of newspapers, *Mundo Obrero* is asking all us workers to go to Madrid next Sunday to support the Republic," announced Fermín. "And if you're in the party it won't cost you a penny."

"Well, count me in," said Nicasio, "that way I can get to see Madrid while I'm there, I've heard it's beautiful."

Everyone turned to the officer next, waiting for him to make up his mind.

"I'd love to go but, please – not on the 'burra' – we'd have to leave days in advance. It's slower than a parade of one legged people" the officer said smiling.

"Oi, if it wasn't for us railwaymen and our revolutionary struggles, Rioseco wouldn't even have a train," replied Fermín.

At that moment, they saw the flowing robes of don Julián coming through the door; he was another regular and one of the canons at Santiago Apóstol. He greeted the regulars, "What a beautiful day God has bestowed upon us all, and with the times we're living in we need it." "Amen," responded Fermín in form of a greeting. The 'parishioners' exchanged a look and with that their previous conversation ended.

Nicasio arrived in Madrid on 10th June 1934. It wasn't a good time to arrive in the city if you needed a job. Rates of unemployment among barbers were at 40%. Nicasio didn't know anyone in the city, but his uncle Eugenio did. His uncle's contact was Tomás Gómez; he had a small barbershop on Calle de Madrid, in the Getafe neighbourhood[76] – about 8 miles from the capital. Tomás had worked with Eugenio in times gone by and was in his debt for some favour or other. So when he received a letter from his old friend, bringing him up to speed with everything, he agreed to give Nicasio an assistant's position in his small barbershop.

Getafe was a typical example of a working town, and living there only reinforced the socialist ideas that Nicasio had brought with him from Rioseco. With his shiny new membership card from the Madrid Association of Hairdressers and Barbers (a member of the UGT), Nicasio started to go to the Casa del Pueblo. The Casa served as a cultural hub for young boys from the country who were keen to expand their horizons. Nicasio was hungry for knowledge and devoured all the revolutionary texts that fell into his hands; most of them from the library on Calle Piamonte, home of the Casa del Pueblo in Madrid. Socialist and Communist newspapers were his essential reading material to round off his revolutionary view of life. He wasn't alone in this; revolutionary ideals were ever-present on the streets and were at the peak of their popularity. The Asturian strike movement[77] was fuel to the hopes for a Marxist revolution that,

---

[76] See map 7.
[77] Known as the revolution of 1934 (5th to 19th October) during the radical CEDA-lead term of the Second Republic. The uprising was cruelly suppressed by soldiers under the command of General Franco.

despite recent setbacks, still burned bright in the hearts of young workers such as Nicasio.

In September 1935, Nicasio joined the *Juventudes Socialistas (JJSS)* or Socialist Youths which at that time had several thousands of members in their ranks. Part of the JJSS's manifesto was the bolshevization of the Socialist Party. So it came as no surprise when the JJSS leaders were overtaken by the Spanish Communist Party and both groups were finally merged to form the *Juventudes Socialistas Unificadas* (JSU) or Unified Socialist Youths.[78] On that same day Nicasio joined the Communist Party, as many young farmers and workers were doing at the time, and he started to read Marx, Hegel, Trotsky and Lenin. His path towards radicalisation as a JSU member reached its high point during the attack on the Getafe artillery barracks.

Given Nicasio's political thought process, a Russian-style Marxist revolution made sense for Spain. The Spanish capitalist system was unfair; it favoured the privileged classes and propped up a regime in which poor people were born into a wretched existence similar to the serfs living under the tsar. His childhood experiences within his own humble family were living proof of this injustice. He was all for a proletarian revolution and he wanted this revolution to break the cycle of centuries of poverty and ignorance of the working classes. He was opposed to a class system where so-called important families imposed their ideological hegemony on the daily life of his country. He was opposed to their oligopolistic businesses, controlling

---

[78] This came to pass in April 1936.

agriculture with their large estates. He was opposed to their monopoly of the banks and businesses. He was against the Catholic Church who supported the moral order of the rich through many a varied tool: confession, religious schools for middle class children, sermons on work, family, good and bad, what you should and shouldn't do, how to treat poor people and so on. The tyranny that had been going on for centuries, and that had ruined towns like Ceinos, had to be eradicated. They had to put a stop to the unemployment that affected 25% of the population, both the workers and their families. They had to put a stop to the illiteracy that held back more than ten million men, women and children. It was deplorable that in a country where 70% of people lived from and depended on the land, most farmers didn't have enough to feed their families. Hunger, unemployment and emigration were endemic. Nicasio wanted the proletarian revolution to succeed for all of these reasons, but mostly because he wanted to create a better Spain.

This chain of thought was interrupted by the Duty Officer barking the order; "Change of Guard." Nicasio looked at the officer and said, "Nothing new to report on the front, lieutenant".

***

Another sad day in Madrid. The sky was overcast and it looked like it might snow. Trinidad went to the window to see what was happening on the streets. The dining room windows were all fogged up, but she wiped them so that she could get a good look outside. Everything seemed quiet out there. There were no gunshots, you couldn't hear the drone of aircraft, but how long before it would all start up again?

The house was cold; their supplies of firewood and coal had run out weeks ago. Getting hold of food was a daily struggle. They hadn't eaten a single bite for two whole days now. Trinidad thought of the last time she had eaten bread. It was when the oil had run out. They had extracted the last few drops from the container using a straw, then spread it on the bread they had managed to get with their ration card.

Hunger was making people more resourceful and the people of the city seemed to be forever coming up with new and ingenious ways to get food. Trinidad thought about that woman yesterday in the queue; pretending to faint because she was supposedly 'with child', but really it was just so people would let her go to the front of the queue. She had been found out when she was helped up from the floor and everyone saw she just had a little cushion strapped to her belly.

It seemed that the war would never end. The front had been stabilised and Franco's tactic of leaving Madrid to starve to death was starting to pay dividends. How long would the General have to wait to get his wish? A wave of pessimism washed over her. Her personal situation was getting to be critical. And yet...

That very afternoon the service doorbell rang. Trinidad wondered who it could possibly be. Emilia was out with Luis but she had her key. Her sister María had told her she wouldn't be coming with the children that night, but maybe she had changed her mind. The farming family had moved to another house to be with people from their village. She looked through the peephole and saw a face she didn't recognise.

She shouted from behind the door, "Who is it?"

"Please, open the door. I have news of don Carlos," came the reply.

Trinidad stood frozen at the mention of that name and for a few seconds she wasn't sure whether to open up or not. She looked through the peephole again to check that the man had come alone. In the end her desire to know what had happened to don Carlos won out over her natural cautiousness and she opened the door.

"Thank you," the stranger said, "are you Trinidad?"

"Yes sir," Trinidad replied.

"I bring you a message from don Carlos. He asked me to tell you that he and his family have sought refuge in an embassy and they are safe and well," the messenger began. "He has given me this envelope with money for you and your colleagues, it's the wages you are owed. You shall continue to receive further payments as long as you look after the flat and make sure nobody takes anything from it. The other condition is that every first Wednesday you must take four changes of clothes and four clean shirts to don Carlos at the address on the inside of this envelope. Is that clear?"

"How do I know you're telling me the truth? How do I know I can trust you?" Trinidad responded.

"You have your answer in the envelope there. Follow the instructions I've given you and everything will be fine," came the reassuring reply.

"And what should I do if I want to contact you?" Trinidad asked.

"You won't see me again, but if you need something then put an extra sock in with the change of clothes and that will be the signal for someone to contact you. You must follow these instructions to the letter so that neither you nor don Carlos are put in any danger. Do you understand?"

"Yes sir, I do" Trinidad nodded.

The visitor looked at her one last time, thanked her and without further ado disappeared closing the door behind him. As soon as he had gone Trinidad opened the envelope. Inside there were ten 100 peseta notes and a commemorative card from Cristo de la Salud de Hervás; she had given the card to don Carlos when she started work at his house. Lastly, the envelope also contained a name and address: Sr. López Sola, Paseo de la Castellana, 55, a place she recognised from street signs she had passed on walks with her sisters.

***

The number of refugees had been steadily rising. More than a thousand people had now been given refugee status. Early on, the admission applications had been submitted in a very humble way; people were overwhelmed with anxiety and fear, they were content with 'a little corner' or 'a chair'. In short, they were prepared to make sacrifices to escape the situation they were fleeing on the outside. However, as time went on and now that those same people were safe in the embassy they started demanding diplomatic protection for relatives, friends and acquaintances. The tone of their exchanges went from "please, I beg of you," to people forcing their way in and saying "I'm here and I'm not budging".[79]

The façade of the embassy was impressive. However, the refugees never got to appreciate this as they were holed up within its walls for months; cooped up in small rooms with 18 to 20 other people, or even 30 to 40 people in the bigger rooms. They were deprived of fresh air, of sunlight and they were unavoidably malnourished. So it was no surprise that they were gradually changing in appearance and that their spirits and health were both faltering. There wasn't enough air, enough space, enough light, enough water, or enough provisions. Everywhere you turned there were long beards and unkempt greasy locks down to people's shoulders, making the refugees look like primitive beings. They were crammed into the corridors, curled up in every corner and sleeping on the floors.[80]

The Decanato dining room housed a sad and sorry-looking crowd. There were decrepit Generals, tired and unwashed men, their skeletal hands limp when they made a request. At lunchtime, they met in the Amadis[81] dining room, where they exchanged information, plans and ideas on how they could be of service to the pro-Franco organisation known as the *Quinta Columna*.[82] *(*Fifth Column*)*

In these dire conditions, the refugees tried to pass the time as

---

[79] *Informes diplomáticos y diarios de la Guerra Civil [Diplomatic reports and diaries from the Spanish Civil War]*, C Morla Lynch, 2010 (pp. 68-72).
[80] Morla, 2010, op cit. (pp 68-72).
[81] *España sufre, diarios de guerra 1936-39 [Spain suffers, war diaries 1936-1939]*, C. Morla Lynch, page 183.
[82] Created by sympathisers of the Uprising within the capital who worked clandestinely towards a victory for Franco.

best they could; talking, telling jokes and playing cards. Don Carlos and his brothers and family, struggled to keep themselves active along with the rest of their companions; doing things to soften the effects of confinement. Don Carlos was a great fan of reading and chess, and he spent hours on these two pastimes every day. Don Antonio gave lectures on engineering and taught German to many of the refugee children. Don Fernando, spent time explaining the progression of the war and the situations of both sets of troops. He did this with the aid of an enormous map laid out on the dining room table, information received from Radio Burgos and details from the newspapers that were published in the Republican area. Doña Concepción helped the nuns take care of the elderly and infirm. Little Conchita played with her cousins and the other girls in the courtyard inside Decanato, but only when there was no threat of bombardment of course.

At times, life for the refugees was worse even than for those awaiting judgement in prison. Quite apart from the daily struggle to survive in a climate of terror, illness and suspicion, life inside the embassy wasn't without its dangers. Many refugees just couldn't take any more, what with the bombardments and the threat of attack from government forces. The phrase "this is no life" was uttered on a daily basis.

Fearing that disaster could befall them at any time, don Antonio had managed to get his wife, his two sons and the rest of his brothers' families on the list for evacuation. Set for the 20th April 1937, the ambassador[83] had succeeded in negotiating this evacuation with the Republican Government.

***

Trinidad stared at the ten 100 peseta notes as if she couldn't believe her eyes. She had never seen so much money. She ran her fingers through the notes and felt a strange sensation that she hadn't had before. This money would allow her and Emilia to buy food on the black market. She would keep Alejandra's money safe until she next saw her, even if that wasn't until the end of the war. That's if they both survived the conflict, she thought.

Trinidad put on her overcoat and went out into the street. She wanted to find out right away which building number 55 Paseo de la Castellana was in.[84] She seemed to remember that the odd numbers were on the other side of the Paseo where all the Embassies were, but she didn't know the area that well. She headed for Castelló to the north, turned onto Ayala and arrived on la Castellana within a few minutes. She walked quickly, not only because of the cold that was nipping at her heels, but because stopping in one place might raise suspicions. She crossed paths with some other pedestrians who, like her, walked hastily by. Before she crossed the road on the Paseo, she quickly looked at the building from the pavement in front. It was a three-storey red brick and granite house; it had a fence, behind which she could make out a garden. A green and yellow flag with a drawing in the middle flew from the first-floor balcony, Trinidad had never

---

[83] The Chilean Ambassador held the position of Dean of the accredited diplomatic corps in Spain and acted as liaison between the foreign accredited ambassadors within Spain and the Republican government.
[84] See map 4.

seen the flag before. She thought to herself, it must be an embassy because it's protected by guards and militiamen. She didn't know whether to approach or not. In the end she decided she would have to if she ever wanted to find out anything and so she took a few steps towards the main door. Before she could go any further one of the guards stopped her, then stood staring at her. She saluted him with her fist raised in the air and asked:

"Sorry comrade, what building is this?"

"This is the Brazilian Embassy comrade. You can't come in without permission."

"Oh, sorry I have the wrong place."

"What are you looking for? Maybe I can help you," said the militiaman with a mischievous smile on his face.

"No thank you comrade, that won't be necessary," and with that she crossed the street in the direction she had come from.

When she got home she told Emilia what happened on her walk. Trinidad had already told her friend about the messenger's visit of the night before, and she had handed over Emilia's share of the money. They immediately started talking about how they might be able to carry out don Carlos's requests.

Emilia started off, "The best thing to do would be to put the changes of clothes in one of those baskets, like the ironing ladies use to take clothes to houses. That way we won't have any problems with the guards."

Trinidad agreed, "Yes that sounds like a good idea to me."

"We've still got two weeks before we have to make the first

delivery, so we have plenty of time to buy the basket," reasoned Emilia. "Would you like me to take the first turn?"

Trinidad shook her head, "No, don't worry, I'll go – I already know the way. You go next time."

"You have no idea how good it is to get those overdue wages," Emilia sighed. "In my condition I should be drinking lots of milk and now at least I'll be able to get hold of it, even if it is through the black market."

"When are you due?" asked Trinidad.

"The doctor told me that, all being well, baby will be here at the beginning of June." Emilia said with a smile.

"Well, tonight we should celebrate the good news. What do you say to truffle chicken with champagne?" Trinidad asked with a mock serious face.

"Ooh yes, with cheesecake and cream - yum yum, how scrumptious!" Emilia laughed.

"Or how about a locust bean consommé with coconut and orange peel?" Trinidad went on.

"Ugh, don't even talk to me about locust beans, you'll give me a funny turn," said Emilia with a grimace. "I've always hated them – I'd rather die than eat another one."

"Right, well today we're going to do something special. I'll pay señora Jacinta the dressmaker a visit, and see if she wants to sell me two eggs on the black market. I'll ask her where I can buy the basket too," Trinidad said enthusiastically. "Yesterday she told me that her husband had taken the Arganda train[85] to look for food and bread in the villages."

***

It was Sunday and the priest was giving mass. The front room in Decanato was full to the brim with parishioners. Don Carlos followed the Eucharist celebration devoutly. It had been a year and half since he and his family arrived at the embassy; this religious ceremony filled him with an inner peace and gave him the strength to survive his captivity. He wondered how much longer he would be confined there and asked God for the strength to withstand this difficult situation with humility.

Every day don Carlos prayed that the war would come to an end; it was taking so many innocent lives. He knew what was going on outside the embassy walls[86] as they had an information service on the inside. He thought of how very grateful he was to his brother Antonio for getting him into the embassy, and to the ambassador for having taken him and his family in. He also thanked the Lord that his house in Castelló was safe, and that none of the girls he employed had come to any harm. He was calmer now. The supply of clean clothes every month, made life more bearable and he promised to thank Trinidad and Emilia for the risks they took in delivering it. When it was all over, he would also explain the subterfuge with the names of the embassies. You can never be too careful in wartime

---

[85] Small-gauge railway that ran between Madrid and Arganda during the war. It was dubbed 'the hunger train' by the people of Madrid because city-dwellers used it to travel to outlying towns in search of food.

[86] It was rumoured that there was a group of spies inside the Chilean Embassy who supported the *Quinta Columna* and kept well-informed of the situation on the outside.

though and he had been advised that this was the best way to protect everybody involved.

A lot had happened in the almost eighteen months that he had been in the embassy. Don Carlos would never forget the feeling of relief in those first few days at Castellana 29. After hiding out at the homes of relatives and friends for so long, arriving there felt like finally coming into "a calm port after having crossed stormy seas."[87]

At first, he and his fellow refugees hadn't thought much about the conditions they were living in at the embassy; given the news of the liberating army's successful advances they hadn't expected to be there long. In October 1936, Franco's troops were on the outskirts of Madrid. Everyone thought the conflict would be over soon and they would be home in time for Christmas. The refugees got a bit of a fright one evening when a bomb hit close by; it felt as though an earthquake had ripped through the building. They were ordered to "get to the basements". Chaos ensued and some people stumbled in their haste to get down there, falling to the floor where they were trampled by those behind them. Others stayed where they were, ducked down on the floor with their hands covering their heads.

Don Carlos had read in the Republican press that the nationalist bombings had killed a large number of civilians, women and children. Reports said that during one daytime bombardment, bombs had fallen on a school during break time while students were playing outside. Fifty of them were killed. He didn't know for sure if this report was true, or if it was pure propaganda, but he saw his nieces

---

[87] A. Núñez Morgado, op. cit. (page 338).

and nephews running around playing in Decanato and he felt for the parents of those dead children.

The endless aerial attacks against the civilian population had fuelled a climate of hatred and a desire for revenge against 'the fascist army', as they were dubbed by the Republican press. In the run-up to Christmas many refugees arrived from the Finnish, German and Italian Embassies, after they had been attacked and hand grenades, weapons and munitions had been uncovered there. At that point, the media campaign against the Embassies was at its peak. The following day the *El Socialista* newspaper published an article entitled "Diplomatic neutrality, yes. Belligerent hypocrisy, no!" Other left-wing newspapers described the refugees as "cowards, reptiles and enemies of the people. Armed to the teeth, they are taking food from the poor whilst holed up in their diplomatic caves like bats. They have yet to do anything for themselves or anyone else."[88] That day the ambassador spoke to them all, saying he feared that in light of this situation refugees might lose their diplomatic protection. His words sparked a panic that spread like wildfire among the group, for surely an attack was imminent. Later on, the crisis abated somewhat but that fear never truly left them.

As the days went by, don Carlos began to wonder what the point of this fratricidal war actually was. He failed to comprehend how a person could hate to such an extent that they could kill another person in cold blood, or burn down convents or kill nuns. They were destroying the Spain that he loved so much. He respected other

---

[88] Op. cit, Morla Lynch, 2010.

people's beliefs but he could not accept these indiscriminate attacks on family, property and religion, and lack of respect for other people. That's why he was in favour of order; of a return to normality that would bring peace and unity back to Spain. He had sheltered in the embassy because he was a pacifist like many other people; he didn't want to fight in a fratricidal war that was destroying his country. It wasn't that he was a coward or a reptile, or an enemy of the people, not when he always helped the poor if he could. This train of thought depressed him and he begged God to end the conflict as soon as possible.

***

Trinidad and Teresa had at long last been able to meet up. It hadn't been easy because Teresa lived in Glorieta de Bilbao[89], a neighbourhood on the other side of the Paseo de la Castellana. It had been ages since the two sisters had seen each other, so they decided to do something fun and go to the cinema. A Laurel & Hardy film was showing and the girls laughed all the way through; it felt good to laugh. Two Russian pilots sat to one side of them; they offered the girls sweets, but the conversation was somewhat stilted as the soldiers didn't speak any Spanish. The cinema was close to Gran Vía, a road that the people of Madrid had christened 'Missile Avenue'. As the girls left the film, they heard sirens and immediately ran towards the metro entrance. They hadn't quite reached the gateway when the missiles began to fall. People screamed and stampeded towards the metro; the sisters managed to reach the entrance without getting hit

---

[89] See map 4.

by any shrapnel, but they were scared stiff. Finally they arrived on the platform but it was full, there was no space to move. The train arrived, and since there was no space inside, the girls had to travel between the cars, something they had never done before. As they travelled down the tracks, the girls looked at one another inside the tunnel and held on for dear life. Danger was a part of their everyday lives in this city so they were used to doing things they would never have dreamt of previously. Their precarious situation in the Metro made Trinidad recall the famous saying about "Pepa" (what the people of Madrid had started to call Death): "Pepa is a chick that's in fashion in Madrid".[90]

After her meeting with Teresa, the bombings intensified to the point that going out in the street became truly perilous. Trinidad carried on taking clothes to don Carlos, risking her life as she did so. The responsibility of delivering the clothes had fallen squarely on her shoulders since Emilia had given birth. Trinidad preferred to make the delivery in the morning, although her walk often turned into a brush with death when the early morning bombing, like the milkman, arrived every day. At midday there always seemed to be a little respite, but it never lasted long. Aerial attacks in the afternoons often coincided with the times people were coming out of cinemas making it the worst time to go out. She could vouch for that after her near miss that day with Teresa.

As she got further away from the Salamanca neighbourhood, there was destruction everywhere she turned. She passed some

---

[90] Montoliú, 2000, op. cit. page 224.

houses that were totally intact, whilst their neighbours had been reduced to piles of rubble and debris. Further up on the very same street, she saw empty buildings that displayed their insides as if they were nothing but doll houses; it was as though they had been cleaved in two by a giant axe. Elsewhere, other buildings were precariously balanced with huge chunks taken out of the upper floors. Lampposts looked as though they had been torn out of the ground; there was broken glass all over the roads, and huge craters dotted the streets, opening up like enormous caves.

Trinidad felt as though she was living on a different planet, seeing so much devastation everywhere. Her peace-loving spirit rebelled and she felt a rage building inside of her against all those who had committed such a massacre. Her Christian beliefs had her searching for any justification for this tragedy. It was just like when she was little and she saw so much death surrounding her family but could see no reason behind it; well, she was struggling in the same way now. How could the self-proclaimed defenders of the Christian faith be capable of committing such violence? What evil lay within them that they would drop bombs and missiles with no thought for where or when they would hit? If God were infinitely merciful, why would He allow this criminal attack on a defenceless civilian population? The continual bombardment was a crime against humanity but it was also destroying the architectural and cultural heritage of Spain. These armies that were saving the Christian faith, and the 'fundamental principles of the movement', were nothing more than evil fanatics who deserved eternal damnation. Her rage helped her to overcome any fear she might have felt as she crossed the streets. She felt all the tears that she could no longer hold back come streaming down her cheeks as she thought about this huge tragedy.

***

The daily news was being read on *Radio Burgos* on 2nd May 1938. As usual, there was a group of refugees gathered around the wireless to listen to the latest from the outside world. The presenter told them of the latest developments, "this afternoon, as a children's festival was being held in the Plaza de Talavera, the red air force dropped bombs killing many people, among them children and the elderly. As a result, we are warning that within 48 hours there will be consequences for a city in the Republican zone."[91]

The following night saw the beginning of an intense bombardment of Madrid. A group of refugees, among them don Carlos and don Fernando, had gone out onto the flat roof of the Decanato to watch the nationalist artillery destroy the Republican strongholds. The noise of the missiles grew closer and don Fernando knew exactly what this meant from his military experience. He ordered: "everyone get downstairs, they're changing targets and fire is coming our way"[92]. They all started the descent to the floors below, but before they could reach their destination there was a huge explosion. Silence fell and then a cloud of dust and smoke started to fill the room on the upper floor where the missile had landed. They heard shrieks and haunting cries of pain as mangled bodies writhed

---

[91] Montoliú, 2000, op. cit. Volume II, page 102.
[92] Montoliú, 2000, op. cit. Volume II, page 102.

on the floor. On the opposite side of the room, other people stood still as if frozen in shock. Further shells landed on the ground next to the building making the room tremble. After the first few moments of confusion had passed, a horrifying scene unfolded before their eyes.

A young boy was sitting bolt upright in his chair held up only by the unconscious vigour of youth, his head had been split open and a mass of brains escaped through the gaping wound. Another boy used his charred hand to hold up a wounded arm with a shapeless mass at the end of it; barely recognisable as a hand. A third victim stood with his clothes torn to shreds, his whole face and body was completely covered in shrapnel and he looked around him without saying a word, as if he was somewhere else.[93]

There were eight victims including don Carlos and don Fernando. The injured lay bloodied and bleeding on stretchers on the floor. Don Fernando's head had been crushed and he cried out in agony. Don Carlos's injuries were just as serious; at first glance he appeared dead. One man's testicles had been blown off and another's hand would need reattaching. The acting Ambassador don Carlos Morla Lynch took the decision to move the wounded to Hospital Francés under consular protection.

The journey from Decanato to the hospital only took 10 minutes, but for those with the worst injuries those minutes were the difference between life and death. The two brothers were hardly breathing when they arrived; their situation was critical. The surgeons

---

[93] Morla Lynch, 2010, op. cit. page 136.

worked against the clock and after a complicated operation they managed to sew up don Carlos's head wound, protecting the previously exposed brain matter. However a few minutes later, following a series of death rattles and convulsions, don Fernando died on the table. The nurses cried as the priest read him the last rites. Fate's cruel irony meant that it wasn't the moors in Africa that had killed him while he served in Morocco, but his own brothers in arms, the very same soldiers that he had fought shoulder to shoulder with.

14. THE LAST DAYS

She didn't know if it had been a dream or a nightmare but it had lasted nearly three years. She replayed the most recent scenes countless times in her mind; people coming out of their homes waving flags and banners to greet the victors. However, it would never wipe out what had gone before; no, that particular nightmare stayed with her still. It had been rather like the scary stories her mother used to tell her when she wasn't behaving herself as a young girl. There were awful images burned into her memory; people killing each other over nothing, children and dogs fighting over a scrap of bread, women crying, fires, destruction and death everywhere she turned.

Trinidad had spent two weeks shut up in the house, terrified to go out on the street and lacking the energy to do anything. The radio, which she had grown to hate, was broadcasting reports that were utterly untrue. Colonel Casado, head of the National Defence Council,[94] had said "life goes on with complete normality. Madrid is completely calm," giving the impression that he was in control of the situation. Trinidad no longer believed anything she heard. Her only reliable source of information had been Emilia, while she had still been around. However, after the fall of Barcelona, Emilia had fled in fear of reprisals against Luis. She had headed for Levante with her

---

[94] In the last few days of the Spanish Civil War Colonel Segismundo Casado struck a heavy blow to the Republican government of Juan Negrín in an attempt to stop him handing over the country to the USSR. Together with Julián Besteiro, Casado tried to negotiate the surrender of Madrid with Franco, to no avail.

husband, her son and her mother-in-law, with every intention of leaving Spain.

Over the last few days Trinidad had been following events in the street through the dining room window. She had watched as the Communist soldiers and Casado's men killed each other in an attempt to gain control. However, it was all for nothing as it would seem the Republic's luck had already run out. Franco's troops were on the verge of breaching the capital and this time they found no opposition as they did so. Well, at least that's what people said although she had to admit the situation wasn't totally clear.

The hunger experienced in the city over the last few months had been devastating. Supplies to the capital had recently been shut off because of fighting between Negrín's and Casado's forces. Trinidad had joined the hundreds of men, women and children all searching for anything edible, even an orange or lemon peel, in the rubbish strewn across the streets of Madrid. When Franco's planes dropped sacks of bread for the starving population Trinidad hadn't thought twice about eating them. After all, at least poisoning was a better way to go than starvation. She remembered seeing an old man die as he tried to eat a bread roll. He was so weak that in his desperate efforts to get the bread into his mouth he had choked and suffocated, his life ending in a bout of violent seizures.

She opened the window a little and listened. She couldn't hear any plane noises. Everything seemed quiet. The cloudless sky was a clear, bright blue. She didn't know whether to go out on the balcony or down onto the street; in the end fear and listlessness stopped her from doing either. She looked at her reflection in the window pane and saw there a thin, exhausted version of herself. She looked like the living dead; only the spark in her eyes remained of her old self. Suddenly, she heard a rumble of sound. It was getting louder and sounded like distant shouting; this wasn't a sound she was familiar with, not one she was used to. She saw that the balcony in the flat opposite her had opened its doors and a red and gold flag, like the King's flag, hung proudly in the breeze. The noise was growing louder, it must be getting closer. Just then she saw crowds of people appear on the streets. More balconies opened their doors and women stood wearing embroidered shawls as though it was San Isidro, and holding banners of all kinds. What had until that point been an indistinct rumble now became a cacophony of voices shouting: "Franco, Franco". This couldn't be happening; it must have been another one of her dreams. She pinched her arm just to check that she was awake. It was real, people were shouting, the nationalists were moving into Madrid. Almost without any effort, she managed to open the door to the balcony and leaned out, then, without really realising what she was doing, she too started to shout.

***

It was eight in the morning and everyone was on their feet at the embassy. You could sense that the end of the war was coming. Some refugees were bubbling with happiness, telling one another jokes. One of them told a joke about Franco and his hatred for politicians. When Negrín, who was also a doctor, meets Franco in Madrid he will say: "I am passing my title on to you" and Franco will reply "Well thankfully I'm neither a doctor nor a politician, but if you want my advice I prescribe that you don't go into politics." Everyone laughed.

In the nine o'clock news bulletin, Radio Burgos reported that the glorious nationalist army was entering the city with the heroic people of Madrid cheering them on. Carlos Morla Lynch, who had been traveling all over the city since six o'clock that morning, could attest to that. "They're coming in through the Hippodrome"[95] he said. This statement was backed up by one refugee who had been up to the flat roof, "Yes, they're already on their way, I saw them". And with that the acting ambassador gave the orders to open the heavy embassy doors. The refugees ran out into the streets and dispersed like a flock of birds. The youngest ones sprinted like wild deer, whilst the older ones among them set out supported by their walking sticks but with a lighter step, as though they had found a renewed will to live. This joy, the shouts and the jubilant exclamations were inevitably accompanied by the wracking sobs of those who now carried a deep pain and hopelessness within. Don Carlos and don Antonio embraced in a long hug at the good news, but their happiness was marred by grief. They couldn't hold back their tears as they thought of their brother Fernando who would never see his men entering the city, the men he had fought so hard for. Holding onto his brother's arm for support, don Carlos walked out into the street and with a tired and weary step he began the walk back to his house on Calle Castelló. The brothers knew that this was a brand new dawn for Spain, but the future would no longer be quite what they had imagined.

---

[95] Where Real Madrid's stadium can be found today.

***

The fall of Barcelona, and then subsequently the whole of Catalonia, was a death knell for the Republican Army. The Somosierra front was one of the few to hold right to the end. The news coming in wasn't good however, despite the political commissars' insistence that the end of the war was still far away.[96]

Nicasio soon saw that his dreams of a Marxist state in Spain would not be realised. It was obvious that the war was about to end, and that his side were going to lose. The front was quiet; they hadn't heard a shot in weeks, but there were rumours that the Republican military command were preparing to surrender.

Nicasio smoked a cigarette and asked his communist comrade:

"Juan, have you heard anything new?"

Nicasio's comrade replied, "Only that we've definitely lost our battle against that fascist Casado."

"How is that even possible when we have more troops than them?" Nicasio replied with a frustrated sigh.

"I have no idea Nicasio. It looks like now that Negrín has gone to France the Party has given orders to stop fighting."

"So this is really over," Nicasio said softly.

"It seems that way," his comrade replied.

Nicasio's anger boiled up, "All that effort for nothing. Our dreams of a proletarian Spain are going to stay that way, just

---

[96] The Negrín-led government had clear Marxist overtones and by March 1939 it had played all its cards in an unsuccessful bid to prolong the war. Following the dictates of the Kremlin, Negrín wanted the war in Spain to last until hostilities broke out in Europe.

dreams..."

"You've got it."

"So what happens now?" Nicasio asked anxiously.

"Are you afraid?" Juan asked.

"Me? No," Nicasio said full of bluster. "You?"

"No, why?" Juan asked, "There's no blood on my hands."

"Yeah, but they know you're a member of the Party and of the Socialist Youth." Nicasio responded.

"It doesn't matter," Juan said assertively. "I didn't kill anyone."

"Don't you believe it Juan," said Nicasio. "They say Franco isn't going to hold back for anyone."

"Lots of our people have already been handed over to the enemy. What are you going to do?" Juan asked Nicasio.

"I'll fight 'til the end," came the reply.

"Me too."

The two soldiers didn't know that Republican Army in the east and the south had already begun its exodus. The news that later emerged about this journey was truly shocking. Long queues of soldiers, women, children, old people and animals lined the snow-covered roads. The fascist aircraft that followed their progress made a hellish noise. How many would make it to their destination alive? As if he sensed what was to come, Nicasio started to recite a verse from his favourite poet[97]:

---

[97] Romance Sonámbulo [Sleepwalking Ballad], Federico García Lorca, Obras Completas [The Complete Works], Aguilar, Madrid, 1964, page 402 [translation taken from online source. http://www.poetryintranslation.com/PITBR/Spanish/Lorca.htm#_Toc485030359

*"How intimate the night became,
like a little, hidden plaza.
Drunken Civil Guards were beating,
beating, beating on the door frame."*

15. VISIT TO HERVÁS

The train slowly climbed the slope; huffing and puffing as though it were an elderly man scaling the last few steps of a very long staircase. The chug of the engine rang out into the distance as it pulled its many carriages up the incline. The train's red nose and black shell could be seen up ahead peeking out of the smoke that it left in its wake. The Jerte valley in all its glory stretched out into the horizon. Cherry blossom shimmered in the midday sun and the scent wafted into the carriages through the open windows. Spring had well and truly arrived and, although it was only April, it already seemed more like the end of May.

The carriages on the train were mostly full; seats were occupied by nuns, cattle farmers and priests. There were also a good number of soldiers returning from the front, their sunburned hue marking them out from the pale, smiling faces of their fellow passengers. There was a sense of optimism and hope in the air. The Civil War had lasted nearly three awful years and a million people were dead or missing; but it was finally over. Now the victors were savouring Franco's triumph. Franco; the saviour of their homeland and defender of traditional values in a 'glorious, great and free' Catholic Spain. The soldiers' conversation and laughter echoed throughout the corridors and mingled with elated cries of "Onwards and upwards Spain" and "Long live Franco".

Further down the train, two women and a man sat unsmiling in one of the third-class carriages; they didn't laugh, in fact their faces were a picture of anxiety. They were members of a country family who had spent the war years in Madrid and were now returning home to check that their parents were safe and well. Alongside them in the carriage there was a priest, two nuns and also a woman dressed in black who looked as though she too heralded from the country.

Trinidad asked the woman, "Excuse me madam, will we be arriving at Hervás soon?"

The black-clad woman, who sat opposite, cast an appraising eye over Trinidad before responding, "Yes, we'll be there in less than half an hour. We've just left Casas del Monte, the next stop is Aldeanueva and then Hervás[98]." The woman placed her bony hands in the lap of her skirt and asked her fellow passenger, "So, is that were you're from?"

The response came, "Yes madam. My brother, sister and I are all from Hervás but we were in Madrid during the war. We're going home to see if our parents are ok."

The woman continued, "So, have you been away for long?"

"Yes madam, for sixteen years"

"Well, I say," the woman's eyes widened; her curiosity piqued, "you must have been very young when you left."

"Yes we were, very young," came the reply.

"I've heard that it was terrible in Madrid during the war, what with all the bombings," the woman continued, clearly wanting to know more.

"You can't even begin to imagine," Teresa said pointedly, voicing her opinion for the first time in this conversation.

---

[98] See map 3.

"So did many people die?"

"Unfortunately, yes, many many people."

At that moment one of the nuns crossed herself and said "May the Lord pardon their sins and take them into His Glory". José III looked at the nun, unable to disguise his anger as he thought of all the friends he had seen die at the front. He had heard people say to his superior in the army, a man they called 'El Campesino'[99], that Spain would never be free until all the priests and the nuns had been kicked out of the country.

Guessing her brother's train of thought, and knowing his opinions on religion, Teresa quickly changed the subject by asking the woman, "And where are you travelling to madam?"

"I'm going to Baños[100]; that's where I'm from. I'm just on my way back from visiting my son in Plasencia."

"Ah lovely! That's a beautiful city and it just so happens to be where I'm from," exclaimed the priest, who had obviously been eavesdropping on their conversation.

Teresa looked at the priest. He reminded her of don Antonio, the priest in her village. He had the same tanned face, grey hair and mocking, false smile. His thick dense eyebrows also reached down to his eyelashes, in the same way as don Antonio's, giving him the look of a Grand Inquisitor as he gazed down at the congregation from his pulpit during Sunday service. He even wore the same round glasses; always smudged and perched precariously halfway down his nose.

---

[99] Valentín González González, nicknamed 'El Campesino', was a Republican soldier who gained notoriety for his cruelty in the Civil War.
[100] See map 3.

The priest on the train had the same fat, greasy lips and teeth that were stained yellow from nicotine. He wore dirty robes and his dog-collar was missing; his cap was crooked, falling to one side of his face. Although he might have wanted to appear serious, he reminded Teresa of the comics she saw in *Sol* newspaper.[101]

The woman replied to the priest's interjection, "Yes – so my son says as well. But I prefer my hometown. Cities are for the young folk, at my age I'm only interested in the quiet life now."

José III took a long hard look at the priest as well; he wondered what a man like this would be doing in Plasencia[102]. José III had never been there himself, but he knew the clergy wouldn't be there for nothing. And he decided that that in itself was reason enough for him never to set foot there.

A sharp whistle pulled him out of his reverie. He noticed the train, which had sped up since it had reached the top of the slope, was now slowing down again as though preparing to stop. And indeed it did a few seconds later; the brakes grinding against the tracks until it came to a complete halt. He looked at the platform and saw it was swarming with brown troops. Police officers from the *guardia civil* were checking all passengers as they got off the train. He worried it would surely be the same when they reached Hervás. A wave of fear and anxiety washed over him; his past affiliation with the red army definitely wouldn't help him there. The station clock struck a quarter to three in the afternoon. The station name was painted on a sign in black lettering: *Aldeanueva del Camino*. José III

---

[101] A liberal-leaning newspaper in Madrid at the time of the Republic.
[102] See map 3.

stared hard at the letters, trying to read the name and sounding out "Al-de-a-nu-e-va" in his head. He was deeply ashamed of the fact that he couldn't read, but he later came to accept that this was simply the way things were for people of his generation. He was one of many young people who suffered from the same problem; in his town only children from rich families had been to school and knew how to read.

"Oh look, we're at Aldeanueva already," said the woman in black. "Not long now until we get to Hervás and then…next stop Baños," she exclaimed, barely able to contain her excitement.

"I am so excited, I can't wait to get there!" said Trinidad with a huge smile on her face. She turned to her sister, "Teresa, do you remember when we left the village?"

"As if I could forget!" said Teresa. "You know, I've thought about this moment for so long now, but I never imagined we'd be coming home under these circumstances."

"Tell me about it, I never thought the war would be so awful and bloodthirsty," said Trinidad.

"All that matters now is that our parents are ok," replied Teresa with a nervous smile.

The woman from Baños looked at Teresa, wanting to reassure her, and said "Of course they'll be ok, you'll see. In my village they only 'dealt with' the reds. If your parents are just simple farmers and they haven't rubbed anybody up the wrong way I'm sure nothing will have happened to them. But… you never know in those villages, there's just so much jealousy; you can never really be sure of people."

"God's mercy is infinite and he always helps those in need," said the other nun, who up to that point hadn't said a word.

José III allowed his attention to drift away from the conversation; after all it was veering off down the religious paths that he so hated. His mind wandered to when he had left Hervás. It was a few years ago that he had been called up to military service, and he hadn't been home since, nor had he seen his parents. However, now he was fortunate enough to have in his possession a written guarantee slip from don Carlos, so that he could take this trip with his sisters. There were checkpoints everywhere now; all run by the police or Franco's army. It was impossible to travel anywhere without papers and if you were caught without them you would be immediately arrested. He also had don Carlos to thank for the fact that he didn't have to go to a workers' battalion like so many of his Republican friends done. He really had been very lucky.

After pulling out of Aldeanueva the train continued on its weary journey through orchards and fields in bloom. The smell of cherry trees, mint and rosemary all drifted through the open window, and the three siblings began to recognise the countryside that opened up in front of them. It was an emotional moment for Trinidad and Teresa; they had dreamt of this return for so long and had at times feared they would never get to see their home again. They saw the orchards of the Romana, and its little houses with their coloured roofs and white walls. They saw the silhouette of mount Pinajarro looming ever larger the closer they got to the village. They had soon passed the white bridge of Peña de los Lagartos[103] and then the station was in front of them. They said goodbye to the other passengers in their compartment and made their way towards the door just as the train came to a stop with a sharp shudder. They hadn't even managed to step onto the platform before the police officers that had been waiting at the station approached them. They looked the new arrivals up and down before saying, "Who are you, and why have you come to Hervás?"

The group showed the guard their identity cards and the guarantee slips from don Carlos, then watched him with a mixture of anxiety and fear. The officer's twitchy eyes rested on each of the siblings as he examined their photographs. He took more time than was strictly necessary looking over the two sisters. His eyes lingered first on Teresa, then Trinidad, his gaze unashamedly resting on their bodies causing them both to blush, uncomfortable under his intense scrutiny. José III who stood next to them felt a creeping anger; he was on the verge of saying something stupid to the officer but managed to restrain himself. At that moment, the policeman saw from José III's documents that he had fought for the Republicans. He looked at the young man and saw that they were roughly the same age. The officer thought that he could very well have been in a similar position had he fallen into the hands of the red army. He winked at José III as if to say, 'Sorry about all that, but at last you've had a bit of luck my friend'.

He then addressed the group, "How long will you be in Hervás for?"

---

[103] **See map 1.**

Teresa answered, "Just for one night."

The officer continued, "And why have you come?"

"To see our parents."

He looked at them again and asked, "Are you Tío Fuste's children?"

"Yes sir, we are."

The policeman showed their documents to his sergeant who, after examining them with interest, said "Tío Fuste is a good man; the pears on his orchard are truly delicious. I was lucky enough to taste them on more than one occasion". He then gave a nod to the policeman who said to the three siblings, "Right, everything's in order, you can be on your way."

They left the station and crossed the bridge over the train tracks, descending through a procession of white, one-storey houses with red roofs. They would have dearly liked to walk through the village itself but their parents lived on the outskirts, and they didn't want to waste any of the precious time they had with them. The smells of the countryside were all around: mint, rosemary, thyme, and the aromas brought all three back to their childhood. Walking towards the fields where they had grown up transported them back to their past. Trinidad remembered all those walks she went on with her goats. Teresa, thought of her time as a nanny looking after the Menglano children. For José III, the smell of cut wood vividly brought to mind to his younger years when he had gone to a workshop to learn how to be a carpenter.

Once they had passed the last house on the path, they crossed the train tracks again, this time going underneath, and then walked into the forest. The noise of the leaves rustling in the trees resounded in their ears as they watched birds wheeling amid the undergrowth. Halfway down the path they crossed the Fuente del Monte Bridge where water from the Gallegos River flowed melodiously over large rocks. They had walked this very same route with their parents countless times. Trinidad thought of all those trips to help her mother wash clothes in the river, or take milk to the village to sell; it made her appreciate how happy they had all been then. She missed that freedom to go where she pleased, the innocence of growing up in poverty that meant she had been happy with just a piece of bread and a few cherries. That wonderful appreciation of all that nature has to offer; she had lost touch with that when she went to the city. All this came flooding back to her, and she knew she had never truly lost her love of nature. Those sixteen years she had spent in Madrid now seemed an eternity and the only thing on her mind was being able to see her parents and throw her arms around them.

As they got closer to the bend in the path that would lead them to the orchard, they heard the gentle sound of bells jangling as the cows moved lazily around in the nearby field. Trinidad's heart started to beat faster. They passed the pond where she had bathed so often, and there in front of them was the house that they had grown up in. The wooden shutters of the window which overlooked the field were open, and a greyish smoke spiralled out of the chimney into the blue afternoon sky.

José III was the first to reach the gate and it opened without a sound, not slamming against the stone wall behind as it so often used to. The three siblings walked under the vine arbours down the narrow path that led to the house. They had barely passed the peach tree when they caught sight of two small figures sitting on a stone bench near the door, enjoying the afternoon sun. There was a woman dressed in black, with completely white hair; and a man in corduroy trousers. The two figures raised their heads in the direction of the group at almost the same time. The three siblings ran towards their parents, who could not believe their eyes. They were trying in vain to get up with the help of the stone wall behind them, so that they could hug their children.

"Mother! Father!" Teresa shouted,. "It's us, your children!"

Their mother could barely contain her shock and wonder as she muttered "In the name of all that is holy!"

"Bloody hell, I can't believe it!" said Francisco with his big blue eyes open wide and a smile that stretched from ear to ear.

Children and parents all came together in a warm embrace as tears sprang from their eyes, then one by one they started to laugh, the joy spreading among the group as though contagious. Then all at once, they started to speak, and little by little the three siblings began to tell their parents what had happened on their journey and everything that they had gone through to come and see them. After her initial surprise Dorotea managed to compose herself and, as she picked up her shawl which had fallen to the floor, she asked her three children the first of many questions.

"So come on you three, tell me what did you do for those three terrible years?" she asked, almost afraid to hear their answers.

José III looked at his mum, smiling, and started to talk.

"Well, as you all know, I had been in Madrid for some time when the war broke out. I joined the army the month after I turned twenty-one and after my training in the *Quinto Regimiento*, I was sent to the Sierra de Guadarrama – it was so cold there!"

Dorotea cried out, "My poor boy!" She couldn't help but think of all those cold winters when he was young; of how he complained because there weren't enough clothes to keep him warm. "You know I thought about you all the time."

José went on, "Most of the men in my company were workers or farmers with communist beliefs, and we were taken to the Guadalajara front to fight the Italian fascists. Many of my comrades died there."

"Oh that's awful! Holy mother of God!" exclaimed Dorotea as she crossed herself. Listening to their son's story made Francisco and Dorotea think of their own brushes with death during the conflict in Hervás.

"My regiment was led by 'El Campesino', who I'm sure you've heard of. He used to execute his soldiers for the littlest thing; we were all absolutely petrified of him," José continued.

Francisco was following his son's story with the same rapt attention as his wife. He looked at his son and said "Yes, I've heard of him; he was very famous here among the socialist farmers. They say he was very brave, but from your tales I now see there was a darker side to him."

"So anyway, about halfway through the war I was moved to the *46ª División* and I fought in the battle of the Ebro, still under the command of 'El Campesino'. It was a huge battle, probably the most significant of the whole war. Many men died; both from our side and Franco's."

Francisco jumped in again, "There was a lot of talk here in the village about the battle of the Ebro[104]. Some people had radios and they used to listen to the 'despatches'; there were lots of different versions of the conflict but of course we only heard Franco's side of it here. We were told that the Nationalists had already won the battle, they even sung about it."

"You're right," José said nodding. "Talking of songs, we used to sing one that went like this…"

If you want to write to me,
You know where I am posted:
The Third Mixed Brigade,
In the first line of fire.

Even if they blast our bridge
And also the pontoon,
You will see me crossing the Ebro River:
In a little sail ship.

---

[104] The battle of the Ebro was the pivotal battle of the Spanish Civil War. Although Republican forces achieved a significant victory early on, their ultimate defeat was inevitable. After four months of fighting, Republican troops were pushed back across the Ebro river. This significant defeat sealed the Republic's fate.

And he went on…

At the Gandesa inn
There is Mohamed, a Moor,
Who tells one: «Come in, fellow!
What do you wish to eat?»
The first course they give
Are fragmentation grenades,
And the second are shrapnel shells,
To refresh one's memory.[105]

The song brought up so many emotions, none of them could hold back the tears. Teresa and Trinidad were crying as they remembered soldiers singing on the streets of Madrid. Francisco and Dorotea were crying for their son and all they had just learned.

After a long pause to recover his composure and get his breath back, José III carried on with his story.

"I spent four months there, not knowing if I would ever make it out of the conflict alive. Finally, I got lucky and managed to get back to Madrid where I spent the rest of the war. When we surrendered I was arrested and I would have been sent to a workers' battalion had it not been for don Carlos, Trini's boss. He gave me a pass so that I didn't have to go and it also meant I got to come here to the village."

"You have no idea how much we both worried about him" Trinidad said. "We found out from one of his comrades that he had

---

[105] Translation taken from https://en.wikipedia.org/wiki/Si_me_quieres_escribir.

been arrested. I went straight to don Carlos who immediately spoke to someone in Franco's ranks and convinced them not to send him to the battalion. It was a real miracle."

"Trini's right," José said, taking up the story again. "You know, I have seen so much death and lived through such a tragic episode in human history. I don't know if I'll ever be able to forget what happened out there at the front, but all that matters now is seeing you both and my sister Josefa."

And with that José came to the end of his story.

Dorotea looked at her son and realised how fortunate they were that he was with them and that she had been able to hold him close once again; it really was a miracle. Throughout the war, she had spent so many sleepless nights fearing the worst and hoping against hope that fate would not take away the only son she had left. She silently gave thanks to God for not letting her down. It was at moments like these that her faith in the Almighty was truly bolstered. "Thank you God for hearing my prayers, and forgive me if I ever doubted your Mercy."

Dorotea stepped forward reaching out to embrace her son, and she held him as tight as she could with her slight frame, it was as if she wanted to stay in that moment forever. Francisco, moved by his wife's actions, also hugged his son as tight as he could.

It wasn't long before Teresa started telling her story, filling her parents in on the most important events of her wartime experience. She begged their forgiveness for not being able to stay in touch with them during the conflict. She told them how they had constantly been in her thoughts, especially in the most difficult moments of the war. She had often thought of her mother, remembering her as she had been during her visit to Madrid before war broke out. These were the memories that had given Teresa the strength to go on, and to believe that she would one day see her parents again.

Teresa's description of events, and what had happened to her, moved both of her parents. Dorotea hugged her daughter close while she desperately searched her skirt pockets for a handkerchief to dry the tears that were running down her face. Francisco's lively eyes shone even more than normal; like stars on a clear summer night. However, his smile, normally so bright, was dimmed as though an eclipse had passed over him.

After a while, when she was sure everyone had recovered somewhat from the emotion that had gone before, Trinidad slowly began to tell her side of the story.

"My story is like Teresa's really. I was terrified most of the time; firstly of the *checas*, then of the military men that guarded the embassy, and in the end, it was the daily bombings that scared me the most. It was risky to even leave the house; you didn't know if you would make it back or be killed in the middle of the street by a bomb. It's like José said, that war killed so many innocent people. Women and children were massacred, even the elderly, not to mention all those young men that were barely even fifteen or sixteen when they left for the front. But, well, thanks be to God that nightmare is over now."

After listening to the last of their children's stories, Dorotea and

Francisco looked at one another and a silent understanding passed between them. All at once they recognised the enormity of the tragedy that had befallen their family; whilst at the same time, they also realised how close they had all come to death, especially José III. They now saw with clarity that all this useless fratricidal war had done was ensure there were more bodies to bury, and even that hadn't been done in a dignified way. It was true that at their age they had lived through a good deal of disasters and tragedies, but nothing of these proportions. All of a sudden, they understood that it was now up to everyone to fix this country of theirs that had been so badly broken by three years of civil war. It was a task that fell to everyone, and it would not be an easy one – especially because of the hatred and misery that the conflict had bred.

Their melancholy train of thought was interrupted by Trinidad. "And what was it like for you both? Tell us everything, we have been going crazy worrying about it."

Dorotea looked to her husband, he was stroking his moustache pensively. After a while, Francisco emptied the last of the water from the clay pitcher into his cup and took a long sip before beginning their story.

"A lot has happened in the village since you all left. During the Primo de Rivera dictatorship, times were relatively good economically in the village. All the problems with the strikes were sorted out and the cloth factories opened again. They were exporting to other countries. I think the Great War helped to sell all our products and standards of living were getting better. We even had a few years of good harvests and we weren't going hungry as before. However, when the King left in 1931 and the Republic was born, we went backwards again. Some people say that it was because the socialists were in charge, but others say it had more to do with exports to Europe grinding to a halt when the United States joined the war. Whatever the real reason is, the left-wing *berzas* and the right-wing *virutas* started getting into brawls on the street."[106]

Teresa couldn't help but smile when she heard these names, it made her think of other similar terms she had heard on the streets of Madrid. However, her smile was fleeting and in no time she returned her attention to her father's story.

"Also, there were lots of strikes, again like we had had in times gone by." At this point Francisco looked at Trinidad, as if urging her to recall all that he had told her about strikes when she was a little girl.

"The old class wars started between the owners and the workers again and we were thrown into another conflict. The Republican government wanted to improve the lives of the workers in spite of the worsening economic situation. They formed *mutuas de socorro*[107] to support those workers that were left unemployed; the town meeting also voted to create a new school group and a secular school for younger children[108]. The religious folk in town didn't like that one bit

---

[106] These were the popular names that each group was recognised by the people in Hervás.
[107] Associations that assisted unemployed workers.
[108] *Represión, silencio y olvido, Memoria Histórica de Hervás y el Alto Ambroz [Repression, silence and forgetting, Historic Memories of Hervás and Alto Ambroz], pp 63-64,* Francisco Moriche Mateos [undated]

and, as I'll get to later, it was the root of a lot of hatred and jealousy during the war. On 29th March 1936, before the war broke out, something happened that really shook up all of the Catholics in the village. Part of the building and the high altar at the Iglesia de Santa María was burned down, it truly was an attack on something sacred."

José III interrupted his father to ask, "Did they catch the people that did it?"

His father responded, "We still don't know to this day who did it, but there's a general suspicion that it was someone from the Left."[109]

He continued with the tale, "When war broke out it wasn't long before the village was taken by forces loyal to Franco, they had come from places like Aldeanueva and Baños. Some socialists and communists escaped into the countryside but even so, forty people were arrested in those first confusing days, all because some big mouth in the village had said that they were sympathisers with the old regime. They hauled out all of the women from the Left, and they shaved their heads, then made them drink castor oil before they were dragged around the village. Children were taken out of school just so they could see this 'spectacle'."

"Oh no! That's terrible" his daughters cried out, almost in unison. Teresa's hand flew to her mouth. "How could something like that happen? Those poor boys and girls, what would they think seeing such an awful sight." She looked as though she didn't want to

---

[109] According to Francisco Moriche [undated] (op. cit.) there are two opposing versions (page 64), one version states that it was the Left that did it and the other version, that it was the Right so that they could then blame the Left.

believe what her father was telling her, "I mean, we saw some terrible things in Madrid, but I don't think I've ever heard anything so disgusting."

Dorotea looked at her daughter and said kindly, "Well my child, that's the way it happened, your father is telling you the truth."

Francisco added, "We didn't go, but people have told us it was awful seeing those poor people so thin, they looked skeletal. The castor oil gave them the runs as they were paraded around, much to the amusement of many of the spectators."

Francisco made sure to pause in his narration here, so that his children could fully take in the tragedy of those female prisoners. Even though none of them had been there to witness this example of vile human cruelty, they could imagine how those poor women felt when they were totally exposed to the vengeance of their neighbours, who took pleasure in insulting and harassing them as they passed, as though they were prisoners walking to the gallows. A shadow of sadness and regret passed over all of their faces as they realised they belonged to a world that would allow such atrocities to come to pass.

After a brief moment of reflection, Francisco carried on, "I haven't told you the worst part yet. Do you remember Quico, Aunt Sorda's boy? You know he was like family to us, ever since José went to Madrid he had been helping me in the fields. What with Quico being so young and having a communist father, well, he obviously grew up to be left-wing too. When Franco's men entered the village little Quico went up to the forests and hid there with the others, he stayed hidden for quite some time but eventually they caught him not far from here. His mother later found out that the Falangists from nearby villages had taken him away in a van and shot him. Nobody knows where he was buried though, that's if he even was. Some of the bodies were just left in the ditch at the side of the Aldeanueva road."

Teresa and Trinidad didn't know Quico, but José had left the village later than them and so he remembered the boy well. Quico had been pleasant and helpful, always ready to work and with a desire to live a better life than his parents. Unfortunately, this wasn't to be; as fate would have it father and son both paid the ultimate sacrifice in defence of their beliefs. May they rest in peace.

"Such an awful tragedy! We miss him terribly; he was such a good lad." Francisco's voice had reduced to barely a whisper, and both he and Dorotea began to get upset again. After a few tense moments Francisco resumed his story.

"It was only because we had always gotten on well with the *guardia civil* that nothing happened to us. The Sergeant and his men came along on various occasions asking if we had seen Quico, but we genuinely didn't know where he was. Of course, even if we had, we would never have told them; they just would have gone and shot the poor boy, which unfortunately they did anyway. Whenever they came, we told them to take whatever fruit they wanted. They and the Moroccan soldiers from Tetuán, the ones that are still stationed in the village, well, they all took pears, apples and cherries. I'm sure you all saw when you arrived at the station that it's packed with troops. They say there are between two and four thousand soldiers here, so we're well 'guarded'".

"Yes father, we were just saying the station was literally overrun with them," answered José III. "They wouldn't let anyone through without a pass. We had one tense moment where we thought they might even arrest us," he said, thinking back to how that officer had looked at his sisters.

"Also, as you can imagine, we were both so scared by what everyone said was happening in Madrid. Your mother spent most nights crying and thinking of you all." Francisco paused here and Dorotea took advantage of the silence to add something.

"You must go and see Josefa; she doesn't even know you're here."

"Mum I'm sure the whole village knows by now," José III said. "The policeman who checked our papers asked us loads of questions and he knew who we were."

Francisco continued with his story, filling in some of the gaps and telling them about other more inconsequential things. Then the three siblings had a rest and something to eat before heading off to see their sister Josefa.

Josefa had married Ángel in 1932 and they had had four children: Manuel (1932), María (1934), Ángel (1935) and José (1937). Josefa herself was a lot like Dorotea. She had inherited her mother's temperament and her work ethic. Just like her mother, Josefa had married young at the age of twenty-one and had had children right away[110]. Of medium build, she had sweet and delicate features; she

---

[110] As the reader will remember Josefa had a total of ten children that she cared for attentively. None of them died in childhood.

was beautiful and her big dark eyes lent an intensity to her gaze.

Ángel was four years older than Josefa and together with his only brother Julio, he worked his father's land. Ángel was Hervás born and bred: he loved wine and women –just like Josefa's father tío Fuste. Also like Francisco, he had a knack for singing and he played the tuba in the village band. Although he was short, he was a good-looking lad and his smile melted women's hearts. When he spoke, he used elegant language with a strong local accent, the words he used could sometimes only be understood by people from the village. His dry sense of humour made him fun to be around, with his tales of the vagaries of village life, of music, religion and, of course, women.

Ángel and Josefa lived in the upper part of the village, on the street that led to the church. When her brothers and sisters arrived, Josefa was already waiting for them outside with her family (the news of their arrival having spread like wildfire just as José III predicted).

"Oh look who it is, goodness me, I'm so happy to see you all!" shouted Josefa as she hugged each and every one of them. "Let me look on youse a while, gosh ya look like death!"

Despite all the time that had passed, Trinidad recognised her younger sister immediately. Josefa had barely been more than a girl of thirteen when Trinidad and Teresa left for Madrid. Josefa called out to her children Manolo and María who were playing in the street; soon the doorway was full of little kids coming to gawp at these strangers. The littlest ones were quickly followed by their mothers who also wanted to say hello to the new arrivals. Teresa and Trinidad didn't recognise Josefa's neighbours, nor did the neighbours recognise the two sisters, but that didn't stop the house filling with well-wishers. Everyone wanted to get a look at these country girls who had come back from Madrid, after all they were the first to make the journey and as such were considered exotic creatures.

After the chaotic arrival, the three siblings stayed to have tea and soon Ángel arrived on a mule carrying a load of firewood. Once all the introductions had been made and the animal had been fed and watered, Ángel rejoined the group. They were by that point embroiled in an animated conversation about everything that had happened in Hervás since the three of them had left the village.

"Well, y'know, since you lot left the village there's been loads of stuff goin' on an everyfink," Josefa told them in the typical local accent.

Trinidad furrowed her brow and a shadow of worry passed over her face. She looked at her sister before saying, "But Josefa, father told us that all the racket of those first few days didn't last long. Was he wrong?"

"Don't you worry ya little heads, things were alright whilst the King was still in power, but when he left there was trouble almost every day," Josefa went on. "But nobody said nuffink about anyfink."

"Wot's more, tío Fuste didn't feel the worst of it, wot with his grub and his fags," Ángel added animatedly, the first chance he'd had to say anything. "My bruvver said fings haven't bin harf as bad in Hervás as fey were in Béjar. There was a right old slaughter-geddon there."

Trinidad looked at him in horror, "Slaughter-geddon! What on earth is that?"

Josefa looked at her blankly, "Well, a slaughter, y'know like what we do to the pigs."

Teresa chimed in, "Well we sure had slaughters every day in Madrid, especially in those last few months."

José III said wearily, "Look, let's change the subject, I've had it up to here with talking about war and death all over the place."

Within a few hours of being back together it felt as though the brothers and sisters had never been apart. They were so happy to be reunited with their family and the atmosphere was almost the same as before they had left the village; but Trinidad knew that somehow it could never really be the same. Living in Madrid had changed her as a person. That brush with the bourgeoisie of her employers, their way of dressing and talking; all of it had altered her to the very core. Listening to her family talk in the traditional way of the village brought her back to her roots, and she was extremely proud of where she had come from. However, just like a plant that blooms when it is transported to pastures new, she realised that her roots were now firmly in the capital. This realisation made her long to be back in Madrid, and to pick up the life that she was entitled to now that the war was over. She took a long look at her brother and sisters, at her family, and she said, "Well come on then, we've got to get going. We've got to be back in Madrid tomorrow"

Josefa looked shocked and saddened all at once, "You're not going already are you? Come on, the fire hasn't even gone out yet".

Trinidad looked at her baby sister, "Yes, we've got to get going, our bosses only gave us one day off."

"Ok then, let's get back to little old Madrid so we can 'have our hair done and get a perm,'" said Teresa reciting part of a song that was popular in the city, all with a posh Madrid accent to impress the others.

They all laughed at her joke. Trinidad, suddenly anxious to get going, rose from her chair and gestured for Teresa and José III to do the same. They said their goodbyes to Josefa and Ángel and started off on the walk back to their parents' finca.

16. REPRESSION

If understanding is impossible, knowledge is necessary, because what happened could happen again, consciences can shrink and cloud over again: even ours[111]

Madrid was a city mired in sadness, however much the ever-present fascist propaganda proclaimed otherwise. The recent war had left its scars and the city bore them for all to see. The joy that its people possessed before 1936 had disappeared somewhere in those war years. Tetuán de las Victorias was a miserable neighbourhood[112] full of rubble and tiny tin-roofed shacks that passed for houses. All the workshops and small factories that had employed so many hundreds of people before the war had now disappeared. Nicasio clearly remembered having attended meetings of the local UGT there while his people were still in power. However, now it was no more than a shanty town, drowning in poverty and plagued by the rats, typhus and tuberculosis that goes with it. The renovation that had been promised in the Plan de la Castellana[113] had still not begun and in the La Ventilla and Valdeacederas areas near where Nicasio lived, there was an abundance of junk shops and people living in shacks despite the lack of sanitation.

Nicasio had found work at a barbershop on Calle Bravo Murillo. From his vantage point there he watched a daily parade of colourful

---

[111] Primo Levi, *Si esto es un hombre* [If this is a Man], page 208.
[112] A working neighbourhood in the north of Madrid. See map 7.
[113] Town planning and development scheme from the 1940s which affected the Tetuán neighbourhood.

characters go by: rubbish collectors, rag and bone men, miscreants and all sorts, trying to wade across the sludge and mire that was building up on Carretera de Francia.[114] Their struggle just another indication of the *Régimen's*[115] desire to punish the working people for their opposition during the war. Many more years would pass before anything came of the plans to redevelop the neighbourhood.

It had now been three years since the end of the war and Nicasio was trying, in vain, to forget all that had happened. The fact that his side had been defeated had left him with a very bitter taste in his mouth. In fact, you could say that his revolutionary dreams had been well and truly quashed by the repression of Franco's regime. Nobody was safe. Even now that the conflict was over, people were still reporting on their neighbours, which resulted in hundreds of executions and thousands of arrests. Nicasio himself had been arrested, as had thousands of other Republican soldiers after the conflict. He had finally been released after almost a year in Madrid where he suffered all kinds of hardship. It was an awful situation. As he described it, "They put us into a tiny room, there were some two hundred prisoners in it, they gave us a small tin of sardines each day and that was all we ate. The hygiene and sanitation situation was deplorable."

Although it had been hard, at least his detention hadn't lasted long, he said to himself. And with that thought he started off towards Ceinos, eager to see his parents. He took the train as far as Medina de Rioseco, but he didn't stay there long once he saw the town was full

---

[114] The old Carretera de Francia road started on Calle Bravo Murillo.
[115] The name given to Franco's dictatorship.

of Falangists. He boarded the *burra* train and got off at Villalón,[116] which was the closest station to Ceinos. From there he walked to Aguilar where his uncle Aurelio lived; they shared the same political ideals.

It was a sunny May morning, and he could see flocks of birds wheeling over the fields; their forms silhouetted against the bright blue sky. The wheat had grown tall that year and the stalks waved in an occasional gentle breeze. On the walk to Aguilar, Nicasio's mind wandered and he thought again of the time he had worked in Medina de Rioseco, before he had left for Madrid. He remembered his childhood and how, like his father and his uncle Aurelio, he had truly believed in the Socialist cause. His belief, paired with his loquacious eloquence, had been enough to attract many fellow townspeople to his cause. Like him, they too had thought that their moment had come when the revolution started. He wondered what had become of them all now; many of them would surely be dead. He feared for his parents and felt a certain anxiety about making his identity known in this defeated town. He had never thought he would be coming home like this.

When Aurelio saw his nephew approaching, tears of joy sprang from his eyes; he had been so afraid that Nicasio had perished in the war. Within minutes of his arrival, the old man related to his nephew what happened to the family and the village during his absence, and offered to go with him to Ceinos. Aurelio had already sent two of his daughters ahead of them to prepare Nicasio's parents in advance; he

---

[116] **See map 9.**

knew they would both need time to take in such happy news, especially Felisa. Soon the whole town knew that Nicasio was home and when he finally arrived at his house, he was greeted by the whole family.

His mother was the first to reach him, "Nicasio, my darling son. Oh, I'm so happy to see you!" she shouted while she hugged him close to her, not wanting to let him go. She was crying tears of joy, "I can't believe it; we thought that we'd lost you forever! Your sisters and I, we prayed for you every night and in the end, God listened."

Nicasio smiled, happy to see his mother again. "I wrote several letters to you all during the war, telling you that I was fine. Didn't you get them?"

His mother looked puzzled, "No, my darling, we didn't get any letters. But then the town's been controlled by Franco's henchmen ever since the war started."

His father beckoned him inside, "Come on in son, we've got so much to tell you."

Nicasio took a long look at his parents; he could see that they had been through a lot. His father didn't stand quite so tall now and he had a hunch that Nicasio couldn't remember seeing before the war. His mother was pale despite the warm summer weather, which told him that she wasn't in good health. He tried to force these worries to the back of his mind, and entered his old family home. It was dark and he was momentarily blinded after the brightness of outside. It took a few moments for his eyes to adjust to the lack of light, but he soon started to make out objects in the entrance hall.

There were the old familiar farming tools and he saw that the picture of his mother's beloved *Virgen del Perpetuo Socorro* still hung on the wall. He went through to the sitting room, where most of their family life had unfolded, and he took a seat on a hard wooden chair.

His family told him of those first few tragic days of the civil war when the *guardia civil* and the Falangists declared power in the name of the rebels. There was a van where they loaded everyone that they had decided to execute. His father had been on that van until, at the last minute, the mayor (a relative and also a Franco sympathiser) intervened on his behalf and tried to save his life. While Nicasio's father was still on the van with the others, one of the henchmen said, "If we only take Francisco off it's going to look suspicious, I mean he's the president of the PSOE". "So, let's take off Secundino and Evaristo as well then," said the mayor, thinking on his feet. And so it came to be that fifteen people were shot that day instead of eighteen, and three less bodies were found at the side of the road near the park in Medina de Rioseco.

Nicasio also listened to his mother tell him how at the very same time, she had been arrested and interrogated by the *guardia civil*. During the interrogation in the prison the policemen started beating her up for being a communist whilst at the same time throwing all sorts of questions at her, "So you go around calling for 'death to the police' do you?"

Felisa looked at them pleadingly, "Why on earth would I say that? My brother's a policeman."

The officers, who were from Villavicencio de los Caballeros,[117] looked at one another before saying to her: "We're going to go and check this out, but if you're lying...well, just you wait."

Felisa did indeed have a brother who had entered the force years before.[118] Having discovered that Felisa was telling them the truth, the officers set her free. However the beating she received had left her with injuries on her back that would take weeks to heal, not to mention the psychological wounds that would never truly leave her. Nicasio learned that it wasn't only his parents that been harassed; his uncle Aurelio had also suffered.

Unfortunately, the family's bad luck had not yet come to an end. Within days of his arrival in Ceinos, while his family were still celebrating his return, the henchmen in the town had a secret nighttime meeting at the cemetery and decided that they had to eliminate Nicasio. The following day, they charged him with being a Communist and he was arrested by the *guardia civil*. He was taken to Valladolid, where he stayed until the relevant reports were sent over from Madrid. Nicasio had no blood on his hands; and at the start of the uprising, he had even saved the life of a lieutenant in Franco's army; so this lieutenant and his boss in Getafe both wrote very positive reports on him. This helped counteract the negative portrayal he had received from those in Ceinos.

During the very brief and perfunctory hearing he received, the pro-Franco judge ordered that Nicasio be sent to a disciplinary battalion. He arrived at Miranda de Ebro[119] on 14th June 1940,

---

[117] A city close to Ceinos where there were police holding cells.
[118] The lack of work in the country meant that sons of farmers often applied to join the Forces, as happened years later with one of Nicasio's brothers.

spending the bitter winter there and living through terrible deprivation. In March the following year his battalion was moved to Igal in Navarra, and they were put to work 'laying roads'.

"As soon as we arrived we were given a hat with the letter "D" on it (which stood for 'desafecto' or hostile to the regime) and they stuck us in these freezing cold barracks, the doors didn't even close properly... [we were then put] in the stables with the cows and horses. In there, it was so warm that there was a terrible flea infestation and we just couldn't stand it. So we asked the lieutenant to take us back out to the snow, we couldn't take it anymore. We were covered in fleas, they were eating us alive. So they took us back to the barracks again, because anything - even freezing - was better than that.

The door to the barracks was tiny, less than two feet high. We slept on a type of bunk bed; and whoever was on the top bed was practically touching the roof. As this was made of asbestos whoever was on top was always freezing cold.

We were starving hungry because the second lieutenant and the corporal (those shameless crooks) sold the battalion's food: oil, chickpeas, anything they could get their hands on. They earned money from selling food on the black market – our food!!

We had been taken there to work on the road that they wanted to build crossing the Pyrenees from Girona to Irún. It was up to us to build the Igal section.

They would bring us out to do a roll call and we would only have a few minutes to get into line once the order had been given. The door was so small that we couldn't all get out at once, it was a matter of going one by one and even then you had to be shoved through. So whenever that whatshisname fancied he would

---

[119] Miranda de Ebro was one of the reception and holding centres used by Franco's machine.

call out STOP! And whoever hadn't been able to get out of the door by then was left outside in the snow. Some of them were barefoot, some had rags on their feet; we were only given one pair of shoes when we arrived and most of them were broken. We didn't even have shoes.

When one of the men took ill because of the cold, we would all make sure to warm him up and to feed him. Some of the men recovered, some didn't. But what was for sure was that the guys that were supposedly taken 'to the hospital', well, they never came back."[120]

In May that year the battalion was moved to Lesaka, near Irún. Their mission there was still to build roads, but this time Nicasio had been able to change his work duty from the hard, physically-demanding job of stone crusher, to that of barber to his company. From there he went to Ensenada de Bolonia in Cádiz until the month of September, when he was transferred again, to Racinos near the capital of the province. He stayed there until June 1942 when he was finally discharged.

The weather, the food and the humane treatment in the Andalusian camps all meant that at first living conditions were much better. According to rumours that floated about among the prisoners, the reason for this was that Franco was scared the Allies would invade Spain when the Second World War was over. Whether that was the real reason or not, life in the prison (at this point they were no longer called concentration camps), became a little easier.

---

[120] *Batallones Disciplinarios (Esclavos del Franquismo), Colección de Memoria Antifranquista: del Baix Llobregat, Volumen I,* [Disciplinary Battalions (Slaves of Francoism), A Collection of Anti-Franco Memories: from the Baix Llobregat, Volume I] pages 52-57 [undated].

It wasn't just physically demanding being in the workers' battalion, it was psychologically gruelling as well. It was torture being deprived of your liberty and being treated like a vile, worthless person every day; after all, the only thing Nicasio had been guilty of was thinking differently. The whole experience had made him think hard about his moral and religious principles. In truth, he had never been a follower of the Church; however his mother had imbued him with Christian values, and these had been put to the test on more than one occasion during the revolution. He had stood up to his comrades when they had wanted to 'disappear' Franco supporters. He was passionate about his beliefs but he also respected the beliefs of others, and he never felt it was necessary to kill someone simply because they didn't agree with him. However, the treatment that he and his fellow prisoners received in the battalion made him see the other side of things: the enemy's side. His forced captivity had also given him time to remember some of his favourite poetry:[121]

Alas! Ah, wretched me! Ah, wretched me!
Heaven, here lying all forlorn,
I desire from thee to know,
Since thou thus dost treat me so,
Why have I provoked thy scorn
By the crime of being born?...

***

---

[121] Calderón de la Barca, *La vida es sueño* [Life is a Dream]. [Translation taken from online source].
http://archive.org/stream/lifeisadream06363gut/lfdrm10a.txt

Must not other creatures be
Born? If born, what privilege
Can they over me allege
Of which I should not be free?
***
/ ...
And with so much more of soul,
Must I have less liberty?

17. IN SEARCH OF A HUSBAND

Life was still hard in Madrid. Food shortages continued to affect the majority of the population and ration books didn't even begin to provide the basics. Weekly rations for one person were ten ounces of sugar, half a pint of oil, fourteen ounces of chickpeas and an egg[122]. Poor people had to be creative with these scant ingredients and so came up with all kinds of new stews: like *arroz de Franco* (rice with fried garlic) and *patatas de pobre* (potatoes, bay leaves, pepper and tomato colouring). People in the city even gave some foods a special name as a joke. This is how snails came to be known as 'garden lobsters', potatoes as 'crop chops' because of how nutritious they were, salted tuna as 'sea sausage', while chunks of cod were called 'little soldiers of Pavia'.[123] Many families had to survive on just one meal a day. Republican currency had been declared valueless and, as that was all most people had, nobody could buy anything. The World War, which was still raging, didn't make it easy to import food from other countries either. Trinidad was lucky in this respect however; they felt the shortages less in her household as they were sent oil, flour and other provisions from don Carlos' properties. Bread was made at home because all the bakeries were closed.

Civilian life slowly returned to normal. After years of loneliness and misery, romance began to blossom again and young people

---

[122] *Los años del miedo (1939-1952)* [The Years of Fear (1939-1952)] , J. Eslava Galán, Editorial Planeta (2008).
[123] *El Madrid de la posguerra* [Post-war Madrid], José Ángel García Ballesteros and Fidel Revilla González, Madrid (2006).

dreamed of getting married, having a home and a family. Teresa was among the first to marry. She met Francisco (who was from Hervás) on a visit to El Escorial, a monastery north of Madrid. They were married not long after they began their relationship. The wedding was held in the Iglesia de la Concepción de Madrid, on 3rd March 1940. Trinidad was the maid of honour and she truly enjoyed the ceremony; it was lovely to see her sister so happy. She thought to herself that, by rights, someday it should be her up there.

Four years later don Carlos also decided to marry. His bride, doña Rosario, was from the Andalusian bourgeoisie and had large properties in Jaén province. Their wedding was held in Madrid and well-known society people from both Madrid and Andalusia were in attendance. Within a year of their marriage their first son, Carlos, was born; shortly followed by Rosario and Fernando.

Life in Castelló was changing quickly for Trinidad. She had gone from cooking for don Carlos and his brother don Fernando to cooking for a newly-wed couple and their family. Doña Rosario gave her instructions on a different meal plan and she tried hard to adapt to her new working conditions. She enjoyed the holidays in Zarauz (Guipúzcoa) where she went with her employers to spend the summer months. In winter she also accompanied them to the olive harvest in Villacarrillo (Jaén). Doña Rosario owned many olive groves and each year she would enlist the help of her family and the domestic servants to harvest the fruit. From December to February Trinidad saw how the whole household, entire families even, lent a hand in collecting this 'green gold'.

The first time Trinidad went to the harvest she was astonished by the number of people involved in picking the fruit. Her employers' country garden was filled with labourers and salaried farmers around harvest-time. They began their work by beating the olive branches, while the women knelt to collect the olives that fell, before placing them in a sort of wooden sieve. They were then put into a large basket to be cleaned and placed into sacks. These sacks were placed on panniers that were transported by mules to the oil press where the olives were weighed. The next step was the grinding of the olives to extract their oil. This whole process was done manually and could take several weeks, depending on the size of the harvest.

What stuck in Trinidad's memory the most was the huge celebration at the end of the harvest. Everybody, including all the workers, joined together in the garden to enjoy a celebratory meal. There was one particular worker, called Antonio; he was really funny and made everyone laugh with his stories and hilarious sayings. It was tradition for someone to tell a funny tale at the end of the meal, and Antonio was always the crowd's favourite.

"Come on then Antonio, tell us one of your jokes!" the foreman shouted.

Antonio replied, feigning shyness, "Oh don't, don Luis, you'll make me blush."

The foreman smiled, "Come on man, don't make us beg!"

And so, wiping his mouth with the back of his hand, Antonio slowly rose from his chair and started:

"So, two drunk Andalusians were talking in a bar. The first one says, 'Julio musht be reeeally drunk. Look he sold the Cathedral for three thousand pesetas!' The other guy frowns and says, 'Don't be shtupid, that's impossuhble, can't be...'. The first guy replies, 'It is! I sweaahr on mi muvver's life, it was me wot bought it!' "

The whole table erupted in laughter, and Antonio encouraged by their reaction, started to tell another one:

"Two girls from Seville meet on the corner of Barrio de la Cruz, one says to the other: 'Did ya know I got myself a boyfriend?.' 'Oh yeah?' says the other girl. 'What's he like?' 'Weeeelll, he's an otolaryngologist.' 'Ooh err, Otala...must be a Basque like mine!' "

Trinidad also remembered another moment when a nervous and sweaty Antonio was struggling to eat his chicken with a knife and fork like those around him were doing. Doña Rosario saw the problems he was having and gave him permission to use his hands, to which Antonio responded:

"Wow, doña Rosario, you're the best thing since sliced bread you are."

And he proceeded to pick up the chicken in his hands and bite into it, exclaiming, "yum yum in my tum," making everyone around the table laugh.

Trinidad smiled every time she heard they were off to Villacarrillo because she knew she would enjoy herself.

Life in Madrid on the other hand was still difficult; most people were living hand to mouth when it came to food. Basic products like bread, milk and oil were in short supply and could only be bought with ration cards or on the black market. Poor families, and those with children, were entitled to eight ounces of bread a day, which just wasn't enough. Children would often shout "Mummy, Daddy, I'm hungry," even though their parents were powerless to do anything to make it better. The black market was commonplace and it was even rumoured that the government actually propped the illegal system up, just so that the people of Madrid at least had something to eat. There were usually one or two black marketeers in each block of houses, and they would always be protected by their neighbours during any police inspection or raid. It was also common to see women standing outside Metro stations selling *chuscos*, (sticks of white bread) which mostly came from soldiers' rations; for the most part soldiers from the upper ranks of the army who had been given express permission to deal in bread. The black market was the subject of jokes and songs like this one:

"Our Father who art in El Pardo and whose name is Franco

Hallowed be thy name if thou givest us white bread,

Give us this day our daily oil that they're taking away from

us,..."

People got by any way they could, despite these hardships.

In March 1942, after she had returned from the olive harvest, Trinidad went to be with her sister for the birth of Mari-Tere; Teresa and Francisco's only daughter. Mari-Tere was born on 21st March 1942 in the Fuente del Berro neighbourhood to the east of Madrid, and Trinidad was her godmother.

Mari-Tere's birth reminded Trinidad of something she had

known deep down for a long time now: she yearned to get married and have children like her sister. Working conditions as a domestic servant had not improved since the end of the war; in fact the discipline that had been lacking during the Republic had come back in force from what Trinidad could tell. She arrived late one day and doña Rosario reprimanded her and was even on the verge of sacking her. "Trini, arriving late is a huge offence and I'm sorry, but if you are late one more time I will have no choice but to sack you," she said. Trinidad took note of the warning and from that day she also doubled her efforts to find a husband so she could become independent. With that goal in mind she started to go out more, and she made sure to go to places where one might find a suitor. The dance hall was still the best place to do this. She was in the hairdressers one day when a friend of hers said she knew of a dance hall where it was easy to find a guy. The dance hall was in the Ventas neighbourhood which wasn't far; they could go by foot or on tram. They decided that that Sunday coming they would go together.

Trinidad thought there was a great atmosphere when they arrived at the dance that night. The band were playing *'Morena Clara'*, by Imperio Argentina; one of her favourite songs. Her friend introduced her to the other girls there and she soon started to feel at ease. Sat amidst the group of women, Trinidad kept a keen eye on the comings and goings of the couples on the floor. The songs flowed and the beat went on, and all the while she watched everything that was going on around her. At one point, the band started to play a *pasodoble* and it was at that moment that a young, good-looking blond man approached her and asked her to dance. Trinidad didn't hesitate, she just followed him onto the dancefloor. She soon realised that he didn't know how to dance, but she helped him and tried her best to look as though she hadn't noticed his ineptitude. At the end of the song the young man walked her back to her seat and they began to talk.

"I haven't seen you here before," he said, "do you come here often?"

She smiled shyly, "No, it's my first time here, and you?"

"I've been a few times before, I like the place – how about you?" he asked, looking at her.

She smiled, "Yes, so do I; the band is great and so is the music."

"Are you here alone?" the young man asked tentatively.

"No, I came with my friend," she replied.

"I'm here alone. Oh, by the way, my name's Nicasio – what's yours?"

"Trinidad."

Meeting Nicasio had been like a wake-up call; it gave her a strength she didn't possess before. From the moment they met she got the feeling that she really liked this young man, and it was a feeling that only grew with time. She knew that he was single, that he professed to be republican, not communist, that he was staying in a boarding house on Calle Bravo Murillo, and that his sister Julia worked in service at Calle Ayala,[124] around the corner from where Trinidad lived. Nicasio had also told her how his parents had been

---

[124] See map 5.

harassed during the war, and that his father had almost been executed. All of these details just made her like him even more.

Ever since she met Nicasio, Trinidad would wait impatiently each week for her day off. The night before she would always sleep badly; she couldn't stop thinking about seeing him and she would go over and over in her mind everything that she was going to tell him when she did. He was always on time and would already be on the corner waiting for her when she walked down the street. Once they had gotten to know each other a bit better, they would go back to the dance where they first met. Their favourite thing to do, however, was to go to the cinema or for a walk in el Parque del Retiro. They never had much time together and so they made sure to enjoy what little they had to the full. They would normally go to one of the cinemas on Gran Vía and, afterwards, if they had time, and the weather was nice, they would go to el Retiro. One day, without realising "we totally forgot about the time" Trinidad would say to her son years later. She arrived half an hour late and doña Rosario, who was a stickler for these things, had had enough of her tardiness. When Trinidad arrived at the flat on Calle Castelló her colleague said that doña Rosario had asked to see her as soon as she arrived. Trinidad hurried in to see her mistress, who was already waiting for her.

With a stern expression she asked, "Trinidad, do you know what time it is?"

Trinidad replied apprehensively, wary of the angry look on her mistress' face, "Yes, I do, madam, it's half eight."

"You know very well that your break ends at eight in the

evening. So, what is the reason for your late return?"

Trinidad replied full of remorse, "I'm so sorry madam, the Metro broke down and that's why I arrived late."

Suspiciously doña Rosario looked at her servant, before asking "Which Metro line was this?"

Trinidad was surprised at the question and answered carefully, "The line that goes from Sol to Ventas."

And just like that, she began to tell a story off-the-cuff that she thought very convincing at the time. However, something must have raised her employer's suspicions as doña Rosario later called the Metro office to ask about the alleged incident. When she found out that both of the Metro lines[125] had been running normally that day, she called Trinidad in again.

"Trinidad, I called the Metro offices and they have informed me that the Sol-Ventas line was running normally all day. So, why did you lie to me?"

Realising that she had made a huge mistake, Trinidad tried to apologise as best she could and this time decided to tell doña Rosario the truth.

"Please forgive me madam, but I went to the cinema with my beau and the film was a lot longer than they said it would be and then we couldn't get on the tram because it was full, so we had to walk. It's the first time that I've come back late and I swear to you that it won't happen again," Trinidad said with a grief-stricken face.

"Let me remind you that this is not the first time that this has

---

[125] In those days there were only two Metro lines running: Tetuan-Vallecas and Sol-Ventas.

happened Trinidad; it is in fact the second time, and I clearly remember telling you that I would not stand for this sort of behaviour. Also, I do not like being lied to," doña Rosario said sharply. She then continued with a softer tone, as though she wanted to lessen the tension, "Look, we've all been in love, and when we are it's easy to lose your sense of time somewhat. So I will let this go, however, I am telling you now that if you arrive late once more I will fire you, I won't accept any excuses next time. Consider yourself warned."

Trinidad looked relieved, "Thank you so much madam, and I apologise again." With that Trinidad left the room, a bit scared at the conversation she had just had with her superior.

The following Sunday she told Nicasio about the conversation and everything that had happened with her mistress. Together they decided that they wouldn't let it happen again. However, the truth is Trinidad didn't really have many more chances to arrive late as the following month everything changed. One Sunday evening, about four months after they first met, the couple were walking through la Rosaleda[126] when Nicasio took Trinidad's hand and looked her in the eyes with such nervous excitement that it startled her. He asked her one simple but monumental question, "Trinidad, will you marry me?" She looked at him in surprise and with a tender expression she replied, "Oh, Nicasio, things are moving so fast!" but the kiss she gave him next left him in no doubt as to her answer.

Trinidad discussed her decision with her parents and sisters (her

---

[126] An area of trees and rosebushes created in 1915 which was part of the Parque del Retiro in Madrid.

mother in particular) and also with doña Rosario who told her: "Trini, men are like bread – you've got to get them while they're hot." Once Teresa and María met Nicasio they gave him their seal of approval, as did Dorotea. And so the wedding date was set for 10th July 1947.

That day the dawn was bright and beautiful. Church bells rang in the air, happy and triumphant. Trinidad, accompanied by her sister Teresa, made her entrance to the wedding march music. There was a new-found happiness there for all to see, she was radiant; she had dreamt of this day for so long. The slow walk to the altar allowed her the time to really take in this important moment in her life. All the guests turned and smiled at her, and she responded showing them her pearly white teeth. She felt supported by her sister's reassuring arm at her side; it gave her the strength to reach the spot at the end of the aisle where Nicasio and the priest were waiting. Trinidad wore a black silk dress with a hat and veil. Nicasio was in a black suit, with a white shirt and black tie. The bride had silver earrings and necklace and she wore a brooch in the shape of a flower. The groom had a white carnation in his buttonhole. The wedding was held in the Iglesia de la Concepción de Madrid[127] and all the happy couple's friends and family were in attendance. The honeymoon was a day out to El Escorial.

Trinidad was so happy that her dream of getting married had finally become a reality. Now she began to think of her future, one that was promising although still somewhat uncertain; one in which

---

[127] **See map 5.**

she could be free. She would be able to come and go as she pleased without answering to anyone. Even though Nicasio's wage as a barber was only 15 pesetas a day, she wasn't worried about their precarious financial situation. The important thing was that she was starting a new chapter in her life, and she looked forward to it with hope and a real sense of optimism.

END OF PART ONE

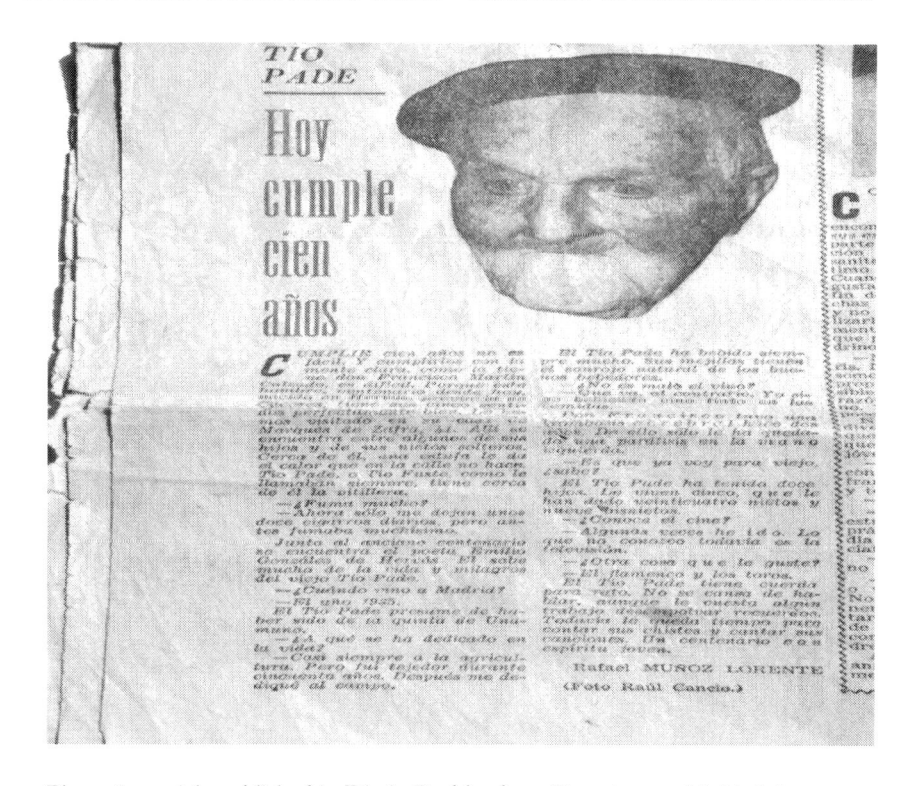

Photo 1 – article published in Diario Pueblo about Francisco on his birthday

Photo 2 – with her family at the Casino's party

Photo 3 – Hervás - calle del Rabilero as it is now

Photo 4 – Hervás, present day, with the Santa María church in the background

Photo 5 – Dorotea and Francisco in 1947 at Trinidad and Nicasio's wedding in Madrid

Photo 6 – what remains of the house in the Romana today

Photo 7 – Dorotea in Madrid with her daughters Teresa, María and Trinidad

Photo 8 – Trinidad in Madrid before the war

Photo 9 – Nicasio (in the back row) with his parents and siblings in Ceinos (1934)

Photo 10 – Nicasio (indicated by the arrow) in the Disciplinary Battalion in Lesaca (1941)

Photo 11 – Trinidad and Nicasio on their wedding day

18. POST-WAR

Trinidad's labour was difficult due to a series of complications; firstly, at 41 years old her age was a risk factor, then there was the fact that this was her first child, and lastly her midwife wasn't very experienced. On top of all that, they were in the post-war period, when the methods and means of dealing with childbirth were less than desirable. All of this made for a long ordeal, during which she wasn't free from danger; and nor was her baby boy who was born with signs of asphyxia. However, after a long ordeal Trinidad was finally able to greet her son in the warm light of a new day. They named him Francisco Jesús, however he would later come to be known by friends and family as Paquito.

He was christened in the Iglesia de Covadonga, on the Plaza de Manuel Becerra in the Ventas neighbourhood[128]. The day itself didn't turn out quite as his parents had planned, as Nicasio argued with some of the guests. Trinidad wasn't at the christening herself, as in those days mothers didn't attend the celebration, so she never really knew just what happened, only that the party ended in a ruckus. She wasn't a superstitious woman but she always wondered if this might be a sign that the arrival of her beloved child, the one she had so longed for during her single years, wasn't going to be quite as calm or sweet as she had expected.

After their wedding, Trinidad and Nicasio decided to rent a flat with Teresa and her husband so they could cut down on costs. It was

---

[128] **See map 6.**

in a four-floor, new-build block on Paseo del Marqués de Zafra; the two families shared a property on the fourth floor where the rent was more reasonable.

Nicasio worked as a barber on Calle del Carnero[129], right in the middle of the Rastro de Madrid flea market, and Trinidad kept the house. She was truly happy now that her dream of being a mother had been fulfilled and her son was growing up healthy. One day when she took her son on the Metro, a woman approached her, she was most likely a Franco sympathiser, and she asked Trinidad with a trace of envy in her voice, "My, what a beautiful boy you have, is he German?", to which Trinidad replied with unmasked pride: "No madam, he's Spanish - he's from Madrid". In Madrid at the start of the fifties being German was still considered something to be proud of, and despite the fact that Germany had lost the war, right-wing people in Spain still admired the Teutonic nation.

Trinidad stayed at home taking care of her son, and enjoying motherhood. Nicasio's salary hardly saw them through to the end of the month, what with the cost of rent and food, and so due to their financial difficulties, when Paquito started school, she decided to go back to work. With the help of her sister-in-law, Julia, Trinidad started as a temporary assistant at the house where Julia worked. It was on Calle de Diego de León and Trinidad walked there up Paseo de Ronda (which is now Francisco Silvela[130]) and she always arrived early. She would work three hours in the morning and two in the afternoon so that she could collect her son from school. She would

---

[129] See map 4.
[130] See map 5.

take it in turns with her husband to walk Paquito to and from school.

Life in Marqués de Zafra was difficult for the new family for many reasons. The country's economic situation was dire and rationing was still in force. Corruption and the black market were still the normal way of doing things. There was an acute shortage of housing which meant that for hundreds of thousands of people getting a flat was no more than a pipe dream. For a poor family it was a gargantuan task just to reach the end of the month. All those Spaniards that had lost the war were still terrified of repression and imprisonment for political motives; it was a real and frightening possibility that hung over them all. Nicasio and Trinidad's conversations during that time centred on some of those experiences, and capture the feelings of the time.

"Nicasio, how are you getting on for tips this week?" asked Trinidad.

Nicasio sighed, "Darling, it's been an awful week; today's Thursday and I've only got one peseta so far. If I get two pesetas by Saturday, I'll eat my hat. Things are really bad. Not a soul is coming in. And what's more nobody has a penny to his name."

Trinidad looked anxiously at her husband, "Well, this week I've really got to go to the pharmacy to buy a bottle of calcium for the boy; it's for his bones, so he grows and doesn't end up stunted. Can't you see how pale he is? Whatever happens we have to get the 4.5 pesetas to buy that bottle."

Exasperated, Nicasio hung his head, "Come on, what do you want me to do? Print the money myself or knock someone over the head and steal it?"

Trinidad wrung her hands as she thought of their money troubles, "Darling, I don't know what we're going to do. The money's just not lasting as long now.[131] And if that wasn't enough I've got to give my sister the rent at the start of the month. I'm the one that will be printing that money. If only don Luis would just pay me what he owes me this month…"

Nicasio's heart went out to her, "it seems like you've got it tough. Don Luis really is stingy. They say it takes a lot of poor people to make one rich person and don Luis is making himself rich with all the maids he has without paying them."

Trinidad smiled a wry smile, "Don't I know it. He hasn't even paid your sister in three months. At least they give her food and board there, if not the poor woman would be out on the street."

Nicasio puffed his chest out before exclaiming, "If my lot had won this wouldn't be happening."

Trinidad, tired of hearing this from her husband, said, "Come on now, give it a rest. The only thing your lot knew how to do was talk and they used up all their energy moving their mouths, just like you! It's no wonder they lost the war!"

Nicasio continued, unperturbed by his wife's reaction, "Well, they were different times. But, look; people are scared to even breathe now. Don't you see that the jails are still full of political prisoners? There are over fifty thousand of them! People were talking

---

[131] In 1948 the cost of living had gone up by 28.6% and the peseta lost 65% of its value. *Madrid bajo la dictadura* [Madrid under the Dictatorship], Montoliú, op. cit.

about it in the barbers, hush hush of course, because if they catch you blabbing about it they'll shove you in the clink."

Trinidad, upset by her husband's outburst, shouted "So what? That's not going to get us any food, is it? All that we should be thinking about is putting some food on the table and saving enough to take the next step to buy a flat, because if I have anything to do with it we sure as hell won't be renting this flat from my sister our whole lives."

Nicasio carried on, "Oh, come on, my love, we've all got it hard enough already! Just look, I'll give you an example and it's from the *Diario Arriba*, no less – you can't get a more pro-Regime paper than that. In yesterday's edition it said that Spain needs half a million more homes. Each year they only build 700 of the kind of flats we could afford (the ones that cost less than 250 pesetas a month), rather than the 6,000 that are actually needed. Another thing, a flat that used to cost 35 to 50 pesetas rent in 1936, is now 227 to 325 a month plus the transfer fees.[132] So, you tell me - what should we do? Unless we win the lottery we'll have it worse than Manolete, the country's unluckiest bullfighter..."[133]

Trinidad shrugged her shoulders, "I know I know, it doesn't surprise me what with the amount of people coming to Madrid from the villages. We'll end up having to live in a shack in el Arroyo Abroñigal[134] just so the Ministry of Housing gives us one of those

---

[132] *Montoliú*, 2010,op. cit. pages 120-26.
[133] Manuel Laureano Rodríguez Sánchez, otherwise known as *Manolete*, a famous bullfighter in the forties.
[134] El Arroyo Abroñigal was at the end of the Paseo de Marqués de Zafra and, at the time in which the story takes place, it housed a municipal dumping ground

subsidized homes."

Nicasio looked at her, "What are you saying?! We should be so lucky, I have it on good authority. The town council is inspecting el Arroyo almost every day and they can't build anymore. Oh yeah, listen to this, according to my sources, one of the teams from the council caught this guy who lives there but has a flat in Paseo de Marqués de Zafra which he's renting out for 800 pesetas a month. Completely shameless, isn't it?"

"No, that's just what it takes to survive nowadays. Black marketeers and Falangists are the only ones who live well in Franco's Spain!" Trinidad said stridently.

The newlyweds' conversations usually revolved around their lack of home, lack of food and how expensive everything was. In fact, their dialogue was so much like a broken record that it must have become ingrained in Paquito's young mind.

The young boy must have been about three years old when, prompted by one of his parents' conversations (having heard his father say so often that he had 'dreams of becoming a baker') and perhaps by his own natural instinct (or even hunger?) he stole some bread from his aunt. He took the bread that Teresa had bought that day, stored in a bag behind the kitchen door and he put it in his mother's bag, where there had been none before. When Teresa realised that her bread was no longer in her bag but in her sister's instead, she asked her why she had taken it. Trinidad, of course, had

---

and it was also where people who came to Madrid and had no home, set up a shantytown. Today it is part of the M-30 (Avenida de la Paz) see *Historias de la Posguerra* [Post-war Stories], Luis Garrido, 1990.

no idea what her sister was talking about and after a short argument it slowly dawned on them what must have happened. The story had a happy ending for Paquito, as instead of getting a slap from his mother, which in the circumstances was to be expected, his aunt gave him a piece of bread as long as he promised never to do it again. Despite his young years the boy kept his promise, which earned him other similar treats from his beloved aunt in the future.

When Paquito turned five and had to go to school, he realised for the first time that he was different somehow because his father had lost the war. Before he had even reached school-going age, his mother had signed him up to Amador de los Ríos school[135] which was conveniently located on their road. The school told her not to worry about the oversubscription problem since they lived on the same road, and so they offered her a place.

However, just a few days before the school year was due to start, Nicasio received a letter from the headmaster telling him that due to excessive demand they would be unable to offer Paquito a place that academic year. Trinidad went to speak to the woman that she had dealt with previously, but was told that this decision had been taken by the headmaster and so there was nothing that could be done. Nicasio asked to come in and speak with him, but was told a meeting wouldn't be possible, as the headmaster was far too busy with the imminent start of the new school year.

Nicasio and Trinidad felt hopeless. Their son had no school place and that meant Trinidad would have to leave work making their

---

[135] See map 6.

financial situation even worse. Teresa offered to look after Paquito while Trinidad went to work but, as so often happens, 'when one door closes another opens' and Trinidad found out that there were still some places left in Escuelas Aguirre school[136]. She wasted no time in going to speak with the headmaster, don Manuel, who was a wonderful person, and also quite liberal as Paquito would find out years later. He must have sympathised with their situation because, after the meeting, he offered Trinidad one of the last available places.

A few days later Trinidad was speaking to a neighbour in the street, who said that she was really happy she had managed to get a place at Amador de los Ríos. When Trinidad replied that her son hadn't been so lucky the neighbour didn't hold back; telling Trinidad that she had heard Nicasio had fought for the Republicans, and said "Oh, of course, well, if your husband is Republican that doesn't surprise me. The headmaster is Falangist and he doesn't want any red children there." Whether it was true or not, in the end it worked out for the best that Paquito didn't get into Amador de los Ríos. Over time they saw that Escuelas Aguirre was an excellent place for children like Paquito.[137] On the few occasions that the two schools played each other at football, Aguirre's team always won, which the family thought was only fair.

Before he went to school, when Paquito was still a babe in arms, his parents took him to Ceinos to meet his paternal grandparents:

---

[136] See map 5.
[137] Don Lucas Aguirre Juárez, founder of Escuelas Aguirre was one of the sponsors of open education in Spain and he bequeathed his fortune so that children from humble backgrounds could receive a liberal and progressive education.

Francisco and Felisa. It was springtime, 8th May San Mamerto Day in Ceinos, and Trinidad was worried about the heat in case it made her son ill. However, she needn't have fretted as they were well looked after by Felisa, who was a great cook. She made them *roscas* that Paquito gnawed at like a mouse, even though he didn't have any teeth yet. Francisco said to Trinidad: "Go powder your nose, the neighbours are coming to meet you."

Grandmother Felisa died in Ceinos in December 1950, the year after that visit. Grandfather Francisco died six years later after a second visit from Paquito –this time with his uncle Paco, Nicasio's brother. Paquito remembered that trip well because it was when he climbed the church tower as a dare from the village boys to prove that boys from Madrid weren't scaredy-cats. However, once up there he found that he couldn't get down because it was really steep and there were no stairs. The children had to call his uncle Paco, who was a policeman and disciplinarian. He was so angry about what had happened that he gave the boy a good hiding once he finally managed to get down from the tower. Paquito remembered that grandfather Francisco was tall and well-built from all his years working in the fields, however that was also what had made him so ill. When Francisco died Paquito was seven and a half years old.

Paquito met his maternal grandparents Francisco and Dorotea at the same time because his mother took him to Hervás to meet them. Grandmother Dorotea died in November 1954 in Hervás but Grandfather Francisco came to live in Madrid for a while and so Paquito had the chance to get to know him better. He died in

December 1966 in Madrid when Paquito was eighteen years old.

19. UNCERTAIN YEARS

As time went on the struggle for food and for a decent home became even more difficult for the young family. Nicasio worked all hours in the barbers; he worked Saturdays, and extra hours here and there on other days when he could. He normally got extra work around Christmas or the festival of San Isidro (the patron saint of Madrid) when people wanted to look their best for friends and family. On Sundays, he even went to cut hair at people's houses and he always got a small tip for his trouble and a glass or two of wine between appointments. However, despite all of his and Trinidad's efforts, they couldn't escape 'that same old story' as he liked to say to his wife. Their hard-earned savings didn't amount to much, and never covered even the most basic of needs, let alone giving them enough to rent their own place and get out of the situation they were in. By the time they had managed to scrape together 10,000 pesetas, the house would cost 20,000; and when they got together that 20,000 for the fees, prices would go up again. It was a never-ending story. The situation got so bad that Nicasio and Trinidad even thought of emigrating to Argentina. Eva Perón had visited Spain a few years before[138] and ever since, Spaniards had pictured the south-American country as a place of modernity, riches and new opportunities; like the America of a century before, somewhere from which they would return with untold riches. Trinidad's aunt Consuelo was a nun in Rosario de Santa Fe, in Argentina, so they decided to write to her and

---

[138] Eva (Evita) Duarte de Perón, wife of the Argentinian president, visited Spain in support of General Franco's regime on 9th June 1947.

ask what she thought of their plans to emigrate. Along with the letter they sent a photo of the three of them, in which they were all smiling, resplendent in their party clothes. However, it seemed even this wasn't enough to impress Sister Consuelo who stated categorically that the economic situation in Argentina was far worse than in Spain and her advice was not to make the trip.

After that scuppered journey to Argentina, Nicasio seemed to sink into a sort of depression that made life a misery both for him and the other members of his (and Teresa's) family that had to live with him. Nicasio was still taking Paquito to school in the mornings at that time, and the young boy noticed that they stopped in more bars on the way there, and his father ordered even more drinks on his empty stomach. Cazalla, (anis), was his Achilles heel. Some days Paquito even arrived late to school, and would have to explain his tardiness to the teacher. On those occasions, his youthful imagination would work overtime to come up with excuses; like 'my mother has been taken ill' or 'the bus was late'. However, the boy kept quiet about the reality of what was happening to his father. He would sometimes try to persuade his father not to go in to the bar; he would say, "Papá. Again? How many bars are we going to stop in? Mamá says that it's not good for you, and you're spending money and then she doesn't have any to do the shopping. Also, my teacher told me that if I arrive late once more he's going to 'take me to meet' don Manuel" (the headmaster). Nicasio would look at his son after this little speech and depending on which side of the bed he had woken up that morning, he would either smile without scolding him, or he would give him a clip round the ear that would sting right up until they reached the school gates.

Even in spite of those difficult days, Paquito loved it when his dad took him to school, because he would tell stories of growing up in Ceinos, and of life before the war. He would also tell Paquito things about what Madrid had been like when he first arrived there and all the places he had worked before he ended up in el Rastro.

Nicasio had started work at the barbershop on Calle del Carnero before he met Trinidad. He loved working in el Rastro because of the swarms of different people that the area attracted, many of whom were his customers. As he told his son, there were antique dealers who bought and sold furniture and other objects of value that were very dubious in origin. Most of these men had shops, galleries or businesses all along Ribera de Curtidores and Plaza de Cascorro.[139] Then there were the book dealers, who Nicasio got on with very well, and from whom he sometimes bought old volumes of poetry or literature. And then there were the scrap dealers, who bought anything and everything, most of it goods that had been stolen by gypsies. These guys would often come into the barbers looking for people that they had dealt with previously, and they would close deals with the gypsies while Nicasio shaved them, or cut their hair. Nicasio would tell his son some of their little stories, making sure to explain what the slang that the gypsies used meant, he also explained that this slang was their language. The following conversation is one which Nicasio often recounted to his son, in a

---

[139] See map 4.

mixture of gypsy slang and Madrid speak:

"Hello don Jesú."

"Hi Curro, I haven't seen you in a while, have you been on holiday?"

"Yes suh, I hightailed it to Pinacedá to see mi old ma"

"Ah, you've been to Andalusia to see your Mum, great. I thought maybe you had been caught by the police and put in the clink."

"No suh, a good gypsy has a good loaf on his shoulders and he knows when things are going south."

"Yeah I know that you can really haul ass when the wolves are circling. So, what have you got for me today?"

"I've got a comfy bed where a Duke slept once – you're going to love it."

"Beds take up a lot of space, even more so Duke's ones – my shop's full right now…"

"Don Jesú, just take a gander at it – it's mint and as it's you I'd give you a good price."

"Curro, I already told you I just don't have room in my shop right now…"

"For the love of god, don Jesú, I've got a wife, girl and five lads to feed!"

"You're beginning to get on my nerves… how much do you want for it?"

"For you, don Jesú, seeing as you're such dapper fella and it's almost a present… *duis gres lúas* or in your language two hundred pesetas."

"Look, Curro, don't try and pull the wool over my eyes, I'm not a bloomin' idiot… a hundred pesetas and that's only once I've seen it."

This was one of many similar conversations that took place every day in the barbers. Nicasio was a fly on the wall for all of them and he learnt something from each and every one. For him, el Rastro was like the university that he had always wanted to go to but never had the chance. Whatever the topic of conversation was he would always get something out of these exchanges, maybe even tips once his clients had sealed the deal and were feeling generous.

Nicasio's political situation was another source of concern for the family, especially for Trinidad. As a result of his sympathies and time spent in action with the Spanish Communist Party before the war, many of the opportunities that he had to slot in somewhere were ultimately foiled. Don Carlos, who was right-wing and had many connections, tried to get him work in many different places. First off, as a porter in the newly-created national railway, or RENFE, then as a messenger at one of the Ministries; however Nicasio's political past was always too big a hurdle to overcome. Trinidad used to say it was as if he had been given a life sentence of poverty.

Nicasio's inability to get a decent, well-paid job had a long-lasting impact on the rest of the family. Paquito's previous negative experience with his local school was unfortunately not an isolated case in their family. The year before something happened at the house which just showed that 'the life sentence' Nicasio had been given followed him wherever he went. One night, when they were all in bed, the doorbell went. Dorotea had come to spend a few days with her daughters in Madrid and she was staying with the family that night. When she heard the bell, the grandmother sat up on the camp bed that she had been sleeping on, in the corridor, and she called out to her family. Trinidad approached the door, and as she looked through the peephole, she saw strange shadows moving about. She called through the door, "Who is it?" and the reply came from the other side "Police! Open up!" Trinidad's blood ran cold and, terrified, she covered herself with a shawl before opening the door.

The inspector identified himself, and showed them his badge from the *Brigada Política-Social* ('The Secret Police', as they were known by most people).

The Inspector asked, "Does Nicasio Vielba Pastor live here?"

Trinidad nodded her head, "Yes sir."

He carried on, "Is he at home?"

Trinidad looked at him warily, "Yes sir, he's in bed."

The Inspector said calmly, "Please tell him to get dressed as he must come with us to the police station."

She was so shocked that she couldn't find her voice, but she went to the bedroom to tell her husband. As he got dressed, Teresa, who was the bravest of all of them, went out into the corridor and asked the Inspector, "What has my brother-in-law done if you don't mind me asking?"

He replied, "I'm sorry, madam, all I can say is that we have received a request for him to appear at the police station."

Teresa didn't stop there, "And then where will you take him?"

The Inspector continued in a calm voice, "He will be taken to the *Dirección General de Seguridad,* or the police headquarters in Madrid. Tomorrow morning you can ring or come into the station and you will be given more information."

Upon seeing his father in handcuffs and his mother and grandmother crying, Paquito too started wailing, saying: "Mamá, why are these men taking Papá away?" And Trinidad, finding a voice amidst the tears, looked at her son and said, "Don't cry my darling, papá is just going out to run an errand, he'll be back tomorrow, you'll see."

Paquito doubted whether his father would be home so soon. Despite his young years he sensed that his father hadn't done anything bad, because he was a good man. He thought that it was actually those policemen who were bad instead. He also got the feeling that his father didn't really want to go with the men that night. However Trinidad was right, even if she hadn't quite believed it herself when she said it, at midday the following day they let Nicasio go. When Trinidad asked him what had happened at the police station, he only said that they had treated him fairly and that when they discovered he wasn't the man they were looking for, they had immediately let him go.

The real reason he had been taken in that night was that somebody had painted a hammer and sickle on the outside of their building, and the 'Secret Police' had records of everyone with political pasts, so they assumed it had been him. In reality their neighbours had painted it, and they had been taken in at the same time as Nicasio. This incident made it plain to Nicasio that his situation wasn't going to improve any time soon.

20. CHILDHOOD MEMORIES

Youth, divine treasure,
You're leaving never to return!
When I want to cry, I do not cry ...
And sometimes I cry without wanting

Rubén Darío

Those uncertain times after the post-war years left an indelible mark on the family, who were still struggling to improve their social and economic standing. The daily life of Nicasio, Trinidad and Paquito, as well as that of Teresa and her family, was a reflection of the struggles that thousands of Spaniards faced daily, as they lived in Madrid trying to overcome the scars left by the Civil War. This struggle was markedly harder for those who had been subjected to repression and hatred by the victors at the end of the conflict. The impact of what happened would be felt for generations; not only did it affect those who lived through the battle but also their children who were born after it. For many children like Paquito, the outcome of the Civil War would mark their lives forever and make them fundamentally reject everything that Franco's Spain stood for.

Looking back with the benefit of hindsight I, Paquito, would like to give the reader my perspective on these years, as I experienced them, and what those uncertain times meant to me.

My childhood days will always be there, hidden away in a very private, very special corner of my mind. The happy sounds of childhood games ring in my ears with an everlasting clarity. I remember the house where I was born with its long, thin staircase, and its plain smooth walls, full of marks and lines; with its high ceilings and its chipped facade…

The flat where we lived was on the fourth floor at the very top of the building. It had three bedrooms, a dining room, kitchen and bathroom; it was large enough for a family with two or three children. However our flat was home to two families. The flat was rented by my uncle and aunt with their only daughter, my cousin Mari. They lived in half of the rooms, leaving the other half for us. Even when I was really young, I remember realising how empty and austere my parents' room was. A bed, an oak wardrobe and a bedside table; furniture that fit into the room and it didn't leave much space for us to move about. I went from sleeping in a cot when I was little, to sleeping in with them, and then I only got a bed to myself once I was a lot older. All of this was in the one room. The other room was used as a living-dining room. In reality, most of our daily (waking) life was lived in that other room, which was also of 'bijou' proportions. The room contained only a round table and a few chairs, as well as a mirrored wardrobe which belonged to my aunt and uncle, and a dolls house which belonged to my cousin. The kitchen and the bathroom were shared by both families.

As is often the case with children however, the house wasn't the preferred place for all my games and adventures. As soon as my little legs would allow I was out into the street; the arena for most of my childhood games. I only had to cross the street and I found myself in front of the lightbulb factory. Its high walls and unobstructed hard floors made it the perfect venue for games of football or hide-and-seek; and so all the kids from the neighbourhood would meet there to play. I remember one kid, Ramón; he was bigger and stronger than me and, whenever we would fight, I would get a good hiding. There was also Javi and José, two brothers who lived on the same floor as me; then there was Isidoro, a puny kid with glasses who lived around the corner. I also remember the girls: Mari-Ester, Marilena and a girl that we called La Pepi, who, much later, became known for her unique talents at the childhood game of 'doctors and nurses'.

Our street was very long and there were an infinite number of places to play. Every little corner was perfect for some game or other. Like on the corner behind Carmen and Flora's egg shop, we would play trading cards, or when it was really cold we would make a fire. In the abandoned lots in front of the new houses, we would hunt for bits of rotten metal and sticks and other rubbish that had been thrown away there. We then used this treasure to make swords and helmets to protect ourselves in the war against our enemy: the boys from Santa Susana[140] or la Colonia Iturbe[141]. Behind those very same new houses we would also play football, with the goalposts marked out on the wall in white chalk.

I was drawn to the street with all its games and the freedom it offered. I remember my mother would often scold me when I returned home late for lunch, or when my clothes were dirty and ripped, or when I was hurt or bleeding from some fight or other with my enemies, or sometimes even from our friendly games. However,

---

[140] A religious school on the corner of Calle Marqués de Modéjar and Sancho Dávila.
[141] A neighbourhood not far from Paseo de Marqués de Zafra.

none of this ever dampened my desire to get back out there. The next day, or even five minutes after one of my mother's reprimands, I would run down the stairs, four at a time, towards the long-awaited street, making the caretaker, señora Longina, utter all sorts of complaints about my behaviour.

The street took on a special quality at night. The streetlights gave off a bleak, grey light, which lent a mysterious air to the surroundings; even more so in winter when it was misty, or when we were in the abandoned lots and it was pitch black. The girls were always scared to play hide-and-seek in those types of conditions; unlike the boys who just thought it was the perfect excuse to test the boundaries of any fledgling romances.

In the summer we would stay out in the street until nearly midnight. One of the boys' favourite pastimes was to hide in a long, narrow alley that ran behind the lightbulb factory; it was the perfect vantage point from which to spy on young couples. Sometimes if we were really lucky we would catch them 'in flagrante'. However we were in big trouble when they spotted us and we would have to run like the wind. We were pursued on more than one occasion by an enraged, half-dressed man ready to pummel us, who kept referring to our mothers in less than favourable terms.

To sum it up, the street was our world, our universe. All of the most important lessons of my childhood were learned on that street…

***

As I look back at what I have just written I wonder if my desire to spend all my time on the street was really just the way things were then or if there was some other reason behind it. My parents' daily fights, which inevitably affected the rest of the inhabitants in the flat, may have had something to do with it. I remember my cousin Mari and I would have secret meetings to tell one another what had gone on.

"Hey Mari, do you know why our Mums aren't talking to each other?"

"They had a fight at lunchtime."

"What about?"

"Well, your Mum arrived late from work at midday and wanted my Mum to let her have the kitchen to herself to make lunch for your Dad before he got home. But my Mum said she would have to wait because she was still using it."

"Well my Mum says it was her time to have the kitchen and your Mum had gotten too big for her boots and wasn't respecting the agreement they had."

"Well, it was because your Mum insulted mine and that's why she didn't want to let her have the kitchen."

"Yeah but it's just because she's really stressed ever since she fought with my Dad last night, all because of the wine."

"My Mum says if your Dad doesn't stop drinking we'll all be on the front page of El Caso"[142]

"I don't like it when my Dad drinks either, he gets in a really bad mood and cuffs me round the ear for no reason – that's why I get out

---

[142] Weekly publication specialised on reporting crimes.

of here and onto the street whenever I can."

"Yeah but I can't do that. My Mum doesn't let me. We have to go to my Dad's workshop to spend time with him there and it's so boring."

"So do you really think we're going to be in El Caso?"

"Don't be stupid, it's just a saying. I know your Dad is a sweetheart when he doesn't drink but lately I don't know what's gotten into him - he's gone a bit crazy."

"It's just that however much my parents save they can't afford a flat. All of their fights are about that. My Mum says to him if didn't have so much pride he could get a better job with more pay. But my Dad says he's not going to be a lackey at his age and when his lot get back in everything will be ok. I don't really know what he means by his lot."

"Me either, but I think he means the communists, the ones that lost the war."

"Do you think my Dad is a Communist?"

"I don't know, but it's what he always says when he's had too much to drink."

"Hey Mari, do you think they'll ever get back in?"

"Who? The communists? I don't think so, at least that's what I've heard my Dad say."

"And how does your Dad know?"

"Well, there are lots of people that come into the workshop, he's made friends with an Inspector from the police who told him that they've got the reds under control."

"Well I've heard my Dad say that the reds have crossed the border and they're already winning the war against Franco's people."

"And how does your Dad know?"

"Just like yours, he's heard people say so in the barbers."

"I just want my parents to not fight quite as much. My Mum has started saying she got married too soon and then she starts crying."

"Well, I think your Mum is a saint; look at the cross she's had to bear."

"Do you think they'll get over it soon and start talking again?"

"Who? Your parents?"

"No, our Mums."

"I think so, it's happened loads of times before and after all, they are sisters."

"You're right, thank goodness, if they weren't they'd always be rowing, not that it would matter to me, it just means I'd be off into the street even sooner."

"Paquito, it's not good for you to be out on the street. You just be careful you don't turn into some good-for-nothing scoundrel from spending too much time out there."

"Hey! What do you mean? I'm just having fun, and anyway it means I don't think about my parents rowing."

"That's not good, you have to study and then go out once you've done that, so you don't end up like your Dad."

"But my Dad's really clever. He just hadn't had any luck because he was fighting on the wrong side in that war."

"My Dad fought against Franco too and he doesn't shout about it."

"That's true. It's like your Dad is mute, I've never heard him talk about politics at all."

"That's because he's not mad like your Dad. He goes from home to work and back again, he doesn't get into anything with anyone, just the way it should be."

"But your Dad likes bullfighting, doesn't he?"

"What does that have to do with anything?"

"Well, he gets annoyed when he goes to the fight and the bullfighters don't do anything doesn't he?"

"And your Dad's the same with Atletico Madrid, his beloved 'Atleti', when they lose he looks like he's going to have a heart attack."

"Yeah, us colchoneros[143] we're that passionate, not like those other posh kids who support Real Madrid."

"Well thank goodness we've got football and bullfighting to distract everyone, what with how hungry we all are, you know."

"One of my friends, Ramón, he's older than me and he says all of this is happening because Franco doesn't want people to talk about politics."

"You see? You're learning bad stuff out there on the street."

"Look, just because you go to a religious school and they teach you all that stuff about religion and the National Crusade. That's just a drag."

---

[143] So called because the Atletico de Madrid strip has red and white stripe shirts reminiscent of the fabric used for mattress covers

"Paquito! Don't say that about my school, you don't know what you're talking about."

"It's true, Ramón's sister goes there too and she talks just like you, and that's why her brother laughs at her."

"I think Ramón is bad news. You shouldn't play with him anymore."

"No, well we don't play much anyway because he's always beating me up, but I admire him, I want to be like him one day."

"Oh look, I think our Mums are talking again, the fight is over already."

"What rotten luck!"

"What do you mean?"

"Well tomorrow is Sunday and it's our turn to use the bathroom."

"Yeah, so?"

"If they hadn't have made up then we wouldn't have used it and I wouldn't have had to have a cold bath."[144]

***

From those years I also remember my aunt Teresa. She thought of me as the son she couldn't have (her first pregnancy was a stillborn boy). She loved me like mad and I always sought to return her affections. Teresa made amazing roscas, small sweet doughnuts, and as soon as I smelt the batter I would come into the kitchen where she would let me lick clean the ladle she had used. When her delicious treats were ready she would always give one to me, but as

---

[144] Hot water cost a lot of money which my family couldn't afford.

soon as she left the kitchen I would sneak another one without my aunt noticing. Of course, she knew my tricks and would count them and when she saw there was one missing she would turn to me with a serious face and say: "You've taken another one haven't you, you rascal?" and I would always say, "No, auntie, you must have counted wrong". And we would look at each other and laugh.

Teresa loved music and she could always be heard singing around the house. When 'La Bien Pagá' came on the radio she would start singing along, giving old Miguel de Molina a run for his money.

Well-paid

Yes, you are well-paid

Because I bought your kisses

And you surrendered yourself to me

For a handful of money

Well-paid, well-paid

You were well-paid, woman'

Later on she would get me to sing one of Antonio Molina's songs and I would start off:

I am a miner

Pick and drill they still my heart.

I am a miner

Beer, wine and rum they help me start...

Señora Magdalena, who lived opposite to us was from Andalusia and she loved Antonio Molina, who was himself from Andalusia. She would listen to me from across the patio, clapping whenever I finished a song. Magdalena would say to Teresa: "you should take him to that competition on the radio, he's got a good voice." But I was scared to sing in public and as soon as I turned fourteen I lost the beautiful birdlike voice I had had before anyway.

It was at that age too that I caught quite a rare illness that stumped the doctors in Spain at that time. I had just returned from a summer spent in Hervás when my temperature spiked to above 40°C. I was initially diagnosed wrongly with typhoid fever and they started me on treatment, but my temperature didn't go down. Trinidad and Teresa took turns looking after me, day and night, but eventually nature took its course and I began to weaken; the doctors feared for my life. After several weeks of treatment and countless tests, the doctors finally, correctly, diagnosed me with Brucellosis.[145] I had drunk goat's milk without boiling it first while I was in Hervás and that was how I got ill.

My recovery was slow with a rest period of six months after I was declared 'well', so I missed nearly a whole year of school. In Escuelas Aguirre they had excellent teachers; some who, like don Feliciano, chain-smoked and would pinch so hard that it left a bruise. Others, like don César, were very demanding and expected their students to excel in exams and win all sporting endeavours. I had the honour of working with the headmaster, don Manuel, in the last year on a project sponsored by the Madrid town council, called *'Madrid de la mano.'* In this project pupils from participating schools had to speak on *Radio Intercontinental*. The night that it was my turn to speak my

---

[145] Brucellosis (also known as Maltese fever) is an illness transferred from animals to humans. It is contracted by consuming infected foods or spending a long stretch of time with livestock.

parents were glued to the radio from start to finish.

I was one of the top students in the class and all the teachers told my parents that I should keep on studying and go on to take my *bachillerato*. Money was tight however, and so instead I started work as an errand boy in a law firm on Calle Sagasta (next to Plaza de Alonso Martínez). They gave me a dark grey uniform with a peaked cap; it made me look older than my years. I earned 500 pesetas a month and the first time I got my pay I was mesmerized by the blue, shiny bank note they had given me. I had been unable to tear my eyes away from the picture on the front of a man in a Basque hat.

My salary, although small, allowed my parents to put away more money, however there was still never enough. The housing situation in Madrid had gotten even worse in the intervening years. Although at the start of the sixties the famous *Plan de Desarollo*[146], tourism and the economy in general had all improved the country's situation, there was still a dire shortage of housing[147].

As time went on my family's financial situation was like a ship that was taking on water. Despite my parent's best efforts to guide that ship into safe harbour, they could still not get enough money together to buy a flat. The situation had reached such a point that they couldn't see a way out and that is when my cousin Mari-Tere found one for all of us. She had just turned twenty, and at that time

---

[146] In the 1960s the "Planes de Desarrollo Económico y Social" [Plans for Economic and Social Development] were rolled out, their aim being to counteract the stagnation of Spain's industry and economy.
[147] Between 1940 and 1975 Madrid's population grew by more than 175 percent.

she was still living in the same room as her parents. She took a brave step that would change our and their lives forever and plug the hole in our boat, to continue with that metaphor. Looking at her decision now, with the benefit of hindsight, the situation was dire indeed and it was desperation that led Mari-Tere to do what she did. She wrote a letter to don Carlos, explaining that the family could no longer live in these conditions and she was turning to him as a last resort to see if he could help. So this was how don Carlos came to offer us the chance to move to a new block of flats that a developer friend of his had just finished, in the Carabanchel neighbourhood.

Don Carlos' kind offer consisted of a concierge job with a fixed salary for my father and free accommodation for the whole family.

21. DREAMS AND REALITY

In 1964 the Carabanchel neighbourhood[148] was part of the newly-emerging *Gran Madrid*.[149] It was an up-and-coming area, favoured by the many out-of-towners who were now heading to the capital from across Spain. Contrastingly, the Abrantes neighbourhood, as it is now known, was a distinctly unwelcoming and somewhat rough area. It was yet to be modernized; during the winter its streets would become treacherous quagmires that were near impossible to traverse, either on foot or by car. The transport situation was dire as well: buses almost never stopped there at peak times, meaning passengers had no choice but to jump on while the vehicle was still moving or risk being left behind. There just weren't enough buses to cope with demand; they were so infrequent and overcrowded. The bus route ran between Glorieta de Embajadores and el Pan Bendito; this was an informal settlement for workers with poor-quality housing at the end of Camino Viejo de Leganés. Homes built in Abrantes had no heating and they were little better than fridges in the dead of winter. To heat them, people used butane gas cylinders or *bombonas,* but these were insufficient to heat the rooms and only served to slow cook a *cocido* (the traditional Spanish winter stew), which was very often the only source of internal heating that people had.

Nicasio, Trinidad and Paquito found themselves in a block on

---

[148] See map 7.
[149] An urban planning project that aimed to make Madrid more like other European capitals, by linking the city with nearby suburbs. Carabanchel Alto and Carabanchel Bajo were annexed to the *Gran Madrid* in 1948.

Avenida de Abrantes. It had eleven floors and its residents were all working people, mainly from Extremadura and Andalusia. Some worked in the Standard Electric factory in Villaverde; others were shopkeepers, taxi drivers or electricians, and there was even the odd small-time military man among them. The residents' level of education was for the most part representative of their small town backgrounds; that's to say, there was the odd person with a secondary school education, but they were in the minority. For many of the residents, this was their first time living in Madrid and having a place of their own. This fact went some way towards explaining why they were so unfamiliar with the needs and demands of the concierge service that was to be offered by the family. Most had no idea what it even meant to have a concierge, let alone how to treat one.

The block's first residents' meeting took place not long after Nicasio and his family had arrived. It was, by all accounts, a lively session; with opinions offered both for and against the idea of a concierge service.

The chairman of the meeting cleared his throat to make sure he had the attention of the rest of the group, "Well, fellow residents, we now come to the next point on the agenda: the role of concierge." He examined the sheets of paper laid out before him on his dining room table; the meeting was being held at his house.

The resident from flat 3D; a short, tubby man with a moustache that made him look like a *guardia civil*, spoke up first, "Mr Chairman, as I expressed during our separate conversation yesterday, I am not in favour of having a concierge - I just don't think it's necessary."

"I agree with señor Letona," said a neighbour from flat 7A. "It's an unnecessary expense and, in my opinion, quite inappropriate. And another thing, just who is this man anyway? I mean, we don't know him from Adam."

The chairman looked over at his neighbour from the seventh floor; a thin man with a nervous disposition. He was a known Falangist and proud of it; as though he didn't realise the war had ever ended.

"Señor Nicasio has been recommended by the builder and he meets all the requirements for the role of concierge," the chairman responded calmly.

"So this is an imposition from the builder; it hasn't even been approved by anybody," the Falangist continued, gesticulating wildly with his hands as though he were giving a speech.

"Which is precisely why this matter has been put on the agenda for today so that the group can talk it through and approve it," the president said with a smile; trying, unsuccessfully, to calm his neighbour.

"Well to my mind, the role is not appropriate and it does not meet with my approval," said the resident from 7A with finality.

"Come on now all of you, let's be reasonable," interjected señor Molledo; a military man on the cusp of retirement. He commanded a certain amount of respect within the group simply by virtue of his military background. "I feel that the role of concierge is indeed a necessary one, and is quite fitting for the time and place that we all find ourselves in. I think we're being hasty in our judgement because we've only been living here a short time and we can't yet appreciate the value this man would bring. In my opinion, it is a worthy position and I support it wholeheartedly. As for señor Nicasio and señora Trinidad themselves, I haven't had many dealings with them yet as they've only just arrived, but they seem to me to be right for the job. They are good people and they too get my support." He took a moment to get his breath back after such a long speech. He then turned to look at his testy neighbour as though to compel him to be reasonable; as he would have done once with a subordinate in the army.

Señor Letona piped up again, "For me the issue isn't whether or not we would like to employ the concierge suggested by the builder, but whether it is in fact necessary to have a concierge at all."

"Look everybody, before I bought this flat I asked whether or not there would be a concierge, and the builder told me he had no intention of having one here. That's the reason I bought my flat in this block in the first place. If I had known otherwise, well - I would have bought somewhere else and it would have worked out cheaper for me. This really is an unnecessary cost," and with that Letona smiled at the military man, and slowly winked; as if they were back in the olden days.

"Talking of costs," said the moustachioed man, "how much will the concierge want?"

The Secretary looked at his papers and answered, "Well, what with his salary, social security, his flat and other costs it will be about four thousand pesetas a month, shared between all the owners."

"That's absurd!" shouted the resident from the seventh floor, "I refuse to pay that amount!" he exclaimed, his face turned an alarming shade of red as he began to cough uncontrollably.

"Señor González, may I remind you that you are obliged to abide by the decisions of the committee and if we do not reach a decision unanimously, then a majority will suffice," the chairman intervened with an air of authority.

"Mr Chairman," González countered, "let the record reflect that I am not in agreement with the simple majority vote, this matter should be debated at a plenary session with all the residents present."

By the end of the meeting, they had not reached a unanimous agreement and so the chairman had no choice but to put the final decision to a vote. As it turned out, nearly thirty percent of residents were against having a concierge.

This result felt almost like a personal rejection to Trinidad and Nicasio; and for the first few months it made daily life very hard and, quite frankly, unpleasant. Trinidad wasn't put off by all the domestic tasks the new job entailed, but the transition was incredibly hard for Nicasio. He used to say, "I've swapped my scissors and razors for a broom." They would divide up the household chores so as to get everything done. They would mop the stairs together once a fortnight, while Nicasio would take care of the rubbish bins and the lift, which was notoriously unreliable. It would break down regularly; Nicasio would have to walk up the twelve flights of stairs to get to the control room in the attic so he could reposition the mechanism by hand and then set it working again. Trinidad, who was more tactful than her husband, would be called upon for the more delicate conversations with their somewhat recalcitrant residents. Gradually, and with a certain amount of trepidation on her part, she won them all over. Nicasio, on the other hand, got in a fluster about every problem that came up; and as a result he would end the day exhausted. At night, when the concierge service was closed, the couple would take stock of their day and think back fondly to when they lived in Paseo de Marqués de Zafra. They compared notes and would come to the conclusion that their situation might well have got worse since arriving in the new flat, instead of better. While it was certainly true that they had more space now that they had their own place, they did not feel truly secure as their tenancy depended on their work contract. What's more, the price they were having to pay in snubs, sacrifices and hours of service was much more than they had ever anticipated. As Trinidad often used to say, "We're like a funeral home; open for business at all hours of the day, even on Sundays and holidays."

On 3rd December 1966, Trinidad received a telephone call that she had been dreading for some time. It was her sister Teresa, telling her that their father, Francisco, had died in Madrid during the early hours of the morning, at the age of nearly a hundred and two. His death meant the end of an important chapter in Trinidad and Teresa's lives. Francisco had been a member of that older generation who fought in the Cuban War of Independence; he was also a legend in his hometown. However, his local fame was not due to his service in Cuba but rather his impressive longevity and his reputation as a

Casanova. When his coffin reached the cemetery in Hervás it was accompanied by all the mothers and daughters that had heard stories of his escapades. Just like El Cid, even after death El tío Fuste continued to win the hearts of women everywhere.

In 1968, Frank (as Paquito soon came to be known) started work in an administrative position in an American military base in Torrejón de Ardoz. With his salary on top of Nicasio's, the family could finally begin to save for a flat. Their long-held dream of owning their own home continued to drive all the family's efforts. At the end of another gruelling day, when Trinidad and Nicasio sat down to rest, they would wonder if that dream might ever become a reality. At times like that, Nicasio, with his flair for poetry, would recite another of his favourite verses:

What is life? Tis but a madness.
What is life? A thing that seems,
A mirage that falsely gleams,
Phantom joy, delusive rest,
Since is life a dream at best,
And even dreams themselves are dreams.[150]

---

[150] *La vida es sueño* [Life is a Dream] by Pedro Calderón de la Barca in the play debuted in 1635. [Translation taken from an online source: http://www.gutenberg.org/cache/epub/6363/pg6363-images.html.

22. FRANK EMIGRATES

Frank was only twenty-three years old; however, his work at the military base in Torrejón, and his stint as a recruit doing national service, had given him a decisiveness and maturity that he would have thought impossible just a few years previously. He could clearly see that Spain's economic situation couldn't offer much to young people like himself. His work at the Base wasn't guaranteed long-term, and what's more, he had heard rumours in the office that the Americans weren't going to stay in Spain for much longer. At a national level there were very few job opportunities and when he had tried to find work before he had not been successful. These were just some of the factors that made it abundantly clear to him that he would need to try his luck on foreign soil in order to progress, both personally and professionally. The four years he had spent at the Base in Torrejón, first as an administrator and then as a computer programmer, had given him valuable experience in a new and exciting industry: computing. IT wasn't a well-known area, but Frank had a strange feeling it was going to be big.

His reliable work for the Americans had earned him the trust and respect of some important military commanders at the Base; and they helped him to enrol on to some American correspondence courses in computing. These studies were officially recognised in the American education system, and so after he had passed his exams, he successfully requested and received a US government grant for foreign students and got a place at the State University of New York at Binghamton.

So one day in September 1972 Frank packed his bags and headed off to the Big Apple. Frank's departure from Spain was a huge blow for Trinidad and Nicasio. Trinidad had only just recovered from a bout of sciatica, that had kept her bed-ridden for six months, and she just couldn't get used to the idea that her son would no longer be living with them. For Nicasio, the loss was more material than emotional. He had appreciated Frank's help in collecting payments for the block's personal physician, an extra job that Nicasio used to do, and which some residents were less than happy about. Frank had lent a hand in other ways too and was undeniably a great help to his father. There was also the matter of the financial help that Frank provided, helping to keep the family's heads above water, so to speak.

In those first few months after Frank's departure, Trinidad and Nicasio lived for the letters their son wrote to them. Further down the line, he started to send them tapes so they could listen to recordings of him talking about all his adventures. Nicasio and Trinidad would listen to the tapes every night after they had closed; the recordings were a great source of consolation and comfort, helping them forget the not so enjoyable 'adventures' of that day's work in the concierge service. For example:

"Binghamton, 23rd February. My dear parents, hello! How are you both? I hope the concierge service has been 'serving you well' since my last tape. I'm ok... I have my intermediate exams in less than a week, so I'm up to my ears in textbooks at the moment. It is freezing cold here right now; last night the temperature outside was -11°F (that's around -24°C) you've practically got to put

on a full ski suit just to walk out the door…

Papá, I'm pleased you're over your chest infection now; and that you're getting used to living without me, Mamá. I hate the separation as much as you do, but it was necessary. Life here in America is like a whole other world, it's by no means perfect but it's such a great opportunity for me to study at an American university. Over here, if you are good, you are valued; if not, you are left at the side of the road. Friends in high places and recommendations don't count for much. Papá says that the neighbours are jealous of me because I'm studying in the United States; that's a shame. But as we all know, people in Spain just can't get their heads around the fact that someone who's not well-off can do what I'm doing. 'The concierge's son conquers New York!' could be one the headlines from those small-town rags in our neighbourhood… So all in all, as Cervantes said in Don Quixote: 'O envy, root of all countless evils, and cankerworm of the virtues!!... [151] *On another note… Papá, you made me laugh when you said the tape player looks like 'a crossword' because of all the buttons. You know, you really have a way with words… Another thing that tickled me was when you said 'we may not have inherited money from the grandparents but they did leave us diabetes'. I love your optimism, 'putting a brave face on it even through the hard times' and all that."*

Nicasio and Trinidad enjoyed listening to every second of the recordings; it was like having their son right there talking to them. The worlds that Frank described were totally alien to his parents; not many people had televisions in Spain then, and Trinidad was transfixed as she listened to her son's voice. She dried her eyes, not

---

[151] *El Ingenioso Hidalgo Don Quijote de la Mancha* [The Ingenious Gentleman Don Quixote of La Mancha], Miguel de Cervantes Saavedra, Ramón Sopena editor, 1931, 2nd part, chapter 8, page 582, What befell Don Quixote, going to see his Mistress Dulcinea del Toboso. [Translation taken from online source < http://cervantes.tamu.edu/english/ctxt/DQ_Ormsby/part2_DQ_Ormsby.html].

sure if her tears were of happiness or sorrow, and thought about how sad it was that young people had to leave their homelands to find a better life. She thought about the fact that both she and her husband had also had to leave their families and emigrate to Madrid when they were young. She wondered if there would ever be a day that young people could earn a decent living in their own country. Why had it been necessary for her, her husband and her son now to emigrate? Was it because they were all from poor families? Or had this always been the way of things? She was still mulling over that disconcerting thought as the first rays of morning sunshine appeared at her bedroom window.

***

Frank's departure from Spain coincided unfortunately with the death of Trinidad's sister Teresa. Teresa closed her eyes for the very last time one fateful June morning: she had died in hospital after a battle with cancer. They had only detected the tumour a few years before, and doctors had been optimistic about her chances after they had carried out a mastectomy to remove it; they had thought she was going to make it. Sadly though, the tumour began to grow again after a few years and in the end it just hadn't been possible to save Teresa. Trinidad mourned the loss of her sister deeply; they had spent the best part of their lives together. Teresa's death happened so soon after the death of her father and Frank's departure that it seemed as if Trinidad's world was tumbling around her, like an old crumbling ruin. She only had Nicasio left now, and cracks were beginning to show in his structure too; his failing health meant that she had to take very good care of him.

As the saying goes, however, 'every cloud has a silver lining'. Trinidad and Nicasio received the good news that Frank had met a woman he intended to marry; her name was Carol and she was a student from England who was studying at New York University. Trinidad's mind was taken up with wedding preparations all through the summer, helping her to forget her troubles.

Quite unexpectedly, it was beautifully sunny in London on the day of the wedding. With his parents by his side, Frank stood eagerly anticipating his bride's arrival and she didn't make him wait long. She made her way into the church accompanied by the traditional wedding march and with four bridesmaids by her side. All heads turned to look at the beautiful bride as she entered; nobody could tear their eyes away from this emotional moment. Carol looked stunning in a white silk dress; she wore a tiara in her hair and a veil atop her head. Frank wore a black jacket with grey trousers and a red silk tie. A single white carnation nestled in his buttonhole. The guests were equally elegant; especially the ladies who all wore hats, some of them wide-brimmed in the London style. The mother of the bride wore a long pale yellow dress and a matching hat. Trinidad also caught the eye of the English ladies in her black and red flowery summer dress with a lace *mantilla* and a comb in her hair.

After the meal came the traditional speeches, which Carol had already made sure to warn her new husband about. Debuting his new very cultured English accent, the groom started his speech by saying "Ladies and Gentlemen... it is a great pleasure to see you all here today…"

After the initial excitement of the wedding, the stark reality of Frank's new life in England began to dawn on him. Work prospects weren't looking good, and he soon discovered that he didn't have legal employment status in the country. This was because the immigration laws in force at the time didn't provide for British female subjects who married foreigners and decided to stay in the UK. Suddenly his dream of being able to live and work in England was looking decidedly shaky.

As a result of this situation, Frank was forced to await the results of the next general election, that was to be held by Conservative Prime Minister Ted Heath, who needed a majority. However, unfortunately for Mr Heath, the numbers did not go his way and, on failing to achieve a majority, and being unable to establish a coalition with the Liberal Party, he was forced to hand over the reins to his opponent the labour minister Harold Wilson. Luckily for Frank, one of Labour's pre-election promises had been to reform immigration laws; putting a stop to discrimination against women by granting residence and work permits to their non-British husbands.

Frank's problems still weren't over though. His happiness was short-lived as the British labour market began to suffer the effects of a global financial crisis. The strikes that had been a huge part of the Conservative government's time in power had come to an end, but the global oil crisis had seriously damaged the British economy. The three-day week, a measure imposed by the Tories to quell an increasingly volatile situation, and to limit the miners' strike action, had left the British economy in tatters. The result of all this was that Frank had to wait a further six months before he was able to find his first job as a programmer at a local business.

His new place of work was some way from his home, and Frank had to commute for over three hours, there and back, taking two buses each way. One day, he sent his parents a short recording telling them about his experiences during his daily commute on the bus, describing for them a world unimaginably different from the Madrid they now lived in:

'It's a beautiful spring day. The bright sun bounces off the rooftops of the nearby houses. It's early. The city gradually rouses itself and begins its morning routine. It's the middle of June. The streets, clean and free from clutter, await with silent anticipation the first ripple of activity that will bring the great metropolis to life. Cars travel slowly around Birmingham City centre.

I see all of this as I wait for my bus, it's just like any other day. A few minutes later the bus arrives. It's a big, white and blue double-decker, just like all the buses that serve this huge urban sprawl.

As I wait for the queue to die down, watching people disappear through the doors, I let my gaze rest briefly on the yellow lettering on the right-hand door; it says, 'Pay as you enter. Please tender exact fares'. *Being the strict rule-abider that I am, I place the exact change for the price of my ticket in a small red till next to the driver.*

Once inside I make a beeline for my favourite seat at the back of the bus; it's on the ground floor next to the emergency exit. From here in my little corner, I can see everything that happens on the bus; it's an ideal vantage point. The bus pulls away...

Every morning as I board the bus my nostrils are filled with the familiar scent of cleaning fluid, and I marvel at the spotless seats and shiny floors that surround me. This experience is reserved solely for the first passengers of the day though, as not long after, the surfaces will gradually be covered with bits of paper and the smell of cleaning fluid will be replaced by other, more human, odours.

Our journey starts at New Street, next to the train station of the same name. As it is so early, (barely half past seven) the bus is half-empty, but that won't last long…

Two stops down the line, the bus will travel through the commercial district. Next to Rackham's department store, lots of passengers board the bus. From here onwards there will be a constant stream of people; most of their faces will be familiar to me, as I see them on the bus to work every day.

As we go up Constitution Hill the bus seems to have trouble going faster than 5 miles an hour. It's only when we've passed the steepest part of the hill and a lot of people have gotten off, that we really seem to pick up any speed again. Constitution Hill is covered with miserable-looking buildings, they take up both sides of the street. The old red or grey-brick structures are stained by the steam and smoke of thousands of industrial chimneys. Their windows are formed of long narrow panels of glass. They are classic turn-of-the-century industrial buildings.

As I look out on the street in front of me, the first groups of workers begin to file in to start their day. They walk slowly, stretching their legs as though the very exercise itself not only stimulates their limbs but also gives them the energy to tackle a new day at work.

The bus continues on its way. The endless stops and the accompanying screech of the brakes help to keep passengers awake. It's hard enough to read, let alone write on this bus; absolutely impossible to snooze. So that leaves chatting or simply watching; I choose the latter...

The bus slowly climbs Soho Hill. We're now arriving in a different area: West Bromwich (WB). Here the bus starts to fill up with a colourful and unique clientele: immigrants. They have arrived here from Asia, Africa and the Caribbean to work, and in search of the financial wellbeing they don't believe is achievable in their own countries. They all share a common past with this great 'metropolis'; their link with the enduring and powerful British Commonwealth.

There are people from India and Pakistan. The women have long, black ponytails, and silk saris covered in sequins are wrapped around their bodies. The men wear turbans and have long, black beards...

There are people from Africa, the women dressed in European-style clothing. Flesh wobbling and knees knocking together as they walk in 'platform' shoes. Their 'afros' displayed like the spectacular tail of a peacock...

There are West Indians, they're the ones who perhaps draw the most attention. The women wear thick-framed glasses and loud, colourful hats. Their constant laughter and chatter in an unfamiliar slang make them the focus of all the other passengers' attention. The men wear Rasta hats and colourful shirts...

In amongst all these people, sat by my side, there is one lone English woman, stiff and silent. She is middle-aged and wears a wig, her face is covered in powder and she wears a white raincoat and blue trousers. She alone stands out from the rest of the tribe...

As we head towards the end of Holyhead Road there is a steady stream of immigrants on their way to work. It's almost eight o'clock. The working day will soon start in nearby businesses. From my vantage point I can see the typical British worker pass by; with his hat and duffle bag...

At the start of Birmingham Road, the bus is once again half empty and the *road starts to get worse. Now it's the early bird schoolchildren who get on the bus. These are the children of immigrants (WB is their neighbourhood). They wear black blazers with their school crest sewn on to their pocket…*

The ticket inspector, in his black hat and uniform, gets on not long after. He listens to his little radio receiver, monitoring what is going on aboard the other services, whilst also checking that the schoolkids have paid their fare.

Once we pass WB, the faces of the passengers boarding the bus begin to get paler. Then, once again, we return to the motorway that we had previously left behind. Two more stops and we will arrive at Wednesbury, easy to recognise by its industrial aroma and black skies filled with smoke and toxic particles.

After that we arrive into Darlston where I work. I get off the bus and say goodbye to the driver, although I'll undoubtedly see him again on my afternoon journey. The bus continues on to Walsall where it terminates. As usual, my second journey of the day on public transport has taken 55 minutes and my mind is already on the return leg."

23. THE TRANSITION

Life in the concierge service was anything but quiet. The meter room in the block's basement, would often get flooded during summer storms. Nicasio would have to call in the firemen, who were over there so often they knew the place like the back of their hands. They would joke with him, saying "Nicasio, mate, not you again – are you trying to become a member of the fire service or something? You know you won't get a discount, right?" To which Nicasio would reply "as if mate, it's these rainclouds – they seem to have a thing for me; they just won't leave me alone". Then the whole day, and sometimes even part of the night, was spent in a cloud of good-natured banter and laughing as the water was pumped out of the basement. All the while Trinidad cried and Nicasio cursed the heavy skies that continued to make their jobs that bit harder.

Spain's political situation in the middle of 1975 was extremely complicated. Franco was in the grips of an incurable illness and the prospect of new political opportunities, long-awaited by many Spaniards, was within reach. However, social tension was also increasing with constant demonstrations by workers, farmers and students. The economy had been moving towards recession for months: inflation was at more than 17%, unemployment was on the rise, emigrants were returning with no work; it was the worst recession in 15 years[152]. The only thing that seemed to be on a positive trajectory was tourism; and even that was starting to suffer due to the growing political uncertainty within the country.

---

[152] *Camb16,* issue 186, July 1975.

After Franco's death Spain entered into a historic period of political transition. During this time, all of the institutions that had served the dictatorship were gradually dismantled until a constitutional democracy had been formed. Nicasio, like many Spaniards, had fought against Franco in the Civil War and so this political change offered him a ray of hope. Might he possibly see his socialist and communist comrades return from exile after almost forty years? Would this new Spanish democracy recognise the rights of Republican soldiers? These were just some of the questions that entered Nicasio's mind during that period of profound change.

Nicasio followed events closely over the next few months. The arrest of Santiago Carrillo in Madrid, on his return from exile, made Nicasio think the worst at first; however his fears proved unfounded when the Communist leader was freed within a few days. It was only when the first PSOE conference since 1939 was held in Spain a few days later, however, that Nicasio truly allowed himself to believe that democracy was a real possibility.

Nicasio also saw a notable change in the behaviour of the residents during those months in 1976. Those who had strongly identified with the Franco regime and had made Nicasio's life a misery, were suddenly much friendlier towards him. Could it be that they were trying to get on his good side after they had heard him muttering "they'll soon see when my lot get back in"?

And Nicasio's lot did indeed get back in. The Spanish Communist Party was legalised and they had their first conference since the end of the Civil War. The country also had its first free elections in almost forty years, which were won by the *Unión de Centro Democrático* or Union of the Democratic Centre; who also won the second set of elections after that. There was a failed coup d'etat and the Spanish Socialist Party, or PSOE, came into power in October 1982, promising to bring about profound change in Spanish society.

Sometime after the PSOE had won the elections, Nicasio's brother-in-law Francisco (Teresa's widower) came to visit. As usual they had a few beers and talked about politics, thinking back to the old days.

"So Paco, what do you think about what's happening here in Spain?" Nicasio asked.

"Ah man, what can I say…? I'm a bit disappointed with the Socialists. See, my daughter and I have spent months now trying to sort out the paperwork for me to get my Republican soldier's pension and I've still not managed it. They pass me from pillar to post, it's been like that for six months…" Francisco said glumly.

"Well, I can't say that surprises me," said Nicasio, "I'm going through the same thing."

"Just when we thought things might be different seeing as our lot are back in after forty years…" Francisco muttered looking off into the distance. "You know, it's as if no one even appreciates what we went through in the war."

Nicasio smiled at his brother-in-law sympathetically, "they were different times Paco. Back then we were fighting for what we believed in; politicians nowadays don't have the same convictions we did, they're just professionals doing a job."

"You said it Nicasio. The only one who seemed at all sincere to me was that Adolfo Suárez, even though he was from the old regime. But you know, what with one thing and another he was given the boot as well."

"Well, it was Santiago Carrillo who gave me hope, obviously he was one of my lot during the war, but in the end even he hasn't done anything for his old comrades." Nicasio said downheartedly.

"Look man, for me the war was like a lottery, I fought on the Republican side because I did my military service in Madrid, if I hadn't have done that, who knows? I could just as easily have ended up fighting with Franco," Franciso admitted.

"Not me. At first I believed in the socialist cause of Pablo Iglesias, just like my dad. Then when I read Marx and Hegel I became a communist; fat lot of good it's done me though!" Nicasio laughed.

"You see, it's just like you and Atletico Madrid, you're a glutton for punishment mate. At least, I had the good sense to support Real Madrid."

"No, no, in football just as in politics I am a product of my ideas. Real Madrid has always been the regime's side; I was never going to be a *'merengue'*. For me, *'los colchoneros'* have always been the people's side; they stand for freedom of ideas."

"Don't talk nonsense man. Not everyone who supports Real Madrid is right-wing. I know loads of Madrid fans who are just workers like me."

"Ok, ok, no more football talk – let's get back to politics seeing as now we can actually express ourselves freely without being scared someone will come and put us in jail."

"Yes, fat lot of good that's done us as well!"

"Whatever man, I'm enjoying the good life now. All my neighbours are green with envy. Looks like now I'm about to retire they are starting to give me a bit of respect, how about that?"

"Well, it's about time – you've had some really tough years here…"

And while the bad times were indeed coming to an end for Nicasio and Trinidad; for others like don Carlos this new political situation was reminiscent of the pre-Civil War years. The same old political parties had returned; there was unrest in the military; ETA terrorism was on the rise. And so, one day in March 1978, after a short illness don Carlos died in Madrid at the age of 75. It was as if he were somehow scared to live through another nightmare like the Civil War. Trinidad and Nicasio found out about his death sometime later and Nicasio wrote to don Carlos's family, passing on their condolences. Even though a lot of time had passed since that period of her life, Trinidad felt as though don Carlos's death closed yet another important chapter in her life story. The protagonists of her life during the war, of which don Carlos was one, had left an indelible mark on her and she would never forget them.

***

The political situation was a frequent topic of conversation in the tapes that Frank exchanged with his parents, and sometimes Mari-Tere joined in too. When he received them, Frank would remark to his wife on the diverse range of opinions that he got from his family on events in Spain at the time. However, it didn't surprise Frank that his parents would have such varying opinions; he knew their respective points of view all too well.

In one of the tapes Frank received in February 1976, Nicasio seemed absolutely delighted with what was going on and he told his son all about it. There was still a certain wariness evident in his tone though, as if he was watching what he was saying in case the police might still open his parcel and intercept the tapes.

"Overall we're well here. I suppose you will have seen on television what is going on over here. Spain must have freedom, and she will. That's what people in the street are asking for: THE PEOPLE DEMAND FREEDOM, FREEDOM! *In our day,* he said referring to the Civil War, *we had no idea how to take advantage of these opportunities. Now we'll see whether or not these youngsters do…"*

Whilst in Trinidad's eyes events had more of a practical than a political slant.

"Things are getting worse and worse here, the price of everything's going up; it'll soon reach the moon. Your father says that workers' salaries will go up as well, we'll see if that's true - we could really do with it. The telephone bills have gone up loads and I'm scared that phoning London will cost us about the same as buying a flat. One of the few benefits of what's going on here in Spain, especially for people in our neighbourhood, is that they're going to pave our street; we've been waiting for it for years. You will have seen from the newspapers we send over that there have been lots of strikes since Franco died. People in Madrid have been getting used to strikes since they started last autumn. Well, bad times always pass don't they, we've got to have faith; faith solves everything. Don't you be worrying

about us, we're fine…"

Mari's version of what was going on in the streets was probably the most realistic.

"Spain is going through some difficult times at the moment but God willing, it will be for the good of everybody. Yesterday, Sunday, there was a demonstration asking workers to go on strike; the government put a stop to it because it was politically motivated, and the impetus didn't come from the workers themselves. The street was swarming with 'grey-shirts' or armed police, and there were lots of people getting into trouble. I mean young people, not even eighteen years old; I don't even think these kids are old enough to know what they want. At the same time as all of this was going on, the extreme right were marching through Plaza de Castilla with cars bearing the Spanish flag…"

24. A NEW LIFE

It was on Nicasio's 65th birthday that his dreams finally came true; the daily nightmare of the concierge service was over. On his last day, he came out with one of his typically witty sayings to mark the occasion; "I'm kicking off my shoes, just like Saint Teresa did, and I don't want a thing from this place, not even the dust."[153]

Nicasio and Trinidad had been waiting thirty-three years for this moment. In the sixteen years that they had lived at Carabanchel, the Abrantes neighbourhood had undergone significant change. Now, the streets were tarmacked, the neighbours were more well-to-do; even the transport had improved, although the Metro hadn't reached them yet. In general, quality of life in the area had got noticeably better. However, in spite of this, the couple just couldn't wait to get out of there and get back to Madrid; to las Ventas, to Manuel Becerra, to Calle Serrano... "*el viejo Madrid*" as Nicasio used to say wistfully.

For the family, including Frank, their time in the Abrantes neighbourhood had been an unhappy one, filled with crises and moments of frustration. Maybe it was because they had been forced to leave their home in Marqués de Zafra to move there, or maybe it was just that the concierge service had been a torture for all of them, most of all Nicasio. Either way, the fact of the matter was that none of them mourned their departure from the block. And though the

---

[153] Nicasio is referring here to one of the myths attributed to Santa Teresa de Jesús.

couple made no attempt to hide how they felt about leaving, it was a testament to their hard work that many of the residents still came out to bid them farewell and wish them good luck.

Their new flat in the La Elipa neighbourhood[154] was modest, but all that mattered to them was that it was all theirs. It was on the other side of the M30 in their old las Ventas neighbourhood and it was close to a Metro station. It didn't take long for them to get used to their new life, and it was a happy time for them both, while Nicasio was still in good health; in fact, it was perhaps the happiest they had ever been.

With their newfound freedom, the couple could travel to England to enjoy spending time with their two grandchildren that had been born a few years previously. For their first trip to the British Isles since the wedding they went to Cambridge. Nicasio fell in love with the city, and marvelled at all the students from far and distant countries. Being there amidst all that young hope reminded him of his youth, when he had first arrived in Madrid so full of dreams; dreams that were later shot to pieces by the outbreak of war. He thought about how he would have loved to study at the University of Salamanca; to get a degree, just like these students he saw here. To his mind this city resembled Salamanca in so many ways. That was all in the past for him, but he was filled with satisfaction and pride at the fact that his son had been able to achieve something he hadn't.

For Trinidad, the best thing about her many trips to England

---

[154] See map 7.

was spending time with her son, her daughter-in-law and her grandchildren. She too was reminded of the dreams of her youth; how much she had wanted to get married and have children. She never tired of seeing her granddaughter's face, and playing with the child filled Trinidad with unbridled joy. It was the same with her grandson, who reminded her so much of Frank as a boy that seeing him flooded her with memories.

Despite the happiness of seeing her grandchildren grow up and seeing her son do so well for himself, there were also some sad times for Trinidad as well. One of those times was when her brother José III died of cancer at the age of 64. He was the second of her siblings to be taken by this terrible disease, and she wondered if he would be the last. Three years later she lost Francisco, Teresa's husband, as he also lost the battle with this awful affliction. She would never have thought that so many of her loved ones, who had survived a Civil War, would later succumb to cancer. Just like when she was a child, Trinidad pondered the 'why' of it all and ruminated on the mysteries of life; in the end she came to the conclusion that only God had the answers.

Another of the dreams that Nicasio and Trinidad were able to make a reality during that time was going on holiday together; something they had never before been able to do. They spent alternate summers in Extremadura and Cantabria. They would often go to Hervás for the public holidays, which fell in the middle of the month. Quite often, when there was space in Trinidad's sister's home (or 'hotel María' as they jokingly called it), they would stay until the middle of September and celebrate the *Cristo de la Salud* festival, in honour of the patron saint of the area.

When they went to Cantabria they made the most of the Sardinero beach in Santander as well as the beaches on the other side of the bay, like Somo and Loredo. Neither of them could swim and they were scared of the waves, but they enjoyed paddling and just soaking up the atmosphere on the beach. Nicasio's sister, Julia, would often join them on these trips. She could swim and would get really excited when there was good weather and the sun was shining; she would start singing: "Wahoo! Wahey! It's beach time today!"

Frank still wrote to his parents as often as he could, telling them about his experiences and describing scenes from his everyday life in his adopted country. Nicasio would read these letters aloud for Trinidad who was a most demanding audience; sometimes making him repeat the most interesting passages over and over again. However, what Trinidad liked best was the tapes her son sent, as she felt her son was actually talking to her, and she was sending him her answers via her reply.

"Hi kids, it's the 8th April today; Good Friday. It's night time here, and I'm finally able to talk to you all now everything's calmed down a bit. We're doing ok here, but your father's health is not getting better. He still has his chest troubles and he sometimes has a bad night, where neither of us can get any sleep. The doctor carries on prescribing him tablets, but they don't seem to do anything. We'll see...

I had a nice time on my birthday but nobody came to visit. As the saying goes, 'everyone in their home, and God in everyone's home'. My niece María (the one from Barcelona) called to wish me well, and my sister Josefa and her daughter Carmen came to see me yesterday and they brought me a bottle of scent as a present. Your presents made me so happy. I love the skirt, I'll wait until I have a special occasion to wear it; and I've already had a chance to show off the scarf as it's still really cold here. The weatherman said it was two degrees in Barajas this morning, and six degrees in Madrid...

Thank you for the photos of the garden that you sent us, we got them with your birthday greetings. I can see you've been working hard on it. If we weren't so far away I would love to lend a hand, you know how much I love flowers. I can see how beautiful it is anyway from the photo...

We haven't made any torrijas *this year, as your father can't eat them because of his diabetes and I wasn't going to make them just for me! You were saying your* churros *didn't turn out well. I'll send over the recipe so you know how to make them properly. Talking of food, your auntie María is in Hervás now but when she comes back she has promised to bring back some* perronillas *(as they say over there) and I'll send them over to you with Mari when she goes over to London...*

I was so happy to be able to speak to you all on the telephone the other day. Even though we've visited you and talked from time to time I still always get emotional when I hear your voice. I miss you so much, especially now that your father isn't well...

I'm getting tired and I don't know what else to say. I'll carry on with the tape again tomorrow..."

***

In June of 1990 Nicasio and Trinidad visited England again. It was to be the last trip they would make together. Nicasio's health had deteriorated terribly; he could no longer enjoy travelling and the plane ride to London was torture for him. The following year, despite the heat in Madrid, they didn't leave the city for the summer. All those years of suffering on the front during the war, in the workers' battalion and then later with the concierge service, as well as the various conditions he suffered with, took their toll on Nicasio. His years as a smoker had left his lungs in a bit of a state and he really suffered during the winters. He had to be admitted to hospital in the winter of 1991 with bronchopneumonia, and he took a while to recover from that illness. After that Nicasio suffered from a barrage of chest complaints and even had to use bottles of oxygen to help him breathe; luckily these were delivered to their home regularly. Trinidad was constantly by his side, helping and caring for him. However Nicasio never fully recovered and towards the end of October 1992 Frank and his family travelled to Madrid to see him one last time, and ultimately to say goodbye. Nicasio died in hospital one week after their visit; he was 77. Nicasio; the idealist, the poet, the dreamer; fiery and proud. His suffering was finally over...

After his death, his sister Amelia sent Trinidad one of the poems he had dedicated to his sister when he visited Ceinos in 1942:

The doves were transformed
Darling little sister
And I was contented
To see the little house;
To see with my own eyes
My own simple fantasy,

All stood in front of my home,
My whole family, together as one
Grandparents arrived,
Uncles and Aunts too,
And you darling little sister
Hugged me tight to you
Amid the tears you said to me:
Don't go, I don't want you to
Don't go back to the battalion
I know it's prison for you.
I bade farewell to you all
With embraces sad and long
And once again I found myself
In that bitter prison

As the saying goes, it never rains but it pours, and as fate would have it Trinidad had also had to deal with the death of her sister María in May that year. María didn't quite reach the age of 100 like their father, but she died peacefully at the age of 96. And so, yet another chapter of Trinidad's family history closed with her death; leaving Trinidad and her youngest sister Josefa as the only surviving family members.

Before going to the cemetery, Trinidad had taken one last look at her dear Nicasio in the funeral home and, kissing him tenderly, she bade farewell to the only man in her life. Once again she would find herself at a crossroads: one chapter of her life had come to an end with the death of her husband; but at the very same time another was beginning, leaving her full of fear and uncertainty…

25. ALONE

Losing Nicasio was a bitter blow for Trinidad. He had been her partner for forty-four years. They had so many shared hopes and dreams, not to mention all those sacrifices and hard times they had gone through together; she felt she was drowning in memories of him. Sometimes, when she got out of bed in the morning, she would walk around the house looking for him absentmindedly, as if he was still there with her. That time was terribly hard for Trinidad, and the only comfort she could find was in prayer.

Her niece Mari looked after her, even asking Trinidad to come and live with her for a little while. However, after such a huge loss, Trinidad wanted to really change her life. And after some thought (although admittedly not much) she got up and dusted herself off, heading towards her future. She decided she might not know exactly what that future held, but it was going to be a happy one.

One day, as she went for a stroll, she met a neighbour who asked how she was getting on. Trinidad responded that she wasn't actually doing that well, but she had decided she didn't want to sit around the house all day crying over her husband. The neighbour asked her what it was she wanted to do then. Trinidad said didn't know exactly but she wanted to fulfil a long-held dream: to learn to read and write and to improve her knowledge of culture in general. Somewhat excitedly, the neighbour told Trinidad about a nearby centre where they gave classes to elderly people. She said the course was called "Starting again." Trinidad liked the name; it sounded hopeful and inspiring and she immediately wanted to know more about it. The following day she signed up for the classes that the City Council of Madrid offered in her neighbourhood.

In no time at all, Trinidad really got into the swing of the course; making friends with her fellow students and teachers alike, who all came to know her as the elderly student. Trinidad would often say to them, "To learn is to live." And, living by that motto, when the teacher passed her an exercise book and asked her to start drawing and trying out her writing, she immediately felt happy. She started to rediscover an imagination and creativity that she thought had been lost to her; she reverted to the young girl who used to look after her animals and play make-believe, or climb trees to get up-close with the birds and wonder how on earth they could fly. Those musings had inevitably led her younger self to wonder what the world might be like when she was older. All she knew back then was that when she was older, she would surely have all the answers to these types of questions.

The centre offered two hours of classes every day, and Trinidad never missed a single one; not even when it was bitterly cold in the winter, not even when it snowed. She was always one of the first to arrive, making her teacher Marisa smile; Marisa made sure to encourage all of Trinidad's efforts. That day the class was going to learn how to change pesetas into euros. There were posters around the classroom showing the price of various products in the two currencies. This was an entirely new concept for Trinidad and she struggled to understand it. She wished she could just do the sums in her head as she has always done before with pesetas, however it was more difficult with the euro. Slowly and with a lot of patience, she started to understand the logic behind the conversion, as did the rest of the class. As they did so, the class also began to realise that the changeover was not going to be good for their shopping bills. In fact, thought Trinidad, everything was just going to get more expensive with the conversion; and in time she was proved right.

On other days they did reading and writing in class. Trinidad's handwriting was not the neatest; she used to say "I'm a bit lazy; I write like a doctor, all over the place", but she persevered with her practice. What she really liked best, however, was their visits to museums or trips outside the city. She loved visiting the Museo del Prado; she was like a passionate art student, taking in absolutely every tiny detail of the paintings: Goya's brilliant colours, the subtlety of Velázquez, and the sad, elongated figures of el Greco.

Her studies had opened up a whole new world that she had never before had the chance to discover. Only at the age of 91 was she beginning to really understand some of the things her husband used to talk about, such as why poetry is so beautiful, why the economy is so important and how amazingly complex the universe is, as well as many other things. It felt so wonderful to finally know and understand such matters. She no longer felt like she was inferior to those around her, and she truly believed that she too could make the world a better place through learning.

This new knowledge and understanding led Trinidad to develop an interest in many different things. She discovered a deep desire to travel and see different places. For years she had dreamt of visiting

Rome and seeing the Pope. As a surprise for her auntie, Trinidad's niece Mari made enquiries and managed to get the Spanish ambassador to his Holiness to write to Trinidad inviting her to visit the Pope in Rome.

It was a beautiful day in June 1997. The sky was clear blue and cloudless, and the bright sun shone into every corner of St Peter's Square. It was 11.45 in the morning and the spectators were beginning to congregate on the terrace. There was a diverse crowd of people from all across the globe: young Americans standing shoulder to shoulder with Japanese nuns; Indian women posing for pictures with their young children and friends; a group of German schoolchildren waving their school flag. An old Italian woman in a wheelchair was escorted to the front of the queue by one of the guards... Everyone was smiling and you could sense the excited anticipation in the air.

Trinidad and her family were seated in the first few rows in the middle of the square. As time went on, more people began to gather and the murmur of voices began to increase in volume. The heat started to become oppressive and Trinidad had to put on the white hat that she had brought with her specifically for this very purpose.

The ceremony started at twelve on the dot. The blare of the Swiss Guard's trumpets sounded and the men made their way in formation towards the middle of the square. They wore Medici uniforms with a helmet and red plume; their blue, red and yellow stripes were topped elegantly with a white ruff and gloves. They lent the ceremony an impressive vibrancy. Then, in the distance underneath a canopy His Holiness Pope John Paul II suddenly appeared. The crowd erupted into applause and cheers for the Pontiff; Trinidad was so excited she started to shift in her seat.

"He looks so handsome", she said in awe.

"Mum, he's so far away still you can't possibly see his face", her son replied smiling; he had accompanied her to the ceremony.

Trinidad's cataracts meant that she could barely see at all but she replied with certainty, "Yes I can; I see him perfectly thank you very much. If you have faith you can see everything, even in the shadows."

The ceremony lasted almost two hours in the punishing heat. However Trinidad didn't feel anything but a burning fire from within. She kept up with all the verses and songs, offering up her own prayers with passion and humility. At the end of the ceremony, the Pontiff got in his armoured car and passed very close to where she was sitting. As one with the rest of the crowd Trinidad rose to her feet and uttered something akin to a prayer of gratitude but it was lost in the noise of the crowd. Her son looked at her from the corner of his eye; her face was smiling and radiant, and tears glistened in her eyes. For her, this was the **absolute highlight** of her visit to Rome.

Her excitement at seeing the Pontiff had given Trinidad just the burst of energy she needed to climb the 450 steps of the tower of St Peter's Basilica. As she climbed the spiral staircase, the young people walking behind her were in awe of her energy and agility. From the top of the dome she stopped to take in the views that opened up in front of her; she may not have been able to see clearly but she felt the warmth of the sun and the breeze caressing her face. In the forefront of the vista, there were the columns supporting the Basilica's roof, forming a perfect circle all around the Square. To the right; the residence of His Holiness with its green garden, full of blooms. In the middle distance, you could just make out the outskirts of the city. Down below, the Tiber glimmered, reflecting the golden rays of the warm sun behind it. Narrow streets and tall houses were dotted around behind the river, like flocks of sheep on a hillside. Even further into the distance, the city stretched out before them with its cypress-covered hills, its churches and bell towers. Residential areas and suburbs lay vibrant in the afternoon sun. Everything was so full of colour and joy and the sounds of a violin playing a Vivaldi sonata could be heard not far away. Trinidad looked out over the countryside and felt completely happy. She thought to herself, "Well, that's another dream fulfilled."

26. FAME

Worry not that no one knows of you;
Seek to be worth knowing.

Confucius[155]

London, 4*th* April 2002

It's nine forty-five in the morning. Frank checks that he hasn't forgotten anything before closing his suitcase. His wife hurries him along, reminding him that the taxi is waiting outside. His children are also waiting for him in the hallway of their family home. Suddenly, he hears them start a rowdy rendition of 'Why are we waiting…,!' in perfect unison. Frank smiles to himself and shouts down to them "I'll be down in a second."

He reaches the ground floor; checks once again that he has everything, punches in the alarm code and closes the front door, locking it behind him. Their regular taxi driver, Alberto, is waiting for them in front of their house. On seeing the family, he waves at them all and immediately opens the door to his Renault people carrier. The whole family get in and then the car starts off on its journey to Heathrow airport.

The sky is a dull grey colour and it is raining on and off. The weatherman on the radio assures them all that it will ease off this

---

[155] Translation taken from online source: http://sourcesofinsight.com/confucius-quotes/

afternoon. The sun might even put in an appearance, he says. The temperature is 12 degrees centigrade. As they pass by various parks on their journey, they can see the branches of the trees sway in the light westerly breeze. There's a lot of traffic on their normal route because they're travelling at a busy time of day; Alberto tells them he's going to try a different route, slightly less direct but quicker. "Ok, that's fine Alberto. Today's a really important day for us though; we can't miss this flight," Frank says, a note of anxiety in his voice.

This is indeed a special trip for the family; they are travelling to Madrid to be with Trinidad on her birthday. It's a surprise; she knows that her son is coming to celebrate with her, but has no idea that her grandchildren and her daughter-in-law are coming as well.

Alberto's new route is, as promised, much quicker and they get to the airport ten minutes early. Baggage check-in goes smoothly, and after a short time in the waiting room, their flight is ready for boarding. The family get comfortable in their seats on the plane and within a few minutes the pilot asks the flight attendants to prepare for take-off.

Frank doesn't listen to the flight attendants giving their pre-flight spiel. In his mind he's already back in Madrid, reminiscing about his childhood and thinking about his life outside of Spain. It's been 30 years since that day in September 1971 when he sat, just like he is now, in a plane waiting for take-off; only that day he was flying from Madrid to New York. Frank allows his mind to wander, thinking about those days that were so difficult for his family, and for his country.

He remembered that long-ago afternoon when he said goodbye to his parents and his Aunt Teresa. She had been like a second mother to him and she arrived unexpectedly at the airport bus stop to say farewell; he never again saw her alive. He was 23 years old then and, like his mother back in 1923, all that he could think about was his chance to start a new life. The many challenges that lay ahead didn't faze him: the difficulties of a new language that he had not yet mastered, of a different culture that he hardly understood, of living in a remote country almost 4,000 miles away on the other side of the Atlantic. Like Christopher Columbus, Frank saw this voyage to America as a way to win respect and admiration from his contemporaries.

Isabel the Catholic Queen had given Columbus his big opportunity, and Uncle Sam had done the same for Frank. The society that awaited him in America in 1971 was built on fundamental values of freedom of expression, meritocracy, respect for people and their beliefs. When he arrived in the United States, Frank studied information technology which was a new profession that not many people were familiar with at that time. After he finished his studies he emigrated to England where at last he found happiness. It was closer to Spain, and to his parents, and he found he could develop professionally, lead a full social and personal life without any political impediments at all. It had been a difficult decision to leave his parents all alone during a time of such political and social change in Spain.

Since arriving in England, Frank had been closely following daily events in his home country. From the death of the dictator, through several free elections, then *la Movida* (a popular and cultural movement practising free expression), right up to Spain entering NATO and the Common Market.

Frank had missed all these significant events that had taken place in his homeland; he was sorry not to have been there with his family and friends during the historic process. However, he knew for certain that the future, both for him and his immediate family, was inextricably linked to England. He had swapped Uncle Sam for Queen Liz and he didn't regret it for a second.

The plane started landing manoeuvres. Frank looked out of the cabin window at the green fields, the new roofs of the modern factories, and the cars driving along the motorway by the airport. He watched as the plane came in to land on the runway at Madrid-Barajas airport.

Frank looked at his son sat beside him, and a fleeting thought passed through his mind; would his son have to emigrate someday too? Would he follow in the footsteps of his father and grandparents before him? In this virtual world that was getting smaller by the day, where both work and the economy were truly global, Frank had no doubt that the future would hold some difficult decisions for his son too.

***

Madrid, 4th April 2002

It was nine twenty in the morning and Trinidad was getting ready to go to class. She picked up her handbag and her backpack, which contained her notebook, all her homework, her pens and her books; then she walked out of her flat and shut the door behind her. Just as she did every other day, Trinidad travelled the short distance between her house and the adult education centre where she took her classes. It was a sunny spring morning; there was a light breeze and the temperature was a pleasant 18 degrees centigrade. While she stood on the pavement waiting for the traffic lights to change, she took in the heady scent of the roses and geraniums planted on Paseo de Marqués de Corbera.[156] She was happy that morning because it was almost her birthday and her son had promised to come over from England for her party the following day.

She walked through the school gates and went to her classroom, just as she did on every other day. She was happy because Marisa, her teacher, was going to ask her about the euro that day and she really thought that, after a lot of hard work, she had finally got to grips with it. She said good morning to Marisa and her fellow classmates then the lesson began.

Trinidad made a valiant effort to tackle the challenges posed by the euro; and Marisa thanked her for the hard work she had put in trying to understand the logic behind the conversion. Everything seemed normal; that is, until mid-morning. The teacher announced to the class that they were going to finish a little early so they could celebrate Trinidad's birthday, seeing as she was turning 95 the next day. A blush crept up Trinidad's cheeks, she started to say that there was no need really, she was grateful for the thought but her birthday

---

[156] See map 6.

wasn't until the next day and... But before she could even reach the end of her excuses, a group of people that she had never seen before burst into the classroom. The centre's headmistress was among them, at least Trinidad recognised her. The headmistress turned to Trinidad:

"Trinidad, many happy returns. I hope that you don't mind but we would like to honour you in some small way for being the oldest student in the whole of Madrid."

Trinidad was stunned for a few moments, she hadn't been expecting any of this. The headmistress then went on to introduce Trinidad to the Culture Councillor for Madrid, and other notable people, who had come to congratulate her. The councilman presented Trinidad with a bunch of flowers and a commemorative plaque that said: "To Trinidad Martín for being the most senior student in Madrid, 2002."

All of a sudden, flashes started to go off as a group of photographers and journalists descended upon Trinidad, while she smiled into the cameras like a movie star. Microphones from a myriad of different radio and TV channels started recording her first words.

"Thank you all so much," she began shyly. "The truth is I wasn't expecting this party at all. I feel like a blushing bride, surrounded by all these photographers and TV cameras. Today is a very happy day for me -gosh it's even better than winning the lottery," she said grinning from ear to ear, as everyone gathered around her.

One of the journalists asked her:

"Trinidad, if you could have studied earlier on in life, what would you have liked to be?"

"I would have liked to be a politician because I talk a lot and don't do much; and my husband used to say that I liked to be in charge, he always said I was just like a sergeant major," she revealed with a touching openness. Everyone laughed at her witty remark, and in a matter of minutes it had been quoted across mass media outlets.

The town councilman looked at her, slightly surprised, but he smiled and demonstrating all the skills of a professional politician said to Trinidad.

"Trinidad, you should stand in my place at the next elections - I am quite sure you would win."

"No sir, you should stand again; I'm a bit old for all this politics stuff."

Trinidad then apologised for the wisecrack remark and said she hoped she hadn't offended the councilman.

The questions didn't stop. Trinidad smiled and enjoyed her moment in the spotlight, answering each question thoughtfully and dealing with the many different topics that the journalists seemed to be interested in. Some of the questions she was asked included:

Journalist: "Trinidad, when your husband was still alive, who wore the trousers in your relationship?"

Trinidad: "My husband wore the trousers, since he was the man, but I took control whenever I could." (*TVE*)

T: "The day I lost my husband I thought I would die. I couldn't stop crying, or feeling sorry for myself. He was everything to me." (*Diez Minutos*)

J: "How does it feel to be able to read and write?"

T: "I wanted to learn so I could be free" (*Diez Minutos*)

T: "For me, being able to learn to read and write was like discovering a new world. Although the bad thing is my appalling memory and my lack of imagination." (*Metro*).

T: "I've got younger since I started to learn," she said pointing to the black shocks in her otherwise grey hair. "I asked the doctor how it could have happened, and he said I was getting younger again." (*Teleindiscreta*)

J: "Your teacher has told us that you have learnt all about the euro."

T: "Oh don't! I've made myself dizzy looking at all those darn numbers!" (*Madrid*)

J: "What message do you have for all those children who don't want to go to school?"

T: "Quit drugs and go and help drug-addicts in the street." (*Teleindiscreta*)

J: "So what do you want to do or learn next?"

T: "I like the internet, so I need to learn how to use a computer. Now, that's another world; people from different places that get to know each other, meet and then get married." (*El Mundo*)

T: "Next I want to go to the moon" (*El Mundo*). "I often dream of going to the moon, but I know that it's an impossible dream because they don't let just anyone go there." (*Pronto*)

After nearly 20 minutes of non-stop questions and smiling, she said goodbye to everyone, telling them she needed to get home before her son arrived from London.

***

It was twelve forty-five in the afternoon when Trinidad arrived back at her flat. Not long after she walked through the door the bell rang; there was someone there to see her. She opened the door; trembling with excitement at the thought of seeing her son. And then there he was; Frank, hugging his mother tightly. When she finally let go of him and looked up, she could hardly believe her eyes as her grandchildren and her daughter-in-law appeared from behind his back. "Oh my goodness, what a surprise!" she said. "Well I certainly didn't expect this, what a day it has been – so much excitement, I'm not sure how much more I can take!"

Since her appearance on television, the telephone hadn't stopped ringing. Everybody wanted to interview her. *TVE* rang to invite her on to their programme "*Así son la Cosas*". No-one in her family had ever been on 'telly' before. The following day *TVE* sent a car to take them all to Prado del Rey. Within minutes, the whole family (including Mari), had arrived at the *TVE* studios. There were barely 10 minutes to spare before they were due to appear on the programme.

The make-up artists worked tirelessly until they were all ready. Surprisingly the only person they decided not to make up was Trinidad.

"Excuse me, miss – why are you not putting make-up on me?" she asked with more than a hint of disappointment in her voice.

"Because you look great as you are, just natural," the make-up artist said smiling.

The whole family was brimming with nerves; but if Trinidad felt nervous, she hid it well. A bell rang and a voice announced that in two minutes they were to move into the main hall where the programme was going out live. Exactly two minutes later a hostess came to collect them and wordlessly asked them to take their seats, they were silent so as not to interrupt the live filming that was going on. The hostess pointed out where each of them should sit, and two minutes later the presenter turned to Trinidad and began the interview. She was being broadcast live across Spain!

"Why did you take up studying?"

"Because I was so fed-up with not knowing what to do. My husband had died nine years before and I was alone because my son lives in England"

"You've only got the one son?"

"Yes just one. The truth is all I was doing was sitting at home crying and I thought this isn't for me, it's no life - I'm going to die of grief. I bumped into a friend one day who suggested I go and take a look at the day centre. So I went one day and the truth is it just wasn't for me; they were all little old men and women and I didn't like it; I wanted something different."

"You are just like my Mum" the presenter said smiling, "she says she doesn't want to go to a day centre because they're all old in there, and she's 81!"

"The day centre wasn't for me, so I asked my friend: do you know if there's somewhere you can go for writing, you know, to learn to read and write? She said yes and so I have her to thank."

"Francisco… Frank, when your mother told you she was learning to read and write, at her age, well - what did you think?"

"Well, it's been wonderful being able to give her this opportunity because she really is a role-model to me; she has been such an inspiration ever since I was born. She has always had a great fighting spirit and a quick mind. Her father died when he was 102 and I think she inherited her good memory from him. It has been truly inspiring for all of the family over in England as well, we are all so proud of her."

"So, she has a good memory, good vision, good hearing…" the presenter said looking over at Trinidad.

"I've always had a good memory ever since I was little. I can still remember the prayers my mother taught me."

"Do you know how to read English Trinidad? Your daughter-in-law Carol is English isn't she."

"Yes, that's my next challenge - learn English, they want me to learn it – at my age!"

"And do your grandchildren speak Spanish?"

"Yes they speak really well, they do well in all their subjects."

"So they got their intelligence from their grandmother then?"

"Yes, it must be because I was born in the land of the *'conquistadores'* you should know that."

"Yes - here in my notes, it says you're from Cáceres"

"Yes, from Cáceres province, where the conquistadors were from"

"And how did you end up in Madrid?"

"Well, at first I went because one of my sisters was getting married. She wanted me to come to Madrid and then I just stayed. I got married to my husband after that; he was from Valladolid, and so I have my life here, and then another life in London as well."

"And do you ever think of moving to London? Or moving in with your niece here in Madrid?"

"My son has said I should go over and stay with them awhile, but that doesn't appeal to me- I'd be like a nun shut up in a convent. I don't know English, I don't know anything – I don't think they'd let me out of the house."

"Why on earth wouldn't they let you out of the house?"

"Well, it's just they say I'll get lost."

"Come on now, I know the streets are not exactly paved with gold over there in England, but people hardly go about murdering one another."

"No, but the family all get up really early to go to work, and don't come home until eight in the evening, so I would be stuck at home like a nun in a convent. There's always the radio, but really - what would I do?"

"Listen, what you do is you watch *TVE* on an international TV station, woman, you carry on watching our show just like you do in Spain."

"They don't get it over there."

"What do you mean they don't get it? They should get cable," the presenter laughed.

"So, María Teresa… Mari, what is your aunt like?"

"She's great, she's not like a normal older person - she's just charming. She's like a second mother to me; she always has been, and well, I'm really proud of her too; she's so full of life."

"I told her to say that." said Trinidad.

"Of course you did, I have a feeling you're always the one in charge," replied the presenter.

"I have here in my notes, to ask you how long it takes you to sign up to the excursions that they have over at the adult education centre."

"I'm always the first name on the list. I go and see the Royal Palaces and all those things and everyone else gets tired and has to sit down, but I stay on my feet because if I sit down I won't get up again."

"Señora, we wish you lots of luck in the rest of your life, we hope you carry on learning, moving on, and that now you put your mind to learning English, and getting to grips with the computer!"

"English will be hard – I don't know how to say anything apart from bye-bye, which means *'adiós'* and *'buenos días'* and I don't know what else."

"How do you say *'buenos días'*?"

"'Morning', *'buenos días'* is 'morning'."

"Well now it's time for you to say 'bye-bye' to everyone"

"Bye-Bye…"

And with a smile, Trinidad bids farewell to all the *TVE1* viewers.

That afternoon, on the way back home, their telephones didn't stop ringing. All the radio stations that had caught on to the day's news and seen the lunchtime news programmes wanted to talk to Trinidad. Her niece, Mari, stepped up as her temporary PR manager. Mari had to have the same conversation with the press over and over, in the end they all knew it by heart; it was like a hit song that sticks in your head because it's on the radio all the time.

"Yes, Trinidad is here but she can't come to the phone right now because she's doing an interview" Mari said for the umpteenth time.

"No, today is impossible I'm afraid, but she has a 'window' tomorrow. Can you remind me who you are and what station you're from? Ah, ok, so that's Olga Delgado from *Radio Caracol* in Colombia; I've made a note of that. Tomorrow at 5.30pm – yes, that's the only slot she has left."

"Yes, you can call her on this number. Ok, we'll speak to you tomorrow". And with that Mari left the phone off the hook before it had a chance to ring again.

Mari read out the list of interviews they have agreed to for the following day. *Radio Nacional de España* was at 10am; then *Cadena Ser* at 10.45; at 12.30 in the afternoon she had *Onda Cero* and at 2pm people from *Cadena Cope* would be calling her. After lunch, at 5pm, she had an appointment with *Los Cuarenta Principales* and then finally *Radio Caracol*. They all looked at one another, their faces beginning to show signs of tiredness; all apart from Trinidad's that is, she was still grinning from ear to ear. Her son had tried to convince her not to do any more interviews but she knew she wanted to accept them; it was her moment of fame. She had become famous; even if it was only for a day while her story was fresh in everyone's minds. It gave her the feeling of being special, just like when she was younger and she was spoiled by her family.

The radio station *Onda Cero* featured her interview on the air, and their presenter Fernando Onega also dedicated this letter to her[157], it was quite long and emotional:

Today I would like speak to you about a woman that not many of you will know; a woman who turns 95 today and has probably been crying over the death of the Queen Mother in England, after all the late Queen was but a little older than her.

I'm talking about a woman who has featured on the news without appearing on Big Brother or The X Factor. For me, ladies and gentlemen, she has been the best part of the news all day, perhaps all year. I only found out about her because Susana Moreno discovered her story in El País. Her story is somewhat like a novel, and it starts like this:

A woman from Madrid decides, at the age of 95, to go to classes and learn to read the letters that her son writes her. That woman is Trinidad - Trinidad Martín, it's a name I will never forget.

She wasn't able to attend school at any time in her long life. At home she relied on both her husband and son who knew how to read; but then her son left for England and her husband died. She was left alone; a widow in the depths of an all-encompassing loneliness; all without the comfort of being able to read a magazine or hear her son's letters read aloud to her.

---

[157] Letter from Fernando Onega to Trinidad (on the radio program Onda Cero – 4th April 2002).

She coped as best she could and in ingenious ways; telling her pills apart by their colour. She only knew Carmen Sevilla's[158] name thanks to the television and seeing her photos. I don't know how she knew which Metro station was which when she travelled around, and I know she had no chance of deciphering the electricity bills, or her bank statement. She didn't even know how much her pension had gone up by. However, most troubling of all for Trinidad was the fact that she had no way of reading her son's letters. Trinidad, my good woman, what you experienced was no everyday loneliness, no – yours must have been the type of mournful feeling that poets write about. It must have been a unique type of loneliness, a loneliness that felt it would be with you today, tomorrow and forever; a loneliness with no reprieve.

But then one day Trinidad rebelled against this consuming loneliness; she told herself she was going to be ok. She decided that she wanted to read her son's letters herself; that a son's letters shouldn't have to be shared with strangers who read them aloud for her. She decided that her son's business wasn't for all to see. And so she signed up to go to school.

There was a photo published of her today, showing her brave, learned face of 95, clutching her schoolbooks against her chest like a young girl. She is proudly holding her handwriting book and her pronunciation dictionary, standing in her classroom at the adult education centre in Elipa neighbourhood.

And that is why I am writing to you Trinidad. Every day in this country we fixate on people who are famous for no good reason; we spend time and energy watching and listening to programmes about people who are nothing but charlatans. They are just living off their story and off the stupidity of the press. Just last night, there was a big public debate about someone whose great

---

[158] A popular Spanish actress, singer and TV presenter.

achievement in life was that they had put parsley in their ears, and still we watched. The shame of it is that all this noise stops us from seeing that on a quiet street in Madrid there is an older woman, an inspirational grandma, who is learning to read at the age of 95. She isn't doing it so she can read her lottery tickets for the big draw, or so she can follow Sara Montiel's[159] exploits in Cuba. She is doing it for the best reason there is and something money can't buy, for the only thing that matters; to communicate with her son.

And so today Trinidad, with your ever-improving handwriting, you are less alone, you are less vulnerable. You can even understand your electricity bills. We should be thanking you and sending you a big hug and a kiss today Trinidad, because you have taught us all a very important lesson.

---

[159] A famous Spanish singer and actress of this period.

27. ONE HUNDRED YEARS

5th April 2007

The party in El Casino was over. It had been a hugely emotional day for Trinidad, but she felt extremely happy. When she got home, alone once again, she thought back to how worried she had been at the start of the day and laughed to herself. The celebration of her hundredth birthday led her to think of her father again. She liked to think that he had been there with her during the celebration today, and with that in mind she started to talk to him.

"So what did you think of the party Papá? Were you proud of me? We both know what we have had to go through to get here, still going strong after 100 years: war, the death of our loved ones, the fight for a better and fairer life... But do you know something? It's been worth it, don't you think? I'm so happy with everything I've achieved. I learned three very important things from you and Mamá: **love**, **work** and **responsibility**. Then from life, I learned about two more: **suffering** and **hope**, and they've been my guide ever since I was a little girl. *Love*; well I've given and shared that with my family, with nature, and with animals. *Work*; I became familiar with that on those first days taking care of the goats, helping Mum to wash clothes and selling milk. *Responsibility*; now that came later – when I left the village to work in Madrid, when I looked after don Carlos's home during the war and then when we struggled to stop them chucking us out of the concierge service. I learned about *suffering* from Mamá who said 'women are put on this earth to suffer.' Do you remember? I can almost see her now, just like I can you. Yes, suffering, well I have lived with that since I saw my brothers die when I was a little girl; and also in the war and after the war with my husband, when we couldn't afford a flat and then, years later, when my son moved abroad. However, for me, the most important thing has been hope. *Hope* is something I also learned about from Mamá; when I saw her overcoming all that life threw at her. Hope is everything. Hope is what gets me out of bed every morning, rain or shine. Hope is what pushes me to overcome – just like Mamá did – and to do things I wasn't able to when I was young, like go to school. And hope is what God gives me when he protects me, giving me health and happiness so I can see the good in life"

She looked at her father and now he was the one smiling, as he remembered the day he saw her leave for Madrid on the train with her sister. Yes, he was very proud of Trinidad. She had shown everyone that it was never too late to achieve your dreams. Hope was indeed a powerful thing and his daughter had it in spades.

END OF PART TWO

Photo 12 – Trinidad holding Paquito in Madrid (1949)

Photo 13 – The old Escuelas Aguirre in Madrid where Paquito was educated

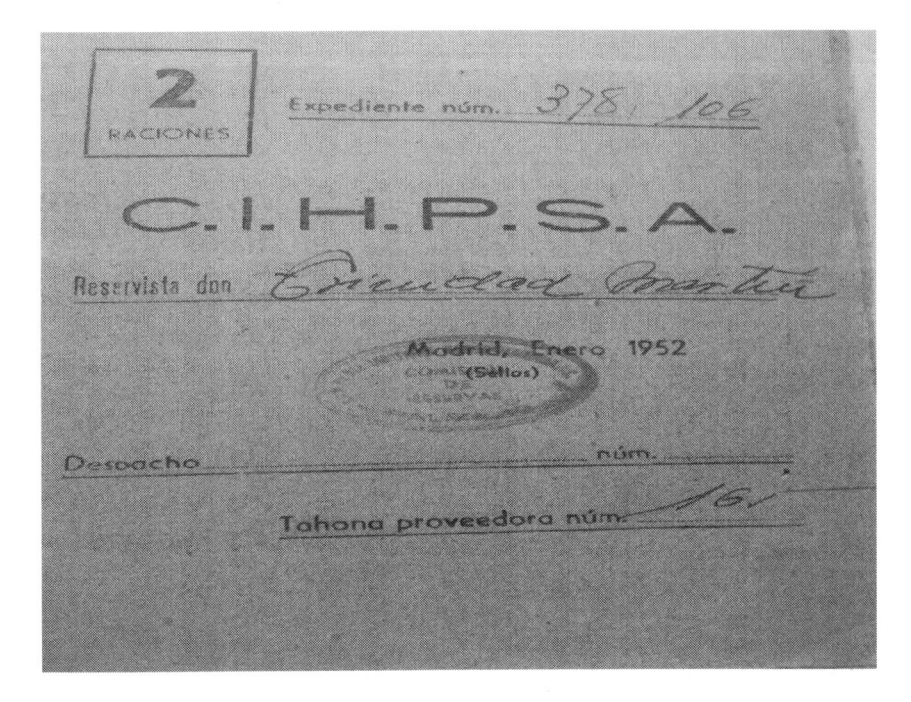

Photo 14 – Trinidad's ration card from the year 1952

Photo 15 – Frank and Carol's wedding with Trinidad and Nicasio in the front row

Photo 16 – Trinidad receiving recognition from Madrid's City Council

LIVING IN SPAIN'S TURBULENT YEARS – THE STORY OF A REMARKABLE LIFE

Photo 17 – Trinidad being interviewed by the media

Photo 18 – at the end her party, feeling proud to have reached the age of 100 like her father before her

EPILOGUE

*No great man lives in vain.
The history of the world is but
The biography of great men*

One possible interpretation of the above quote from Thomas Carlyle[160] is that only the biographies of great men are worth writing. Another, perhaps more acceptable interpretation, is that the history of humanity is only written by heroes and famous people.

My humble aspirations when writing this biography of my mother, and telling the story of my family, was to help bring their 'history' to light. Not because they had been heroes or famous people as the quote suggests, but because the story of their lives deserved to be told. Of course, in part, I did so to contribute to the knowledge and enjoyment of the readers, but also because, as Disraeli once commented; "biography is life without theory".[161] Biography pure and simple, what we write in our daily lives, this is what deserves to be told.

When I started this project five years ago, all I had was what I had heard my family say and what my parents had told me since I was born. Of course, it must be said I do have first-hand knowledge of some parts of the story where I feature as one of the characters. Then, finally, for the more objective sections of the story, I relied on

---

[160] Thomas Carlyle. *"On Heroes, Hero-Worship and the Heroic in History"*, Fredrick A. Stokes & Brother, New York, 1888. p2.
[161] Disraeli, Benjamin extract from *The Mirror of Literature*, Amusement, and Instruction Volume 20, No. 556, July 7, 1832.

what information I was able to source from archives and libraries. After my father died and my mother was left alone, I had many a conversation with her, in which she would talk to me about her memories and I would make sure to record it all on the tape recorder. Most of her tales were later corroborated by the stories of other friends or family.

It has been a fascinating journey writing this book; one sometimes filled with surprises and contradictions, as José Ortega y Gasset once said, the biographer attempts to piece things together,[162] but for the most part, the things I have learned fitted with the details I had already.

It was while attempting to find out definitively when Trinidad left Hervás, that I stumbled across my first surprise. My mother had always maintained that she was 14 when she went to her sister María's wedding in Madrid. She also told me that she and her sister Teresa went alone. That journey to the capital was a seminal moment in my mother's life, so I felt it was of the utmost importance to the story that the facts be correct. One obstacle in my search for the truth here, and perhaps why it took such a long time to resolve, was the difficulty locating María's marriage certificate. When I finally found the document it said she was married on *29th December 1923*. Which would mean that my mother had been 16, and not 14 as she had told me. Her aunt Felisa had also signed the register as one of the witnesses, which proves that the sisters hadn't travelled to Madrid

---

[162] The Dehumanization of Art and Other Essays on Art, Culture, and Literature (Princeton Paperbacks, 128), 1968.

alone at all, but with their aunt.

Another piece of information that my mother gave me, and which I'm sure she believed to be true at the time, was the name of the embassy where don Carlos and his family spent the war. She always maintained that it was the Brazilian Embassy, however I later found out it had actually been the Chilean Embassy. The reason for this erroneous detail in her own version of her story is actually explained within the book; my mother never really knew the true location in which don Carlos was hiding, hence the confusion. As for the rest of her life story, all that she has told me has been checked and was found to be true.

My father's story was much more difficult to piece together, perhaps because he died before he could tell me many of his tales, or perhaps because I never asked.

It came as a surprise that Nicasio had belonged to the Spanish Communist Party (PCE), The General Workers Union (UGT) and the Unified Socialist Youths (JSU) before the war. His affinity with the PCE had been well known in our family, but we were not aware of the fact that he had actually been a member. Confirmation of this fact came when I received his personal file from the *Archivo General Militar de Guadalajara* [Guadalajara General Military Archive], as well as the judgement against him by the much-feared *Tribunal Especial para Represión de la Masonería y del Comunismo* [Special Courts for the repression of Freemasonry and Communism].

My research into the Civil War leads me to believe that it was not uncommon for young people of the Republican Army to belong to these left-wing organisations. As Trinidad says: "...everyone's either a socialist, a communist or an anarchist nowadays.... The first question anyone asks is always, what party do you belong to?".[163]

However, I discovered much later on in my research that Nicasio truly believed in these left-wing parties; his wasn't a casual membership. The socialist beliefs instilled in him by his parents left an indelible mark on his impressionable young mind. His Marxist beliefs grew with the revolutionary fire that he lived through in Medina de Rioseco in 1934 and were finally consolidated when he arrived in Getafe at the very start of the war. However, what happened when the war finished...? Well, he had done nothing. He had no blood on his hands from the conflict (fortunately) so the courts pardoned him in 1949; he kept his beliefs, talking about them with his family on occasions (during moments of depression, or when he had been drinking); he got excited when Santiago Carrillo returned to Spain and the PCE was legally recognised and... then he remained inactive for the rest of his days.

How should we interpret his political philosophy? I think that, like many others of his generation, Nicasio was an idealist. He fought for a better world, one in which poor people could have opportunities without having to rely on the rich. Nicasio had learned the value of education from his mother and he wanted the children

---

[163] See Chapter 12.

of poor families to have access to it. He had a great artistic sensibility and loved poetry. He was a dreamer. Marxist ideas 'rang his bell' —as he often used to say. Was it a mistake for him to dream of creating a world where the poor were less poor and the rich were less rich? Maybe, but if it was, it was a mistake that he never regretted.

My mother, on the other hand, was different. From a young age, she was more interested in topics like religion or nature, than politics. Although she expressed sympathies with the constitutional monarchy system when she was young —maybe influenced by her father- she was never truly interested in it. She made her stance on politicians very clear: they "talk a lot and don't do much"[164]. Her beginnings in a rural, farming environment, where hardly anyone went to school, stopped her from having an educated view of the society in which she lived. However, even without this basic knowledge, she was able to survive and respond to the faith that don Carlos had placed in her. At the same time, I have no doubt that her religious beliefs and principles guided her and allowed her to overcome the worst days of the Civil War, with all the dreadful hunger, fear and death that she had to face.

One of the most remarkable times in her life was when, after the death of my father, she decided to fulfil a dream she had had since she childhood: to learn to read and write. By the time she achieved her aim it had been 90 years in the offing, and her achievement was recognised by the *Ayuntamiento de Madrid* [Madrid City Council]. In

---

[164] Chapter 26.

the European Year of Culture (2002), when so many children who had the chance to go to school chose not to, she showed them all the way. Her excitement at being able to read the letters I had sent her from England, her willingness to work and to push herself, when most of her contemporaries were in nursing homes, caught the public's imagination (both in Spain and abroad) when they learned of her story. What an amazing inspiration!

After her hundredth birthday party, Trinidad continued to display an impressive zest for life. Her excitement for learning and keeping up with the latest things lasted three more years. Her good health continued on, like an unstoppable Swiss clock. Her smile and her sense of humour did not dim: much to the delight of both young and old. Her granddaughter Isabel calls her a truly 'unforgettable grandma'.

In the summer of 2010 whilst on a visit to Ceinos de Campos (where she had been wanting to return for a while) she suffered a fall, and although she was taken straight to hospital, she died in Valladolid on 16th July. She lived **one hundred and three years, three months and eleven days**, beating her father's record, and achieving just one more of the goals that she had set herself.

London, 2016

APPENDICES

MAPS

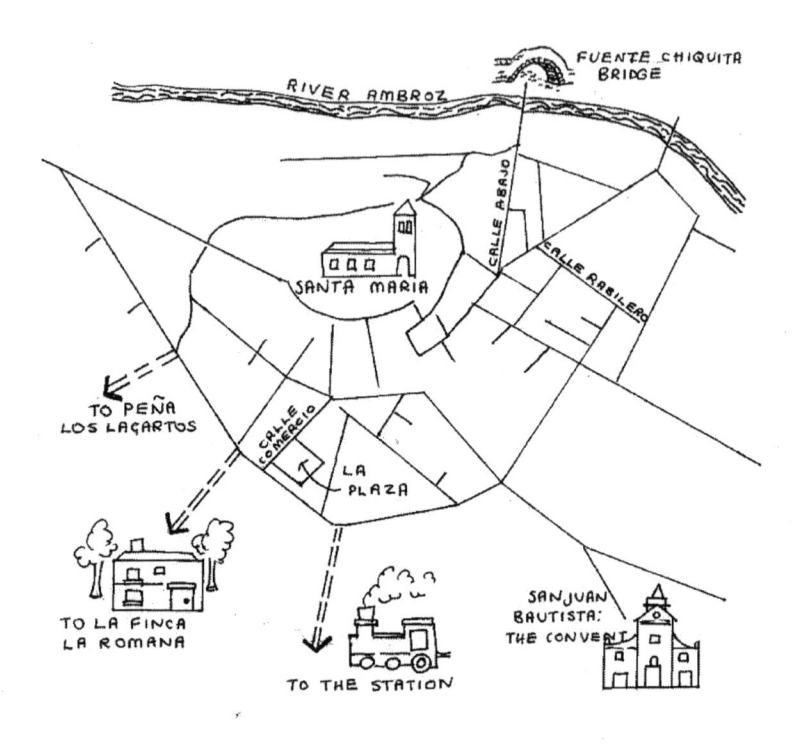

Map 1 – Hervás – locations of the key places mentioned in the book

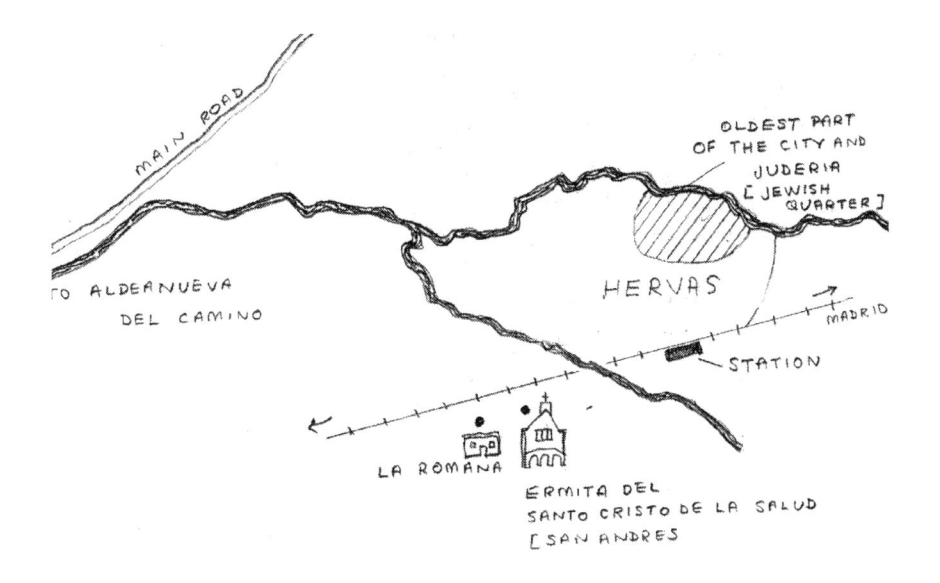

Map 2 – Hervás and its environment

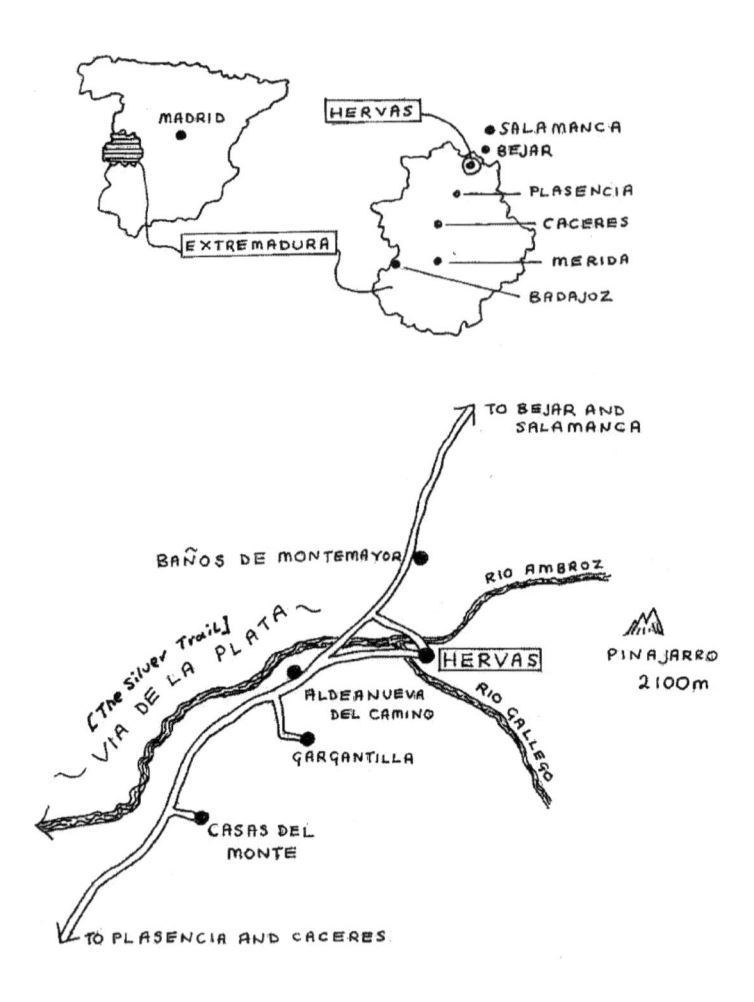

Map 3 – the location of Hervás and the region of Extremadura

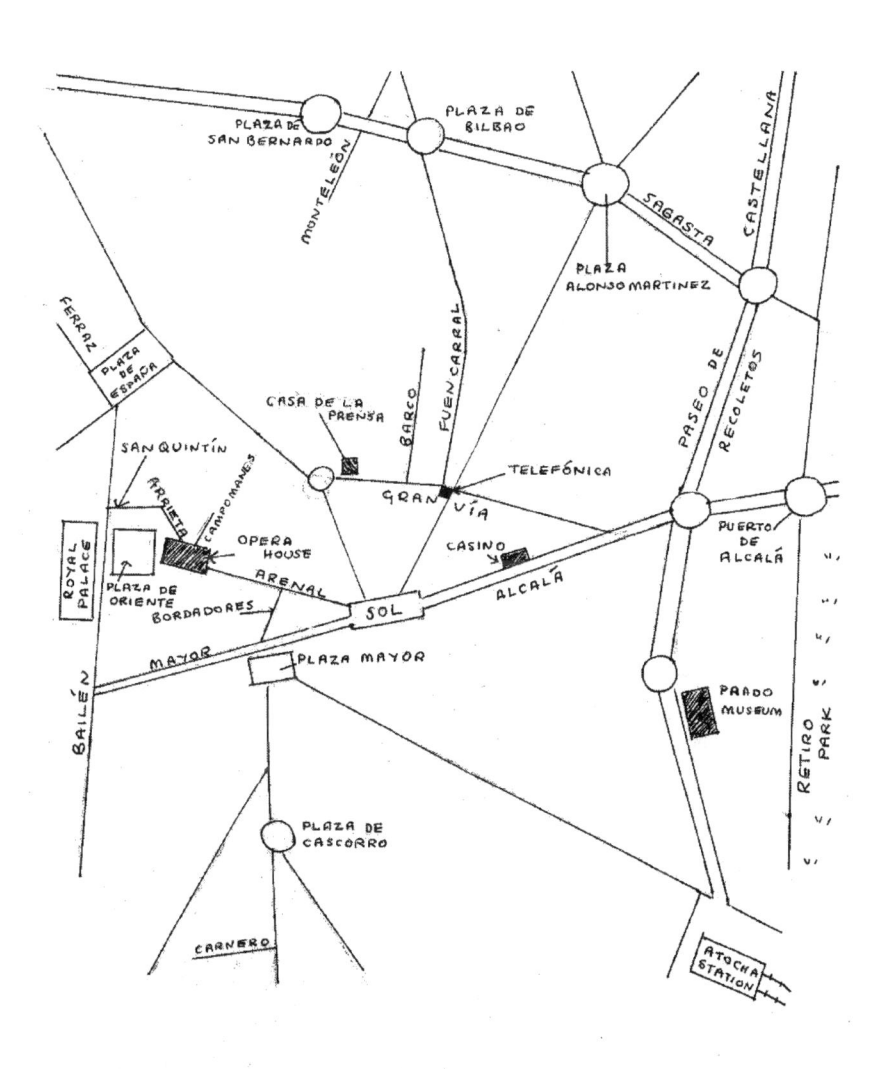

Map 4 – Madrid centre

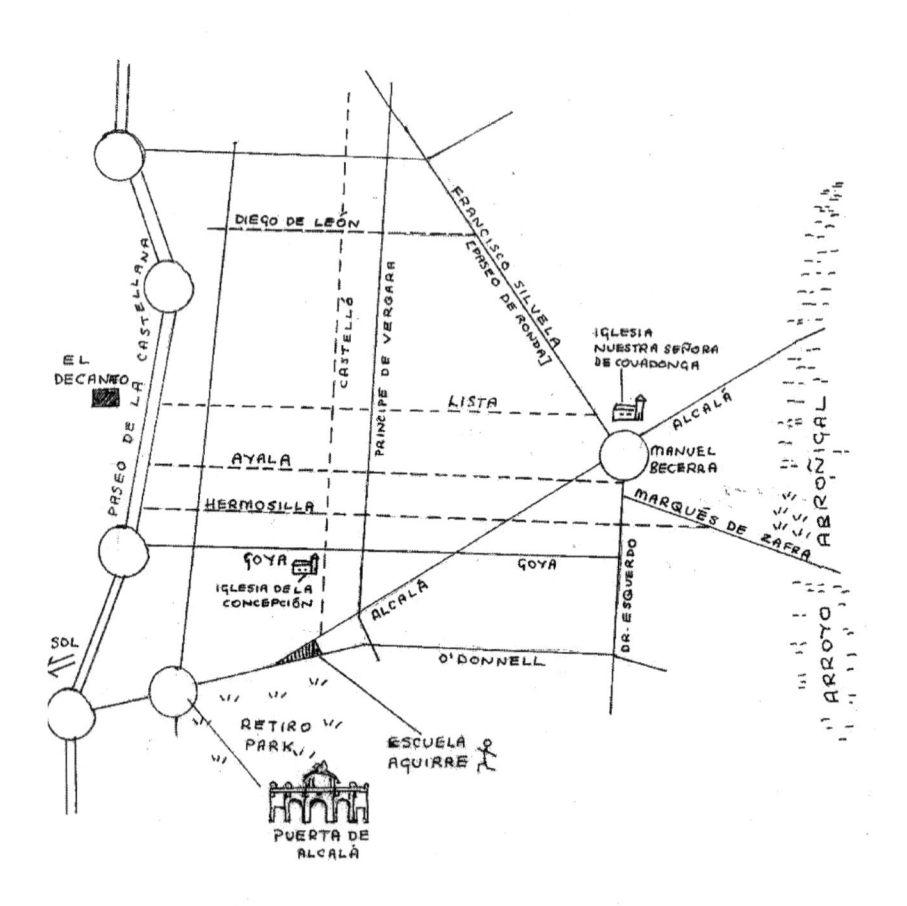

Map 5 – Madrid Salamanca district

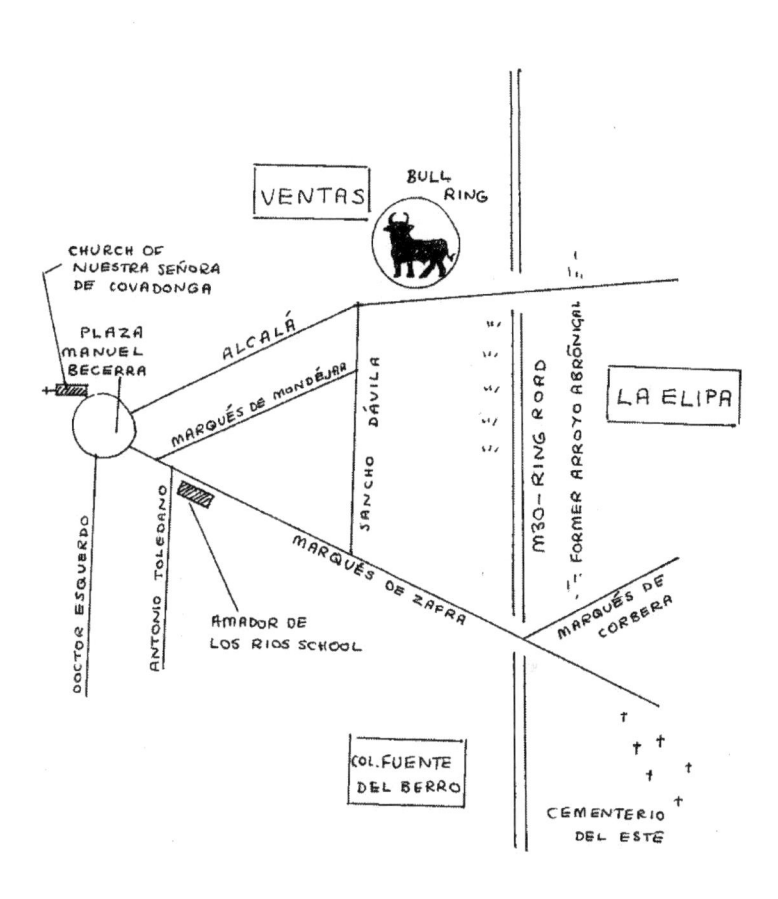

LIVING IN SPAIN'S TURBULENT YEARS – THE STORY OF A REMARKABLE LIFE

Map 6 – Madrid Ventas district

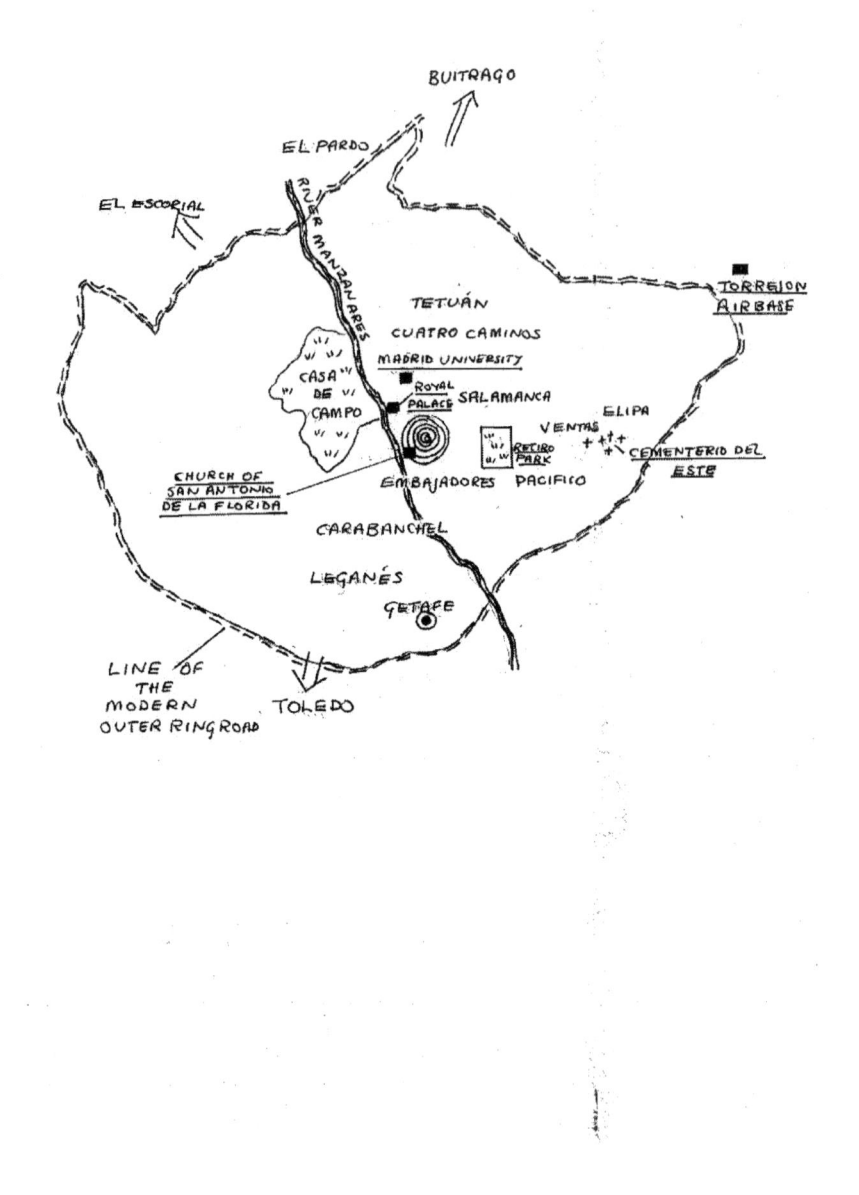

Map 7 – Madrid and its environment with the location of places mentioned in the book

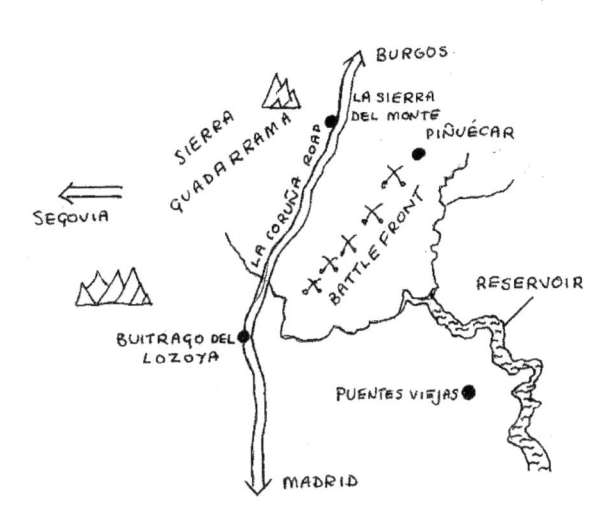

Map 8 – Somosierra Battle

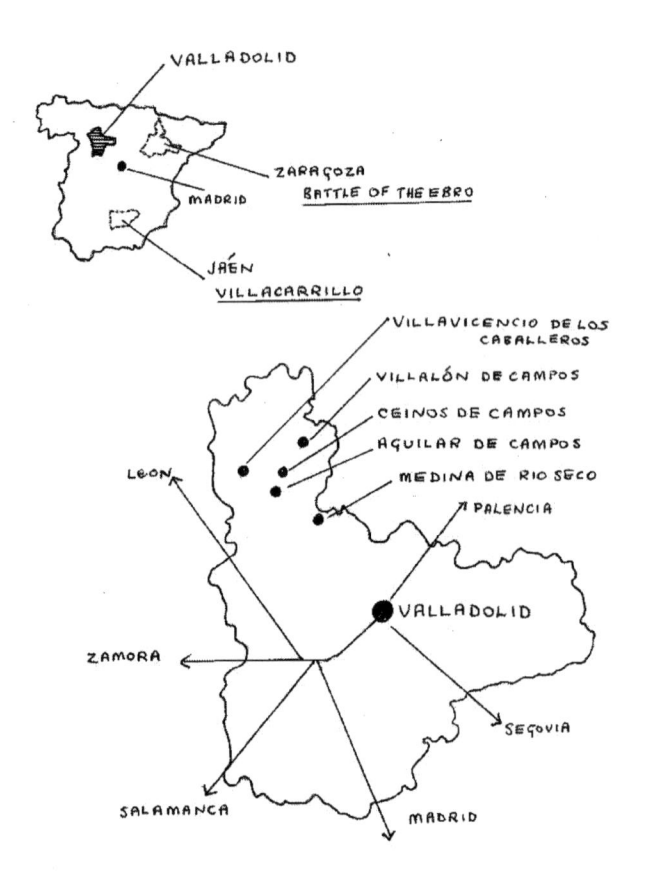

Map 9 – Ceinos and its environment

CHRONOLOGY

Date	Local	National	Global
1865	Francisco Martín Calzado is born		
1871	Dorotea Gómez Montero is born		
1892	Francisco and Dorotea are married		
1900	The factory where Francisco works burns down; it may have been set intentionally		
	Strikes and conflict between factory owners and the textile workers of Hervás		
1904	Hervás – According to the local newspaper *El Ambrot* the town had an illiteracy rate of 50%	3rd January, the "caso Nozaleda" blows up in the face of the Maura's government	War breaks out between Russia and Japan (Russo-Japanese War); Russian defeats in Yale and Port Arthur
	Labour disputes between the owners and workers in the	11th September, first official day of Sunday rest in Spain	Re-election of Theodore Roosevelt

	cloth factories, lasts 9 months A large part of the population (day-workers) go hungry and a 'cocina económica' [food kitchen] or 'tienda asilo' [welfare shop] is set up to alleviate hunger in the winter months		
1905	Trinidad's sister Teresa is born Huge conflicts in local textile industry.	31st May Anarchist attempt on the life of Alfonso XIII in Paris.	Political and social unrest in Russia; 'Red Sunday' killings in St Petersburg Tsar Nicholas II awards Russia a constitution.
1906		8th April Algeciras Conference. Spain and France divide up Morocco 31st May Attempt on the life of Alfonso XIII and his wife in Madrid on their wedding day	The first Russian Duma is convened; unrest and strikes in Russia; cruel repression by the Tsars causes thousands of deaths in Moscow

1907	Trinidad is born		
1912	Trinidad's older brother, José II, dies following an accident in which he broke his back and spent 3 years in a box. Official cause of death is tuberculosis	12th November. José Canalejas, President of the Government is assassinated in Madrid	
1914	Grandmother Petra and Grandfather Ruperto die, they are both 75 years old	5th August Spain declares itself a neutral party in the First World War	First World War
1915	Trinidad's second oldest brother Francisco, dies in Hervás, after a machinery accident in the textile factory where he works

Trinidad's younger sister Petra dies

Trinidad's brother José III is born

Nicasio is born | | |

1917		13th August General strike across Spain	Russian Revolution
1920	Trinidad's older brother Jesús, dies in Hervás, he caught pneumonia after bathing in a pond in the woods	15th April *Fundación del Partido Comunista Español*, stems from *Partido Comunista de España*.	
		4th September Millán Astray creates *La Legión*, riot squad in the Moroccan Army	
1923	Trinidad and Teresa arrive in Madrid in May to attend their sister María's wedding	13th September Coup d'Etat. Start of the Primo de Rivera dictatorship (1923-1930)	
1930		28th January Primo de Rivera relinquishes power	
1931		Second Republic Alfonso XIII flees Spain	
1933	Trinidad starts as	12th January	

	a maid for don Carlos on Calle de Castelló	*Matanza de Casas Viejas*. Attacks on the Azaña government
		29th October José Antonio Primo de Rivera founds the *Falange Española* in Madrid
		19th November Victory for right-wing parties in elections; Lerroux forms government with the blessing of Gil-Robles and la CEDA
1934	Nicasio arrives in Madrid and lives in Calle Madrid in Getafe where he also works as a barber	4th October Lerroux allows ministers from CEDA to join the government. This is the start of the workers rebellion in Asturias and the Catalan rebellion in Barcelona, the so called October Revolution
1936	Nicasio joins the *1ª. División en la Brigada Mixta, número 26*	16th February Electoral victory for the *Frente Popular*.

	stationed in Somosierra for the entire Civil War as a watchman.	Azaña becomes President of the Republic with Casares Quiroga as Prime Minister	
		12th July Murder of Police Lieutenant José Castillo	
		13th July Murder of Calvo Sotelo	
		17th July, Civil War starts	
		Neighbourhoods in the West of Madrid are partially destroyed by bombings in Civil War	
1939			Hitler's troops invade Poland, triggering the start of the Second World War, followed by the occupation of Paris in 1940
1941			US enters into the war
1942	Trinidad's niece María Teresa is		

	born	
1945		End of the Second World War, with the release of atomic bombs over Hiroshima and Nagasaki. It was calculated that over one hundred and thirty thousand people may have died as a result of the two blasts
1946	Trinidad meets Nicasio at a dance	
1947	Trinidad marries Nicasio	
1948	Trinidad's only son Francisco Jesús is born	
1954	Trinidad's mother Dorotea dies	
1964	Trinidad's family move to Carabanchel	
1966	Trinidad's father Francisco dies	

1968	Frank starts work at the military base in Torrejón	
1972	Frank leaves for State University of New York in September	
1973	Teresa (Trinidad's sister) dies	
	Frank marries Carol	
1975		Franco dies. The monarchy is restored and a period of political change brings Spain closer to democracy
1978	Don Carlos dies	The Constitution is approved and there is a democratic regime in Spain
1979	Trinidad's grandson Carlos is born	3rd April. First Municipal Elections of the Spanish democracy. Enrique Tierno Galván is voted

		mayor by the PSOE and PCE coalition
1980	Trinidad and Nicasio move to their new home in the Elipa neighbourhood	
	Trinidad's younger brother José III dies	
1983	Teresa's husband Paco, dies	
	Trinidad's granddaughter Isabel is born	
1992	Nicasio dies	
	Trinidad's older sister María dies	
1997	Trinidad visits Rome to see the Pope	
2002	Trinidad turns 95 and is recognised by the City Council of Madrid for being the oldest student in the city	The euro, enters into circulation in 12 countries of the EU

2005		Global sadness at the death of Pope John Paul II
		Terrorist attacks in London (7th July).
2007	Trinidad turns 100 and celebrates by inviting all of her family to a party at El Casino in Madrid	
2010	Trinidad dies	

MAIN CHARACTERS (in order of appearance in the text)

Trinidad	main character
Mari-Tere (Mari)	Trinidad's niece
Francisco (1)	Trinidad's father (also known as Tío Fuste)
Nicasio	Trinidad's husband
María (1)	Trinidad's older sister
María (2)	Trinidad's niece, resident of Barcelona
Manolo	Trinidad's nephew, resident of Hervás
Josefa	Trinidad's sister, resident of Hervás
Julia	Nicasio's sister
Paquito (Frank)	Trinidad and Nicasio's son
Dorotea	Trinidad's mother
José I	Trinidad's older brother, died in infancy
Felisa (1)	Trinidad's aunt, resident of Hervás
Evarista	Trinidad's paternal grandmother
Sebastián	Trinidad's paternal grandfather
Ruperto	Trinidad's maternal grandfather
Petra	Trinidad's maternal grandmother
José II	Trinidad's brother, died at the age of 6
Francisco (2)	Trinidad's brother, died at the age of 16

Don Antonio (1)	Hervás parish priest
Saturnino	husband of Felisa, Trinidad's aunt
Eugenia	Felisa and Saturnino's daughter, died at the age of 9
Jesús (1)	Trinidad's brother, died at the age of 19
Demetrio	husband of María, Trinidad's older sister
Paquita	Demetrio and María's daughter
Doña Luisa	the mistress of the first house Trinidad worked in
Fernanda	Trinidad's colleague
Don Luis	the master of the second house that Trinidad worked in
Alejandra	Trinidad's colleague from the house in calle Castelló
Don Saturnino	the master of the third house that Trinidad worked
Felipe	Trinidad's first suitor
Doña Luisa	Don Saturnino's wife
Don Carlos	master of the house that Trinidad worked in during the war
Don Fernando	Don Carlos' brother
Emilia	Trinidad's colleague from the house in calle Castelló

Doña Concepción	Don Fernando's wife
Luis	Emilia's husband
Conchita	Don Fernando and Doña Concepción's daughter
Don Antonio (2)	Don Carlos's brother
Francisco (3)	Nicasio's father
Felisa (2)	Nicasio's mother
Eugenio	Nicasio's uncle
Tomás Gómez	Nicasio's boss at the barbers in Getafe
Juan	Nicasio's comrade in arms
Ángel	Josefa's husband
Aurelio	Nicasio's uncle
Francisco (4)	Teresa's husband
Doña Rosario	Don Carlos's wife
Antonio	worker at Don Carlos' olive grove in Villacarrillo
Consuelo	Trinidad's aunt who is a nun
Jesús (2)	furniture seller in el Rastro
Curro	gypsy
Magdalena	Teresa's neighbour in Madrid
Don Manuel	headmaster of Escuelas Aguirre school

Don César	teacher at Escuelas Aguirre school
Don Feliciano	teacher at Escuelas Aguirre school
Señor Molledo	resident in the avenida Abrantes block
Señor Letona	resident in the avenida Abrantes block
Señor González	resident in the avenida Abrantes block
Carol	Frank's wife
Carmen	Ángel and Josefa's daughter
Marisa	teacher at the adult education class Trinidad attends
Alberto	taxi driver in London
Carlos	Trinidad's grandson
Isabel	Trinidad's granddaughter
Fernando Onega	journalist from Onda Cero

BIBLIOGRAPHY

ALVAREZ PALACIOS, F., *Novela y cultura de posguerra [Post-war Novels and Culture]*, Cuadernos para el Diálogo [Essays for Discussion], Madrid, 1973

ARCADI ESPADA (EDITORES), *Dietarios de posguerra [Post-war Ledgers]*, Editorial Anagrama, Barcelona, 1998

AYUNTAMIENTO DE MADRID, *Madrid, Información sobre la ciudad-1929 [Madrid, City Information- 1929]*, Madrid: El Ayuntamiento, 1929

AYALA VICENTE, FERNANDO, *La violencia política en la provincia de Cáceres durante la Segunda República (1931-1936) [Political Violence in the province of Cáceres in the Second Republic (1931-1936)]*, Brenes: Muñoz Moya Editores Extremeños, 2003.

BATALLONES DISCIPLINARIOS (Esclavos del Franquismo), Colección de Memoria Antifranquista: del Baix Llobregat [DISCIPLINARY BATALLIONS (Slaves of Francoisim), A Collection of Anti-Franco Memories: from the Baix Llobregat], Volume I, pages 52-57, [undated]

BAREA, ARTURO, *La Forja de un Rebelde [Forging a Rebel]*, (Volume I), *Buenos Aires: Editorial Losada, 1951*.

BAREA, ARTURO, *La Ruta* [The Way], (Volume II), *Buenos Aires: Editorial Losada, 1951*

BAREA, ARTURO, *La Llama* [The Flame], (Volume III), *Buenos Aires: Editorial Losada, 1951*

BAROJA PIO, *La Lucha por la vida – La Busca* [The Fight for Life – The Search], Barcelona: Planeta, 1961

BEEVER, ANTONY, *The Spanish Civil War*, Cassell, 1982

BRAVO MORATO, FEDERICO, *Historia de Madrid* [History of Madrid], Volume 2-5, Madrid, Fenicia, 1968

BUCKLEY FERGUS, REID, *Servants and their masters, a novel,* Hodder and Stoughton, 1975.

CALDERON DE LA BARCA, *La Vida es Sueño* [Life is a Dream], E.D.A.F, Madrid, 1964, pp 236-237.

CAMB16, Number 186, July 1975

CARLYLE THOMAS, *On Heroes, Hero-Warship and the Heroic in History,* Frederick A. Stokes & Brother. New York, 1888

CARR, RAYMOND, *Estudios sobre la Republica y la Guerra Civil* [The Republic and the Civil War in Spain Macmillan, 1971], Aeriel, 1973

CARRILLO, SANTIAGO, *Memorias* [Memories], Barcelona: Planeta, 1993

CERVANTES SAAVEDRA, MIGUEL, *The Ingenious Gentleman Don Quixote of La Mancha,* Ramón Sopeña editor, 1931, 2nd part, chapter 8, page 582

CERVERA, JAVIER, *Madrid en guerra: la ciudad clandestina* [Madrid in wartime: the secret city], *1936- 1939,* Madrid: Alianza Editorial, 1998.

CHAVES NOGALES, MANUEL, *A sangre y fuego* [Blood and Fire], Madrid: Espasa, 2006

CHAVES PALACIOS, JULIÁN, *Violencia política y conflictividad social en Extremadura: Cáceres en 1936* [Political Violence and Social Conflict in Extremadura: Cáceres in 1936], Diputación de Cáceres, Institución Cultural El Brocense, 2000

CHAMORRO, VICTOR, *Guía secreta de Extremadura* [Secret Guide to Extremadura], Madrid: Al-Borak, 1976

CIERVA DE LA, RICARDO, *Historia de la Guerra Civil Española* [History of the Civil War], San Martin, 1969

DÍAZ VIANA, LUIS, *Canciones Populares de la Guerra Civil* [Popular Songs of the Civil War], Taurus, 1985,

DÍAZ PLAJA, FERNANDO, *La vida cotidiana en la España de la guerra civil* [Everyday Life in Spain during the Civil war], Madrid: EDAF, 1994

DÍAZ PLAJA, FERNANDO, *La posguerra española en sus documentos* [Post-war Spain as told by documents], Barcelona: Plaza & Janés, D.L., 1970

DISRAELI, BENJAMIN, *The Mirror of Literature*, Amusement, and Instruction Volume 20, No. 556, July 7, 1832.

ELORZA, ANTONIO y Marta Bizcarrondo, *Queridos camaradas: la Internacional Comunista y España, 1919-1939* [Dear Comrades: Spain and the Communist Internationale, 1919-1939], Barcelona, Planeta, 1999

ENGEL, CARLOS, *Historia de las brigadas mixtas del Ejército Popular de la República* [The History of the *brigadas mixtas* of the people's army of the Republic], Madrid: Almena Ediciones, 1999

ESLAVA GALAN, J., *Los años del miedo – La Nueva España (1939-1952)* [Years of Fear – The New Spain (1939-1952)], Planeta, 2008

FERNANDEZ QUINTANILLA, EUGENIO, *Ayuntamiento de Madrid. Información sobre la ciudad. Año 1929: Memoria* [Madrid City Council. Information on the city. Year 1929: Memory], Madrid: s.n., 1929 (Imp. Municipal)

FERNANDEZ GARCIA, ANTONIO, *Historia de Madrid* [A History of Madrid], Madrid Complutense, 1994

FLOREZ MIGUEL, MARCELINO, *Crisis Agraria, Emigración y Lucha de Clases (El Caso de Villalón de Campos, 1880-1930)* [Agrarian Crisis, Emigration and Class War (the Villalón de Campos case, 1880-1930)], Volumen I, El medio rural español: cultura, paisaje y naturaleza [Volume I, The Spanish Rural Environment: culture, countryside and nature], Universidad de Salamanca, 1992, pp. 313-321

GARCIA BALLESTEROS, JOSÉ A. et al, *El Madrid de la posguerra* [Post-war Madrid], Universidad de Mayores de Experiencia Recíproca, Madrid (2006)

GARCIA LORCA, FEDERICO, *Romancero Gitano* [Gypsy Romance], Obras Completas [The Complete Works], Aguilar, Madrid, 1964, page 402

GARCIA VALDECASAS, ALFONSO, *El hidalgo y el honor* [Nobleman and Honour], Madrid: Revista de Occidente, [1958] (Clavileño)

GARRIDO, LUIS, *Los niños que perdimos la Guerra* [Children we lost the War], Edimundo, 1987

GARRIDO, LUIS, *Historias de Posguerra* [Post-war Stories], Madrid, Vosa, 1990

GARRIDO, LUIS, La *Década Oscura 1940-1950* [The Dark Decade 1940-1950], Maeva, 1987

GIRON DE VELASCO, J.A., *Si la memoria no me falla* [If memory doesn't fail me], Planeta, 1994

GÓMEZ VUESTA, CRISTINA, *Ecos de victoria: propaganda y resistencia en Valladolid, 1939-1959* [Echoes of Victory: Propaganda and Resistance in Valladolid, 1939-1959], Diputación de Valladolid, 2010

GÓMEZ PORRO, F., *La conquista de Madrid, paletos, provincianos e inmigrantes* [The Conquest of Madrid, rednecks, countryfolk and immigrants], Silex, Madrid 2000

GONZÁLEZ DE HERVÁS, EMILIO, *Mis Versos de Ayer y Hoy* [Verses of yesterday and today], Librería Raíces (Alicante), 1971

HORN, PAMELA, *Life below stairs in the 20th Century,* Stroud: Sutton,

2001

JAUREGUI, FERNANDO, *Crónica del Antifranquismo* [Chronicles of Antifrancoism], Barcelona: Argos Vergara, 1983

LEVI PRIMO, Si *esto es un hombre* [If this is a Man], Turín: Enaudi, 1947, p. 208

LLARCH JOAN, *Campos de Concentración en la España de Franco* [Concentration Camps in Franco's Spain], Producciones Editoriales, 1978

MACIAS PICAVEA, RICARDO, *La Tierra de Campos. Novela original* [Tierra de Campos. An original novel], Madrid, 1897

MARSAL, JUAN F., *Pensar bajo el franquismo: Intelectuales y política en la generación de los años cincuenta* [Thinking under Francoism: Intellectuals and politics in the fifties generation], Barcelona, Península, 1979

MARTIN GAITE, C, *Usos Amorosos de la Posguerra Española* [Amourous Uses in Post-war Spain], Anagrama, 1994

MATTHEWS, JAMES, *Reluctant Warriors,* Oxford University Press, 2012

MIGUEL DE, ARMANDO, *Cuando éramos niños* [When we were young], Barcelona: Plaza & Janés Editores, 2001.

MOLINERO C., SALA M., Y SABREQUES J., EDS., *Una Inmensa Prisión – Los campos de concentración y la prisiones durante la guerra civil y el franquismo* [An Immense Prison – Concentration Camps and prisons during the Civil War and under Franco], *Crítica Contrastes*, 2003

MONTOLIÚ CAMPS, PEDRO, *Madrid bajo la Dictadura, 1947-1959: trece años que cambiaron una ciudad* [Madrid under dictatorship, 1947-1959: thirteen years that changed a city], Madrid: Sílex, 2010

MONTOLIÚ CAMPS, PEDRO, *Madrid en la Guerra Civil, La Historia, Volumen I, y Los Protagonistas, Volumen II* [Madrid in the Civil War, The

History Volume I and the Protagonists Volume II], Madrid: Sílex, 2000

MORICHE MATEOS, FRANCISCO, R*epresión, silencio y olvido, Memoria Histórica de Hervás y el Alto Ambroz* [Repression, Silence and Forgetting: Historical Memory of Hervás and the Alto Ambroz], Asamblea de Extremadura [undated]

MORLA LYNCH, CARLOS, *Informes diplomáticos y diarios de la Guerra Civil* [Diplomatic reports and diaries of the Civil War], Espuela de Plata, 2010 (pp. 68-72)

MORLA LYNCH, CARLOS, *España sufre, diarios de guerra 1936-39* [Spain suffers, diaries of war, 1936-39], Renacimiento, 2007 (page 183)

NODO (Noticiario Español [Spanish News]), Years 1943-52

NUÑEZ MARGADO, AURELIO, *Los Sucesos de España vistos por un diplomático* [Events in Spain as seen by a diplomat], Talleres Gráficos Argentinos, L. J. Rosso, 1941

OLIVARES ANGEL J., *Historias del Antiguo Madrid* [Stories of Old Madrid], La Librería, página 321

ORTEGA Y GASSET, JOSÉ, *The Dehumanization of Art and Other Essays on Art, Culture, and Literature* (Princeton Paperbacks, 128), 1968.

PANIAGUA, JAVIER, *España: siglo XX, 1898-1931* [Spain: twentieth century, 1888-1931], Madrid, Grupo Anaya, 1989

PETTIFER, JAMES (Ed.), *Cockburn in Spain: Despatches from the Spanish Civil War,* Lawrence and Wishart, London 1986

REDONDO CADEÑOSO, JESÚS ANGEL *Protesta y violencia de los campesinos castellano-leoneses: la Tierra de Campos (1900-1923)* [Protests and violence of the people of Castilla y León: la Tierra de Campos (1900-1923)], Diputación de Palencia, 2011.

REID BUCKLEY, FERGUS, *Servants and their Masters, A Novel,* Holder and Stoughton, London 1973

REVISTA DE FERIAS Y FIESTAS [Fairs and Fiestas Magazine], Hervás, 1964

SANCHEZ BUENO, JOSÉ LUIS, *La provincia de Cáceres, situación socio-económica y condiciones de vida (1883-1902)* [The Province of Cáceres, socio-economic situation and living conditions (1883-1902)], Revista de estudios extremeños, ISSN 0210-2854, Vol. 58, N° 1, 2002, pp. 93-138

SENDER, J, RAMON, *Réquiem por un campesino español* [Requiem for a Spanish peasant], Ediciones Destino, 1984

SERASUA, CARMEN, *Criada, nodrizas y amos, El servicio doméstico en la formación del mercado de trabajo, 1758-1868* [Maids, wet-nurses and masters, Domestic Service in the formation of the labour market 1758-1868], Siglo XXI Editores, 1994

STONE MARILYN, *Women at work in Spain: from the Middle Ages to early modern times, New York: Peter Lang, 1998*

TOMÁS, SALVADOR, *La guerra de España en fotografías* [The Spanish War in photos], Barcelona Marte, 1966.

TUÑON DE LARA, MANUEL, *La España del Siglo XX – De la Segunda República a la Guerra Civil* [Twentieth Century Spain – From the Second Republic to the Civil War], Laia, 1974

VELASCO ZAZO, ANTONIO, *Frases y Modismos* [Sayings and Idioms], Madrid: Librería General Victoriano Suárez, 1951

VIZCAINO CASAS, F., *La España de la Posguerra, 1939-1953* [Post-War Spain, 1939-1953], *Espejo de España, Planeta,* 1975

VIÑAS, ANGEL, *El Honor de la Republica* [The Honour of the Republic], Barcelona: *Crítica, 2009*

VIÑAS, ANGEL, *El Escudo de la Republica* [The Shield of the Republic], Barcelona: *Crítica, 2007*

VIÑAS, ANGEL, *La Soledad de la Republica* [The Isolation of the Republic], Barcelona: *Crítica, 2006*

BIBLIOGRAPHY (WEB)

Una escolar de 95 años [A 95-year-old schoolgirl], Susana Montero, 'El País', 4th April, 2002.
http://www.elpais.com/articulo/ultima/escolar/95/anos/elpepiult/20020404elpepiult_1/Tes

Ahora quiero viajar a la Luna [Next I want to go to the moon], Roberto Becares, 'El Mundo', 5th April 2002
http://www.elmundo.es/elmundo/2002/04/04/madrid/1017930714.html

Sola en casa... a los 101 años [Alone at home... at 101 years old], M. J. Alvarez, 'ABC', 23rd June 2008
http://hemeroteca.abc.es/nav/Navigate.exe/hemeroteca/madrid/abc/2008/06/23/054.html

1904: rebelión en Tierra de Campos [1904: rebellion in Tierra de Campos], Jesús-Ángel Redondo Cardeñoso,
Espacio, Tiempo y Forma [Space Time and Form], Ángeles Lario (ed.) Historia Contemporánea, Revista de la Facultad de Geografia e Historia, Serie V22, Madrid, 2010
http://uva-es.academia.edu/Jes%C3%BAs%C3%81ngelRedondoCarde%C3%B1oso/Papers/429323/1904_rebelion_en_Tierra_de_Campos

ABOUT THE AUTHOR

Frank Vielba is a retired IT Manager who is interested in family history writing and research. Before his retirement, he published in a different genre *Reducing the M and A Risks: The Role of IT in Mergers and Acquisitions,* Palgrave Macmillan; (31 May 2006). He is currently researching and working on another book to do with family history. He is married and lives in London.

Printed in Great Britain
by Amazon